So Just How Funny Are You?

I know I can teach you comedy, but I can't teach anyone how to be funny. You either have a sense of humor or you don't. And just because your wife laughs at you doesn't mean that you are a funny guy. She might be having an affair and figures the least she can do is laugh at your dumb jokes. Or, even worse, you could be like my mother, where the phrase "tough audience" takes on a whole other meaning. For instance, I would tell my mother a joke, such as . . .

"Women are bad in math. How can you be good in math when your whole life you're told this (holding up two fingers a few inches apart) . . . is eight inches."

Instead of laughing, my mother would say:

But, Judy, that's not true. A lot of women are very good in math. I'm good in math. Your grandmother is good in math. Our neighbor Florence is good in math . . ."

I could never teach my mother to be funny. Then again, she could never teach me how to do the dishes.

How do you know if you're funny? Take the Funny Test and see!

QUANTITY SALES

Most Dell books are available at special quantity discounts when purchased in bulk by corporations, organizations, or groups. Special imprints, messages, and excerpts can be produced to meet your needs. For more information, write to: Dell Publishing, 1540 Broadway, New York, NY 10036. Attention: Special Markets.

INDIVIDUAL SALES

Are there any Dell books you want but cannot find in your local stores? If so, you can order them directly from us. You can get any Dell book currently in print. For a complete up-to-date listing of our books and information on how to order, write to: Dell Readers Service, Box DR, 1540 Broadway, New York, NY 10036.

STAND-UP

COMEDY:
The Book

Judy Carter

DELTA

A DELTA BOOK
Published by
Bantam Dell
a division of
Random House, Inc.

Book designed by Sheree Goodman

The Trademark Dell ® is registered
in the U.S. Patent and Trademark Office.

ISBN: 0-440-50243-8

Printed in the United States of America
Published simultaneously in Canada

September 1989

20 19 18

To Linda Adelman, who taught me that all is possible

Grateful thanks are extended to the following interviewees whose cooperation helped to make this book possible:

Jerry Seinfeld, Larry Miller, Mark Breslin, Cynthia Szigeti, Mary Downey, Dennis Danziger, Dennis Erdman, Bob Fisher, Charlie Fleischer, Richard Gordon, Jan Smith, Kelly Goode, Monica Piper, Buddy Morra, Gary Mule Deer, Jeanne Y. Robertson, Lou Ross, Valery Pappas, Paula Poundstone, Mark Russell, George Schlatter, Silver Saunders Friedman, Carrie Snow, Charlie Steadham, Taylor Negron, Fred Travalena, Lotus Weinstock, Robert Wuhl, Marty Klein, Marsha Meyers, Emily Levine, Joanne Parrent.

The following magazines were consulted in the research process: *Just for Laughs, Rave Magazine, Comedy USA,* and *L.A. Weekly.*

Special thanks to:
My agent, Annette Welles, for believing in me.
My editor, Chuck Adams, for saying yes.
Judy Brown for her meticulous research.
Abby Belkin for her support.
And especially to all my students who made this book possible.

Contents

CHAPTER 2.

CHAPTER 3.

CHAPTER 4.

CHAPTER 5.

CHAPTER 6.

CHAPTER 7.

CHAPTER 8.

CHAPTER 9.

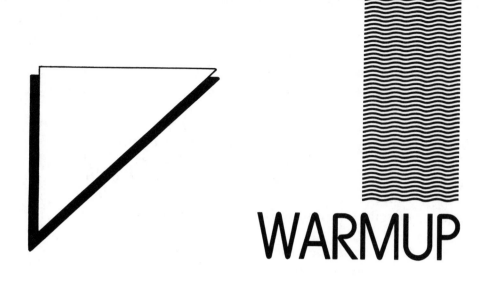

WARMUP

Dear Reader,

It's true. I can teach anyone with a willingness and a sense of humor the secrets of making people laugh. You don't even need to know how to write jokes, because this book is chock-full of exercises that will teach you how to turn your own life experiences into comic routines. So if you have a life—you have an act.

Why put together a stand-up comedy routine? Especially if you're not planning a comedy career? Because in the very process of creating an act you can become a funnier, wittier, and more confident person in your professional and social life. Sooner or later you're going to find yourself having to speak in front of people, and if you're like most of us, public speaking isn't at the top of your to-do list. Whether you are speaking to the PTA, the PTL, or the PLO, why not get some laughs? Humor is a powerful tool. In business, ideas presented with humor gain more support, and after five, the person who gets more laughs gets more dates. And

for those of you who never intend to perform, Chapter 9 provides special techniques to punch up your business and social life.

Humor is therapeutic. Even if you have no intention of ever getting up on a stage, learning how to turn negative, painful life experiences into comedy routines will give you a new perspective on life. Once you can laugh at something, you can stop crying. Student Peggy Lawrence got great material from going through a divorce:

66My ex-husband and I had a communication problem ... he wouldn't even tell me who he was dating!99

Training your mind to focus on the funny, not the fatal, can help you heal even the most open of wounds. I know, because for the past ten years I have made a living doing stand-up. I have performed on over forty-five major TV shows, three Showtime comedy specials, and have toured the United States playing colleges and nightclubs, opening for everyone from Pat Boone to Prince. I am a regular in Atlantic City, where I was nominated for that city's "Entertainer of the Year." I have also performed at the Sahara-Tahoe, Sahara–Las Vegas, and Medora-North Dakota. (Well, some places are better than others.) I have made a lot of money doing what I love to do—make people laugh. I may not be famous in Price, Utah, but then again I have never had to get a job at K mart.

Before I was a stand-up, I taught high school, which is great preparation for anyone considering a career in stand-up. If you can make a room of jaded eleventh graders laugh, you can work any room anywhere. I quit teaching and, not having the slightest idea of what I was doing, I put together a comedy act. A pretty bad act at first, which gradually got better. I learned the principles of making people laugh in ten years of trial and error, luck, and a lot of bombing. A *lot* of bombing. You, however, won't have to go through that because I am sharing the secrets of how to make people laugh that took me from being an underpaid teacher to making the big bucks in Atlantic City. Okay, I don't get the summer off, and okay, comics don't get tenure, but working twenty minutes a night—as opposed to eight hours a day and supervising detention—isn't too bad.

Putting an act together isn't a mystical process. Anyone can learn the basic principles to making people laugh. For the past few years I have taught these principles to hundreds of students in my comedy workshops in Los Angeles. Throughout this book, I will be quoting students who, just like many of you, started out with little or no material. Many former students tell me that their newfound sense of comedy has helped them get employed, get noticed, and get laid. One student, a lawyer, felt that his trial litigation had improved. (At least he kept the jury awake.) Another student found that after learning how to make an audience laugh, he no longer was tongue-tied on dates. An overweight, shy student found new self-acceptance and confidence by learning how to laugh at herself. Others, including housewives, accountants, college students, and ex-cons, became working comics and are making money doing stand-up. They all came to my classes because their friends, co-workers, or cellmates said to them, "You're so funny, you should be a comedian."

Judy Carter

Do you think you are funny? Have you ever pictured yourself onstage, driving an audience mad with laughter? Or having them rolling in the aisles during your speech to the American Legion? Do you dream of being the center of attention? Having people love and adore you? Impressing an audience, your boss, or your date with quick, witty comebacks? Would you like to do stand-up comedy?

Then read on . . .

What are you? Crazy?

Do you have any idea how scary it is to stand onstage all by yourself trying to make people laugh? Why not take up a less dangerous activity, like jumping out of an airplane? Join the Green Berets, work for a bomb squad, but *don't* be a stand-up comic.

Congratulations! If you got past that last page and still want to take a crack at making people laugh, then you have what it takes and this book is for you.

As I mentioned, the two requirements for making people laugh are having the desire and having a sense of humor. You probably have the desire since you've made the effort to take this book off the shelf and turn a few pages. For that I commend you. For me, just making the decision to open a book can be an exhausting experience. So . . . how do you know if you have comedy potential? Turn the page and find out.

SO JUST HOW FUNNY ARE YOU?

I know I can teach you comedy, but I can't teach anyone how to be funny. Either you have a sense of humor, or you don't. And just because your wife laughs at you doesn't mean that you are a funny guy. She might be having an affair and figures the least she can do is laugh at your dumb jokes. Or, even worse, you could be like my mother, where the phrase "tough audience" takes on a whole other meaning. For instance, I would tell my mother a joke, such as

> **66Women are bad in math. How can you be good in math when your whole life you're told that this (holding up two fingers a few inches apart) . . . is eight inches.99**

Instead of laughing my mother would say,

> **66But, Judy . . . that's not true. A lot of women are very good in math. I'm good in math. Your grandmother is good in math. Our neighbor Florence is good in math . . .99**

I know I could never teach my mother how to be funny. Then again, she could never teach me how to do the dishes.
   How do you know if you are a funny person?
   Take the funny test.

The Funny Test

Check √ if answer is yes.

☐ 1. Are you Jewish, Black, or Italian?
(NOTE: If you answered yes to this question, skip directly to Chapter 2.)

☐ 2. Do people at work (or in the unemployment line) laugh at your jokes?

☐ 3. Do people often repeat your lines?

☐ 4. Do you notice the absurdities of life?

☐ 5. Do you find people's shortcomings amusing?

☐ 6. Do you joke about your own shortcomings?

☐ 7. Are you quick with sarcastic comebacks?

☐ 8. Were you the class clown?

☐ 9. Did you secretly think you were funnier than the class clown?

☐ 10. Do you find TV commercials funny when they aren't supposed to be?

☐ 11. When people laugh at your jokes, is it more satisfying than: eating, drinking, or making love?

Turn the page for your score.

If you answered "yes" to any of these questions, you have comedy potential. If you thought that taking this quiz was really stupid, then you are a very cynical person like myself, and not only do you have comedy potential, you are perfectly suited to a career in comedy.

From this point on, each of you will be doing the same thing: developing a stand-up comedy routine. It's the *process* of developing an act that you will take with you long after you write it or perform it.

Step by step, I will show you how to create an act, perform it (even make money with it), and apply it to everyday life. If you read each chapter thoroughly and do all the exercises, I guarantee that you will have an act and be on your way to performing on the *Tonight Show, Star Search*, or at least in someone's living room.

This book is actually two different books—one that you read and one that is a personal workbook you write in. If possible, create a comedy support system by working through this book with a comedy buddy. I highly recommend the buddy system and use it in my classes. You are going to be doing your act to people, and it will be too much of a shock if you've just done your act to your mirror. The only equipment you need other than this book is:

1. A hand-held tape recorder—Carry it with you everywhere.

2. Pen and notebook—A small pocket notebook.

3. Food in the refrigerator—For comfort.

4. A little courage—*See* chutzpah.

5. Lots of chutzpah—*See* courage.

COMEDY GLOSSARY

ff*Hey, man, I really killed. I slaughtered them. I murdered them . . .*™™

No, this is not a psycho killer bragging about his latest murder victim. This is *comic talk*. Here are some comic-talk terms I will be using throughout this book.

I Killed: *I did great.*

I Died: *See* "I Bombed."

I Slated Them: *I made them laugh.*

Rolling in the Aisles: *The audience laughed.*

Doing Filler: *I ran out of material and winged it* (i.e., "*So where are you guys from?*").

Over Their Heads: *Too hip for the room.* What happens when you do your Sartre routine about *Being and Nothingness* when playing the Elks Club.

Doing Panel: Sitting next to Johnny Carson trying to disguise the material you're doing as chitchat. *"No, Johnny, I'm not seeing anyone now. I just have these L.A. Teflon affairs . . . nothing sticks! And how's your life?"*

Gig: A job.

Setup: The explaining part of a joke. *"Last night someone asked me to get married . . ."*

Punch: Where they are supposed to laugh. *". . . My mother!"*

I Crackled: *"I got nervous and started speaking in tongues."*

I Bombed: *See "I Died."*

Blue Material: Talking about the pink parts of your body and/or anything coming in and out of holes.

Independent Contractor: How comics are booked so the government doesn't partake of their paychecks.

Mike Too Hot: Volume too loud.

Setlist: Piece of paper that has the order of jokes.

Spot: Your place in the lineup.

Chunk: A collection of jokes arranged together about a specific topic.

Closer: Headliner, does between forty-five minutes to an hour.

Middler: Does twenty to thirty minutes.

Opener: Opening act who does ten to twenty minutes; usually doubles as MC and also has to empty ashtrays.

I Had to Work the Room: *"I got them but it was tough."*

On a Roll: The audience is with you and you can do no wrong.

Comedy Condo: A cockroach-infested apartment where a club puts up out-of-town comics.

THE SIX LAME EXCUSES FOR NOT GETTING ONSTAGE

"SURE I'M FUNNY AT PARTIES, BUT ..."

Excuse #1: "I'm Scared"

The number-one obstacle to doing comedy is FEAR. And it is a very appropriate reaction. Let's face it, if standing alone on a stage, in front of strangers, doesn't frighten you, then something may be very wrong. See a doctor.

It's okay to be nervous. It's very human. Every successful performer wrestles with fear, so don't let it stop you from pursuing your dreams. In the years I've been performing, I can't think of one time when I haven't been nervous. The trick is to go on *in spite of* feeling afraid. Usually the fear goes away as soon as you step onstage.

Don't panic. Fear is such a powerful issue with my students that I have devoted an entire chapter to it, including exercises for controlling it. Look at the bright side: At least performing will keep you regular.

Excuse #2: "I'm Shy"

Well, so am I. Most stand-ups are very shy in their personal lives, and going onstage is a great outlet. You shy people have a lot of stuff to let out, and the stage gives you an arena in which to vent your repressed criticisms of the world. I find that the quieter the person is offstage, the more he or she has to say onstage. Once they actually get the chance to be heard, my shy students are the ones I can't get to stop talking.

Excuse #3: "I'm Just an Ordinary Schlump"

So what? Prior to having successful careers in comedy, Jay Leno fixed cars and Roseanne Barr was a housewife with three kids.

❝I've been married fourteen years, and I have three kids. Obviously, I breed well in captivity.❞

—Roseanne Barr

Roseanne Barr

Brian McLaughlin

You don't have to be a worldly person to do comedy. People don't go to nightclubs to hear intellectual pondering. They want to laugh. The challenge is to find the humor in your most ordinary experiences. Being astute and clever helps, but let's face it—this is America, a place where complete nerds achieve high levels of fame and fortune.

Excuse #4: "I'm Ugly, I'm Fat, I'm . . ."

Darryl Hannah may be really gorgeous, but can she make people laugh? Okay, who cares, right? Stand-up is one of the few places in showbiz that accepts people of all shapes and sizes. In fact, a physical distinction can even be the basis of your act. Phyllis Diller and the late, great Jackie Gleason, among others, made careers out of being fat or unattractive. Comedian Geri Jewell develops her act around having cerebral palsy:

> **❝I don't understand why people will go out of their way to drink, so they can walk like me!❞**

The very characteristic society sees as imperfect can work to your advantage. Chapter 2 teaches how to turn those extra pounds into extra laughs.

Excuse #5: "I Don't Know How to Write Comedy Material"

Stand-up isn't about writing words down. It's about "talking" words—performing. Stand-up is a live performance, not a book for leisure reading. For that reason, I discourage my beginning students from writing down their material. In Chapter 2 there are exercises on how to create your material by talking into a tape recorder. If you can talk, you can create material.

Excuse #6: "When I Get in Front of People, I Tend to Spit"

See a shrink. Stand-up is not for you.

Stand-up is tough stuff and it takes a lot of hard work. But the rewards of doing comedy are immense. There is no greater feeling in the world than the feeling of an audience who is with you, understanding you, and loving you. Moments like that make all the struggling worthwhile.

Andy Warhol once said that in the future everyone will be famous for fifteen minutes. With this book, when your fifteen minutes come up, at least you won't be boring.

STAND-UP COMEDY:
The Book

CHAPTER 1

GETTING STARTED

What Makes People Laugh?

> *Words with 'K' in it are funny. 'Cupcake' is funny ... 'Tomato' is not funny. 'Cleveland' is funny. 'Maryland' is not funny ...*
>
> —Neil Simon, *The Sunshine Boys*

What is funny?

I'm constantly amazed at what people think is funny and not funny. Some people will laugh at a guy slipping on a banana peel. Some people will only laugh at Hitler slipping on a banana peel. So, what is funny? If someone laughs, that's funny.

An audience will laugh at anything, everything, and nothing at all. Trying to figure out an audience is like trying to figure out what to cook your family for dinner. No matter what you make, someone will hate it.

1

I've seen so many comics come offstage after a killer set depressed because all they saw was the one guy in the third row who didn't laugh at the fourth joke. All the laughter in the room was drowned out by one man's silence. And it doesn't matter that this guy wasn't in the mood to laugh because he just lost his entire family in a fire and stopped in for a drink before killing himself. We still blame ourselves for not pleasing everyone, every time.

Believe in Yourself

Manager Buddy Morra, who discovered David Letterman and also handles Robin Williams and Billy Crystal, among others, says that: "you shouldn't give an audience what *they* want. Give them what *you* want. Most comics will go down to the audience level to make it work, when in fact what you should be doing is bringing the audience to your level."

The first time Morra saw David Letterman, he instantly knew that David would go on to doing his own show, because he had his own identity. Morra feels that's what sets apart comics who are special from those who just try to please. You've got to believe in yourself.

It's hard to swallow the idea that you can't make everyone love you. This one's worth repeating: You can't and won't be able to make everyone love you. You must go onstage with a passionate desire and the intent to communicate your thoughts and feelings, not just to make people laugh.

Five Big Secrets to Making People Laugh

Secret #1: Don't Tell Jokes

People confuse stand-up with telling jokes. When I go to a party and tell people that I am a stand-up, they inevitably say, "Really . . . tell me a joke." When I tell them that I don't know any jokes, they don't get it. "But you're a stand-up comic, right?" Now when I go to parties I tell people that I'm a Kelly Girl.

Joke-telling is the old Catskill school of comedy.

❝Two Jews walked into a bar . . .❞

The new school of comedy is personal comedy. Your act is about you: your gut issues, your body, your marriage, your divorce, your drug habit . . .

Try to find the jokes in Sam Kinison's act. There aren't any.

❝If you ever think about getting married, sir, just remember this face— ahhhhhhh!❞

Sam goes nose to nose with the customer and screams.

Sam Kinison

Bonnie Schiffman

Kinison's humor comes from having an extreme attitude

3

Paula Poundstone

about women, Vietnam, and starving kids. His consistent, angry attitude is the driving force of his success.

My students who pick topics that are truthful and even painful for them are much more successful than those who pick topics they think are jokey or weird. As a matter of fact, the more candid the material, the better it is. People love to laugh at another person's heartache. I'm not sure why. Maybe because they're so happy that it's not happening to them.

Paula Poundstone, the Sylvia Plath of comedy, does a chunk of her fumbled suicide attempt.

"I tried using carbon monoxide, but my building has a big underground parking garage so it was taking a really long time. I had to bring along a stack of books and some snacks. People would go by and tap at the window and say, "How's that suicide coming?' And I'd say, 'Pretty good, thank you, I felt drowsy earlier today.' "

Garry Shandling's grief over his rejections by women have made him a comedy millionaire.

"I broke up with my girlfriend. She moved in with another guy, and I draw the line at that."

4

One of the main misconceptions about being funny is that you have to be a real together "up" kind of person. Not true. It is far more interesting to watch someone struggling with his or her problems than some spiritual, flawless know-it-all. Have you noticed that there are not too many monks who are stand-up comics? Remember . . . the more miserable your life, the better your act. The trick is to be willing to expose yourself as much as you can without getting arrested.

Secret #2: Don't Tell Stories

Funny stories usually don't work. The most common mistake my students make when starting out with ideas for their act is telling stories about something "funny" that "really" happened to them:

66No, no, listen . . . this is really true.99

Stories might be true, but they are rarely funny and inevitably end with

66Well . . . I guess you had to be there.99

Another reason stories don't work is because night-club audiences most often are drunk and have short attention spans. Any piece that goes longer than five lines without a punch is going to be in trouble.

Bob Fisher, owner of L.A.'s   Garry Shandling

Ice House and booker of seven comedy clubs, will not book storytellers who go three to five minutes without a punchline. "I look for the setup/punch kind of comic as opposed to a storyteller, because I need a comic who will give the audience a certain number of laughs per minute."

Stories also don't work because they are frequently told in the past tense:

> **"So there I was in a department store. And this lady walked up to me and asked me if I worked there. So I told her 'Yes,' and 'All the televisions are free today.'"**

Here is the same material delivered by comic Bob Dubac, in present tense, not in story form:

> **"To have some grins and loosen up, I recommend going to a department store and pretending you're an employee. When someone comes up and asks you, 'Do you work here?' tell them 'yes' and that all the televisions are free today. Sit back and watch the fun."**

Keep away from telling stories. What's funny is simply the way you look at even the most mundane events, such as Larry Miller's observations about phone cords:

> **"How does that phone cord always get so tangled? How? All I ever do is pick it up, talk, and hang it up. I don't pick it up, do a cartwheel and then a somersault, and then hang it up."**

Secret #3: Don't Try to Be Funny

> **"You don't have to act like an asshole to get laughs."**

> **—Anonymous**

6

If I told you right now "Be funny," what would you do? A lot of people might start making stupid faces, jump up and down, and do something that would get them committed to a mental hospital.

Being funny has nothing to do with acting weird or outrageous. The weirder you are, the less people will understand you, and no one laughs when confused. As eccentric as comics like Howie Mandel and Sam Kinison are, they make enormous efforts to communicate their ideas clearly. Acting stupid might be funny if you're performing for five-year-olds, but kindergarten gigs don't come along too often and the pay is lousy.

Novice comics tend to "try to be funny." Go to an amateur night and watch comics. A guy comes onstage pretending to be cool. He does his first line and no one laughs. So he tries harder to be funny. He's talking louder, he's waving his hands around, he's become a desperate man. Suddenly you feel that if you don't laugh, this guy will go home and kill himself and it will be your fault. It's no surprise that from this point on nothing he does is funny. The harder he tries to be funny the more you pray, "Please God, make him stop!"

If you go onstage desperately wanting a guffaw, a chortle, or a tee hee, you're liable not to get it. Nothing turns people off more than when they think someone wants something from them. Whether it's love or laughs, it needs to be given freely. Just as people who are the most desperate for love end up living alone in Winnebagos, comics who are the most desperate for laughs end up keeping their day jobs.

Secret #4: Be Serious

Comedy is a serious business.

The perfect act is funny to the audience and serious to you. Imagine you are a paid whore . . . a comedy prostitute.

Steven Wright

In other words, the only one who's got to like it is the one paying. If it's funny for you and not for the customers, then you didn't do your job.

A comic who has made a dedicated commitment to his or her act can make an audience laugh just on the strength of confidence alone. It doesn't really matter what's being talked about. Whether discussing the pope or polyps, or even the pope's polyps, it is the *commitment* of the comic to his or her material that carries the act. The commitment to communicate, to get ideas across, will provide all the fuel you need. The desire to communicate is the only sane reason to ever get on any stage—ever.

Why? If *you* don't believe in what you're talking about, neither will the audience. The topic you pick doesn't have to be serious, but your attitude about it does. Whether talking about love or lint, talk to your audience as if your words are going to change their lives. Don Rickles cracks up an audience just by talking intensely in gibberish. It is his ultra-serious attitude about nonsense that makes the audience laugh.

Comic Steven Wright has taken seriousness to new dimensions with his just-out-of-the-grave, deadpan delivery:

❝I'm living on a one-way, dead-end street. I don't know how I got there.❞

8

Secret #5: Relax

Remember . . . it's stand-up comedy you're doing, not brain surgery. Relax and have fun.

The way to make people laugh is to:

▶ Relax and be yourself
▶ Find importance in your material
▶ Have fun

If you really understand these principles, you are ready to begin.

Workshop #1:

When you watch a good comic, you should never be aware of the structure of his or her act—you should be too busy laughing. Good comics appear to be talking spontaneously, off the top of their heads. "They just get up there and are funny." What many people don't realize is that all working comics structure their acts into very specific comedy formulas.

Many years ago I appeared on a new comedian's special for HBO. Also appearing on the bill was a new comedian named Robin Williams. I was quite curious to see him rehearse, because like most people, I was under the impression that his act was totally improvised. Not true. During the rehearsal, as I overheard him talking to the director, it very clear that his entire act had been mapped out.

❝First I will start on the stage and do my 'death of a sperm,' and then I will go into the audience, do my Shakespeare parody, and then . . .❞

9

Robin does improvise during his act, but upon close examination, his act has a beginning, middle, and end, and every piece is broken down into a setup/punch format. What makes him brilliant is his ability to make every chunk seem to be totally impromptu.

This exercise will reveal to you that a comedy act is a highly structured piece of material where every attitude, word, and moan is meticulously worked out. Analyzing proven comedy material can be a great learning experience. Understanding someone else's act will bring you closer to discovering your own.

Robin Williams

1. Tape a comic you enjoy. (Watch TV or rent a videocassette featuring your favorite comic.)

2. Play the tape over and over again.

3. Write down answers for the following questions.

   A. What is the overall emotional attitude (i.e., Is the comic angry? Frustrated? Confused? Worried? etc.)? Write it down here:

   _____

   _____

   _____

   B. List the topics (subjects) covered in the routine (i.e., dating, marriage, restaurants, etc.).

   _____

_____

_____

_____

C. What do you like and/or dislike about the comic?

_____

_____

_____

D. Memorize three minutes of the comic's act and say it out loud.

NOTE: You should *never*, I repeat, *never* perform another comic's material publicly. This exercise is designed to help you get the feel of what good professional material sounds and feels like. Performing someone else's material for even one other person is stealing and will get you nowhere fast.

Now . . . before we move on to creating your own act, there is one little demon to take care of . . .

Dealing with Fear

"Remember, comedy doesn't kill."

People say to me, "I could never do stand-up. I'd be too frightened." So what else is new? I wish these people could see the miserable wreck of a person I am before I go on. In all the years I've been performing, I have never gotten over stage fright. It doesn't matter whether I am appearing before a small group of people, in front of a screaming mob of thousands, or just thinking about performing, I still get vicious anxiety attacks. I feel absolutely petrified and I'm convinced my death is nearby.

Paula Poundstone, a successful comic who has done countless appearances on Carson and HBO specials, equates stand-up with skydiving. "The first time I jumped out of a plane, something major did go wrong and I thought I was going to die. And after I landed safely, my first thought was that this was exactly the same feeling as doing the *Tonight Show*."

Unfortunately, there is no cure for stage fright. The good news is not only does it go away as soon as you land onstage, but there is a way to make fear more manageable—and it's legal.

Before I learned how to manage my fear successfully, I tried everything to stop my performing terror. Alcohol and drugs were a disaster. They made me forget my act and retain water.

There may not be a cure for fear, but there is a way to not let it rule your life.

The trick to dealing with fear is to go on in spite of feeling afraid. The first time Arsenio Hall heard his name being introduced from a stand-up stage, he ran in terror out the door. Even though his fear persisted, he worked up the courage to try it again. Years later he ended up headlining in major clubs, starring in movies with Eddie Murphy, and hosting his own talk show.

Stand-up takes courage. This is what separates the men from the boys, the women from the girls. This is what is commonly called "putting your dick on the line," or your ovaries or whatever you have.

The first day of every new class I ask my students, "How many of you are frightened to death to get onstage?

Bonnie Schiffman

Arsenio Hall

The entire class raises their hands. They admit they're terrified. They want a cure. I don't have a cure. Disappointed, some students drop out. Others want their money back. And the brave ones hang in there for the ride. The way I see it, if you like roller coasters, you'll love stand-up. Remember? You get in line, thinking that this is going to be fun. As the line moves, you start to sweat. You begin thinking that this was really a stupid idea. You're at the front of the line. You get in the car. Your heart is pounding. You might die. You panic, want to escape. The coaster starts crawling up that endless first hill. You've stopped breathing and blinking and then—wheeeeee! When the ride is over you get off and can't wait to do it again.

Medical science has shown that fear and excitement produce the same physical reaction—the runs. People who avoid risk-taking lead dull lives. They want to protect themselves from feeling afraid or out of control. Yet it is precisely this out-of-control feeling that creates excitement and makes a performer exciting to watch. After years of this craziness, I realized that if I didn't feel a little frightened, it wouldn't be exciting. The rare times I go onstage without feeling scared I actually worry. In fact, the day I'm no longer nervous will be the day I quit stand-up and take up something really frightening—like getting married.

Stand-up is a great high if you can get past that critical voice that tells you to stay in bed with a quart of Rocky Road. If you are like most funny people, you have a critic inside of you that yaps away every time you try something new. My inner critic has been yapping away for the last ten minutes: "You can't say 'dick' in a book. Now you'll offend everyone. Stop writing and get married already."

As you can imagine, this critic of mine (Slash, as I like to call her) is no pleasure to live with. But like my shadow, we're stuck with each other. I have come to realize that I will always have a critic who talks to me as if I were the scum of the earth. My salvation has been to stop pretending she doesn't exist. I now accept my critic and actually find her comments to be quite funny—sometimes. I guarantee that when you start creating material, your critic will come blasting at you to stop. This is when most people give up. Before you go on, I highly recommend that you do this critic-controlling exercise.

Workshop #2

≈≈≈≈≈≈≈≈≈≈≈≈≈≈≈≈≈≈≈≈≈≈≈≈≈≈≈≈≈≈≈≈≈≈≈

DEALING WITH YOUR CRITIC

When I try to ignore my critic, her voice just gets louder. So I make a deal with her. I give her uninterrupted time to speak with this condition: She takes a hike while I am creating. It works.

NOTE: Do this exercise anytime you are having an anxiety attack or writer's block.

First, take your critic for a walk. Letting your critic fully express itself can release fear and restore your creative process.

Take a walk around the block and criticize yourself aloud, while you walk. (Do this in a place where you won't run into people you know and get mistaken for a bagperson.) Give your critical voice a real name. Let everything hang out.

Or: You can take a walk and talk out loud to your critic as if it were a frightened little person. Reassure it that everything is going to be all right. Make deals—bribe it.

"Okay, Slash, I'll go on a diet, if you first let me finish this chapter. Okay?"

I have come to the point where I find my critic a hoot— the same way that I find all paranoid psychos humorous.

Then *dialog with your critic.* Bringing your critic out of the closet and getting to know it in the light will make it

14

less menacing and, perhaps, even provide you with comedy material. So, get out your paper and pen. It's time to hear what your critic has to say. For three to five minutes:

▶ Write down *everything* it says, just like a court reporter—evaluating nothing, record everything.

▶ Write your response. Dialog with the bully. To really distinguish between the two voices, try writing as the critic with your right hand and as yourself with your left hand.

▶ Reread what you wrote and ask yourself:
a. Does your critic's voice sound familiar? If so . . . who does it sound like? (my boss, a nun, my mother, my brother, etc.)
Write your answer here:

_____

_____

b. What kind of relationship do you have with your critic? (mother-son, father-daughter, tormentor-victim, teacher-student, etc.) Write down all your thoughts. Some will sound vague. That's okay.

_____

_____

_____

_____

c. Is your critic reasonable? Does it ever stop criticizing? How do you reason with it? How do you ever shut it up? (Include drinking or eating if that's part of your anesthesia.)

_____

_____

_____

_____

_____

The goal of this exercise was to release your demons and put *you* in charge of your creative process. Once we relax and stop battling ourselves, our inner critic can provide us with a wealth of comedy material. The next chapter will show you how to turn your critic's voice into comedy material.

Summary

Remember these rules and you will be off to a good start:

1. Be serious about what you say onstage.
   Make a commitment to your material.

2. Don't *try* to be funny.
   Expect nothing from the audience.

3. Don't tell jokes or stories.
   Be yourself.

4. Control your critic.
   When fearful, dialog with your critic.

5. Relax.
   Have fun.

Now let's move on to creating your killer act.

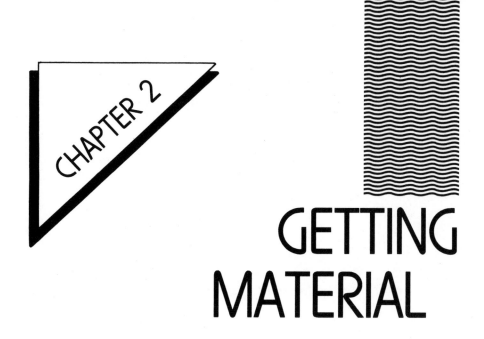

CHAPTER 2

GETTING MATERIAL

❝Can we talk . . .?" "Sure . . . but what about?❞

You've Got Tons of Material: Your Life

You don't have to look in the newspaper to find material. All the material you'll ever need is inside of you. It's just a matter of discovering it, punching it up, and delivering it. Even if you've never been onstage before, I'm sure you have done an act. Remember that party where you started trashing your ex-spouse, got on a roll, and had your friends rolling in the aisles? Or how about when you killed in your therapy session despairing over your weight, or cracked up your mailman complaining about your bills? All of that could be material for an act.

In this chapter we are going to gather your subject

matter, your raw material. In Chapter 3 we will make them into funny routines. So, how do you begin? The way to start developing material is to find

- ▶ —your attitude
- ▶ —your issues
- ▶ —and the connections between the two.

Finding Your Attitude

❝I don't get no respect . . .❞

—Rodney Dangerfield

When a singer sings, he acts out his feelings. Good comics don't simply tell jokes, they act them out with a very specific emotional attitude. Attitude is the heartbeat of an act. Material cannot be emotionally neutral. Your subject matter has to disgust you, pain you, thrill you, because audiences don't respond to words, they respond to feelings.

Every piece of material has a specific attitude, such as "I'm WORRIED about . . ." or "I LOVE . . ." or "I'm ANGRY about . . ." This Margaret Smith piece comes out of how she feels about her manager:

> **❝I** hate *my manager. He's always giving me advice like 'Wear red lipstick up there. Look pretty.' What if I'm not funny and it's coming out of these big old red lips? It's like being a crummy outfielder with a paisley mitt.❞*

Spacy student Valerie Webber worries about odd things:

> **❝I'm** worried *about lapels. They have a buttonhole, but no button. And what are those notches*

for? If you put them together, do they make a box? Who invented this, Jean-Paul Sartre? Lapels! Lapels! Lapels! Life is one big mystery."

And student Roseanne Katon *loves* being Black:

"**I love *being Black because it makes my white friends feel so liberal. I rent myself out every Martin Luther King Day as an audio-visual aid. It makes me feel special, like the last raisin in a bowl of oatmeal.***"

Attitude should not be confused with persona. Most comics have a different attitude for each piece of material, and during their act they will jump from something they're *angry* about to something they're *proud* of to something they're *worried* about.

A persona is when a comic has one specific emotional attitude for their entire act and all of the material hangs on that hook.

For example:

Rodney Dangerfield—"I don't get no respect . . ."

Jay Leno—"Here's something stupid . . ."

Richard Lewis—"I'm in pain . . ."

Every "joke" they tell illuminates their particular M.O. or point of view. You can always identify a successful comic's persona. That's the one thing that is never fuzzy.

Margaret Smith

19

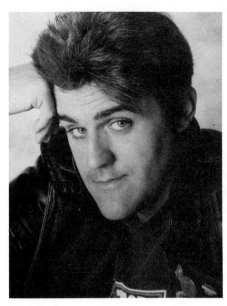
Jay Leno

❝I call my doctor up. Told him I had diarrhea. He put me on hold. Story of my life . . . no respect.❞

—Rodney Dangerfield

❝I saw a stupid ad for a new improved microwave oven that can cook a meal in ten seconds. Are there really people who say, 'Hey, I've been home for ten seconds, where the hell is dinner!?'❞

—Jay Leno

❝I'm in pain . . . I should produce a show at Radio City: Night of One Hundred Anxieties . . . My mother brought a Jewish satellite dish, it picks up problems from other people's families . . . For the holidays I bought her a Menorah on a dimmer and a self-complaining oven . . .❞

—Richard Lewis

Buying comedy material before you have a specific persona will be a waste of money. When comedy writers create material for other performers, they first must familiarize themselves with the comic's persona. Material that is perfect for Richard Lewis would most likely die in the hands of Jay Leno. People who steal material make the mistake of stealing the comic's lines without his persona. I was performing at a fund-raiser and this blond, blue-eyed teenager had memorized Bill Cosby's act verbatim. He totally bombed. Even though he delivered the material word for word, what was missing was Cosby's attitude: his childlike enthusiasm for the world he lives in. People who steal material are destined for doom. They are avoiding the real work of stand-up—digging deep into themselves and discovering their unique way of looking at the world.

Richard Lewis

Many students want to know right away what their overall attitude should be. Unfortunately, your overall attitude, your stage persona, is not something that you can consciously plan. Rather it is something that will evolve as you uncover your issues. So for now, don't worry about it.

In the next section you will begin the process of digging up a lot of topics and trying on different attitudes.

Here are some of my students' topics along with their corresponding attitudes:

TOPICS	ATTITUDE
Chain letters	LOVE
My podiatrist	LOVE
Barbara Bush	ADORE
Lint	WORRY ABOUT
Liver spots	WORRY ABOUT
Being a nerd	PROUD ABOUT
Free hot dogs	FRIGHTENED ABOUT
Fur bikinis	FRIGHTENED ABOUT
My mother's eczema	HATE

TOPICS	ATTITUDE
Mimes	HATE
People who unwrap hard candy in the theater	HATE

Picking Your Topics

Times have changed since Lenny Bruce. Nowadays, there's very little a comic *can't* talk about onstage. We all know what we can't talk about on TV. George Carlin did a routine about the seven dirty words. If you feel strongly about something and talk about it with commitment, you can blab about anything. Don't check out to see if another comic is talking about it. Go ahead. If you feel uneasy about certain topics, avoid them. It all has to do with you feeling comfortable and committing to your topic. Here are some guidelines.

Topics That Will Make People Throw Things at You

1. *Racist jokes.* Don't put down Blacks, Jews, Hispanics, Orientals, and so on unless you happen to be Black, Jewish, Hispanic, Oriental, etc. The world doesn't need any more racism and you don't need your nose broken. This also includes putting down men if you're a woman and vice versa. Instead of "Women are all ball busters," try "I'm frightened of strong women ..." Expressing your inner fears rather than complaining about others makes better material and makes you more likable.

2. *Diseases.* Don't use cancer, AIDS, or any other terminal disease as a topic unless you want a depressed, teary-eyed audience.

3. *Gross images.* Avoid creating graphic imagery such as anything dripping out of bodily holes. The audience might be eating.

4. *Dirty words.* It depends on why you're using them. Comics such as Kinison, Pryor, and Carlin use them to good effect, but more often lazy comics use dirty words because they can't figure out how to make something funny and they think that expletives will help. In many cases unskilled comics will use expletives as a way to camouflage their lack of real passion.

A dirty act won't help you get work. Comedy club owners, such as Jan Smith of L.A.'s Igby's Comedy Club, are reluctant to hire a "blue act," especially as an opener, because it sets the tone for the show and makes it difficult for others to follow if they're not in the same blue vein. Instead of literal off-color terms, I encourage my students to come up with euphemisms.

Comic Jordan Brady has a chunk of material in which he substitutes a sound effect for the word "fuck."

> **❝The only thing I like about porno movies is the early seventies jazz theme music (SAID IN JAZZ RHYTHM): 'bau chick a boom bau.' When you heard that music, you knew what was going to happen. The housewife is all alone, the gardener comes in for a drink of water, and . . . 'bau chick a boom bau.' He could have drank from a hose, but he wanted some: 'bau chick a boom bau.'❞**

This joke was used on the CBS morning show as an example of how Jordan works clean.

Dirty words can become crutches for the lazy and desperate comic. But if that's your style and you don't want to get on TV, what the fuck, use them.

Who Are You?

The way to put together an act is to discover what you feel strongly about in:

▶ Your *outer* self (physical appearance)
▶ Your *inner* self (personal issues, i.e., childhood, parents, school, relationships)
▶ The world you live in (social commentary, politics, etc.)

The following workshops deal with identifying your outer- and inner-self issues. (Social commentary and political humor is much more difficult and will be dealt with in Chapter 4.) I will be asking you some very personal questions. It is essential that you tell the truth. Material based in truth helps establish a personal relationship with an audience. Later, in Chapter 3, you will learn how to exaggerate the truth to make it funny, but right now, be *honest* and *believable*. The "funny" will come later.

I am also going to ask you for a lot of information. Fill in as many items as you can because developing material is like breeding Siamese fighting fish. They need to lay two thousand eggs because only ten baby fish will survive. Don't try to be funny right now. Don't judge yourself, just follow the instructions.

Negative Personality Traits

Is there something about your personality that you are embarrassed about? Do you have a psychological trait, or a character defect, or just some weakness that you try to cover up? Something that you would be ashamed to reveal on a first date? Are you a compulsive eater? A loser? Egotistical?

24

Seemingly negative traits are breeding grounds for good material. Jack Benny built his entire act on being *cheap*. Many male comics talk about being *losers with women*.

> **❝I have low self-esteem. When we were in bed together, I would fantasize that I was someone else.❞**

> —Richard Lewis

Everyone has traits that are not socially acceptable. The more embarrassing it is, the better comedy it makes. People come to a club and pay a two-drink minimum to hear things they just think about. What is appropriate behavior in real life is perfectly okay for the stage.

> **❝I thought I had PMS—premenstrual syndrome. But my doctor said, 'I got good news and I got bad news. The good news is you don't have premenstrual syndrome. The bad news is you're a bitch.'❞**

> —Rhonda Bates

Keep in mind that your negative traits need to be believable. An audience will not buy a gorgeous hunk of a man talking about how unsuccessful he is with girls. Nor will they buy a thin woman talking about how fat she is, unless she is speaking about it with sarcasm. Even if you perceive yourself as fat, or ugly, unless others do, you will confuse the audience. You need to establish credibility with an audience. You need to be authentic and convincing. Tell the truth.

> **❝I had to move to New York for health reasons. I'm extremely paranoid and New York is the only place my fears are justified.❞**

> —Anita Wise

Remember . . . you don't need to make things up, because truth is entertaining enough.

Workshop #3

〜〜〜〜〜〜〜〜〜〜〜〜〜〜〜〜〜〜〜〜〜〜〜〜〜〜〜〜〜〜

NEGATIVE PERSONALITY TRAITS

'Fess Up Time

Write down negative personality traits. The more negative, the better. Keep in mind that you are writing down *psychological* traits. Keep away from writing down *physical* traits, such as nail biter, thin, dandruff, and so on.

Here are some examples from my students: compulsive eater, bitch, nerd, compulsive talker, neurotic, loser, alcoholic, liar, slut, wimp, confused, self-absorbed asshole.

1. _____

2. _____

3. _____

4. _____

5. _____

Is there something about you that makes you unique? Do you have an unusual occupation? Student Belinda Ware's act was based on her strange job.

> **❝I'm a gravedigger at Forest Lawn. It's not so bad. My customers don't talk back.❞**

Student Joan Gibson was a truck driver:

> **❝Some people don't think women can be truck drivers. Hey, I can downshift, hold my water for three hundred miles, and grow hemorrhoids just as big as the next guy!❞**

Do you have a curious religion?

> **❝Telling your parents you want to be a comedian is rough, especially when they're Mormons. I remember sitting them down and saying, 'Now look, Mom, Dad, Mom, Mom, Mom . . .'❞**
>
> **—Dave Markwell**

Do you have a handicap? Hearing-impaired Katherine Buckley got into the semifinals of a comedy contest her first time on stage, partly because her material dealt honestly and openly with her disability, while putting a twist on a traditional comedy topic, dating:

> **❝I haven't had a date in two and a half years, but maybe that's because I haven't heard the phone ring.❞**

27

Or is there something unique about your family? Student Linda Adelman based her act on a very chancy topic, that her parents are Holocaust survivors:

66. . . so I wanted to please them, but no matter how hard I cleaned my house, when they came to visit the first words out of my father's mouth were 'I smell gas!'99

Comic Blake Clark bases his act on being a Vietnam vet:

66I'm writing a book about my experiences during the Vietnam War to be called, A Guide to the Bars and Taverns of Montreal.99

Do you have a *unique characteristic*? If so, write it down here:

_____

_____

_____

If you don't have any unique character traits, don't worry, just move on to Workshop #5.

Workshop #5

OUTER SELF

A great way to open an act is by making fun of the most obvious—what you look like. Are you thin, fat, ethnic, and so on? It can be something as simple as your hair. One of my students had an abundance of hair. She came out onstage, took a moment, and then said with a straight face,

❝I hate my hair.❞

It brought the house down. No joke, no punch, just the point-blank simple truth delivered with a strong honest attitude of "I hate . . ."

Another student was very wimpy-looking. His first words onstage were,

❝Okay, I'm a nerd . . .❞

Then he went on to talk about how proud he was to be one.

❝. . . who else would take you to the airport at one in the morning!❞

His attitude was "I'm proud . . ."

Another student was very, very tough-looking. She was a 200-pound security guard with a fresh knife wound down her face. Her first lines after staring at the audience for a full minute were

❝Okay, so I'm not a fuckin' debutante.❞

Her attitude was "I'm angry . . ."

Other outer-self items from my students have included: "I'm Japanese . . ."; "Large shoulders . . ." (a student wearing large shoulder pads); "I'm butch . . ." (a masculine-looking girl); "I'm Black . . ."; "I'm middle-aged . . ."; "I'm handicapped . . ."; and "I'm tall . . ."

Now it's your turn. What is the first thing that someone notices about you? Is there something about you that stands out *visually*? If you don't know, then ask a friend. Ask your comedy buddy, friends, or strangers on the street. Strangers are the best source of information, because that is what an audience is—a group of strangers. Whatever it is, it just *has* to be true and *obvious*.

Here are some more examples from my students: fat, thin, big hair, big head, big nose, sexy, gorgeous, poor dresser, Black, Caucasian, Latino, etc.

Write your response here:

1. _____

2. _____

These outer-self traits are not funny right now, but they will be the springboard for material in Chapter 3.

If this outer-self workshop hasn't harvested any material, not to worry. Many of my students don't have outstanding physical traits to joke about either.

A Day in the Life of Your Inner Self

What personal issues are you struggling with right now? What do you hate? What worries you? What frightens you?

As you go through the day, observe what thoughts seem to flash repeatedly through your mind. Notice what your mind seems to dwell on. What relationships are you thinking about? Mother? Father? Accountant? Dog? What bothers you? Visceral issues for my students run all the way from nuclear war to hickeys. Carry around a small notebook. Don't censor or judge what you are thinking, just notice it and write it down.

A terrific time to do this writing activity is when you first wake up. I find that my writing is not as restrained if I do it first thing in the morning. And I mean *first thing*, before you get out of bed, before you have coffee. Put this book and a pen right next to your bed. If you can't function at all before you drink coffee, then make some the night before and put it in a Thermos by the bed. When you do this exercise you might be astonished at what comes out of you:

"I hate fuzz on record needles, parking tickets, the circus . . ."

"I'm frightened about Q-tips, airplanes, the dark, dying . . ."

"I worry about food with eyes, getting old, my face shrinking . . ."

Workshop #6

Make a list of things you hate. Things that disgust you. Pick topics that are the most personal. A *father* is better than an *uncle*. Topics that have been a breeding ground for good jokes have been: plastic surgery, blind dates, men who spit, hair growing in unusual places, bimbos, proctologists, the way my father eats, my mother's psoriasis . . .

Carry this list with you throughout the day and jot down at least ten things you hate. Don't cross out anything. Be brutal, irreverent, and as *specific* as possible. Hating "the way your mother gets out of bed" is better than hating your mother. Hating brussels sprouts is better than hating vegetables. Don't fill in the list all in one setting. Be genuine and have patience while you gather the seeds of your act.

1. *I hate*_____.

2. *I hate*_____.

3. *I hate*_____.

4. *I hate*_____.

5. *I hate*_____.

6. *I hate*_____.

7. *I hate*_____.

8. *I hate*_____.

9. *I hate*_____.

10. *I hate*_____.

Workshop #7

Once again, be as specific as possible. Worrying about liver spots is better than worrying about aging in general. Write down all those oddball things that worry you:

1. *I worry about*_____.

2. *I worry about*_____.

3. *I worry about*_____.

4. *I worry about*_____.

5. *I worry about*_____.

6. *I worry about*_____.

7. *I worry about*_____.

8. *I worry about*_____.

9. *I worry about*_____.

10. *I worry about*_____.

Workshop #8

Write down all those things that frighten you. Remember that these need to be items that truly do frighten you. Keep away from typical items, such as nuclear war, and find those little unusual items such as potato bugs, fur bikinis, chain letters, car mechanics, dying in an airplane . . .

 1. *I'm frightened about* _____.

 2. *I'm frightened about* _____.

 3. *I'm frightened about* _____.

 4. *I'm frightened about* _____.

 5. *I'm frightened about* _____.

 6. *I'm frightened about* _____.

 7. *I'm frightened about* _____.

 8. *I'm frightened about* _____.

 9. *I'm frightened about* _____.

10. *I'm frightened about* _____.

Workshop #9

Adding Attitude

Before you arrange your items into stand-up material, you need to get the feel for talking about your topic with a specific attitude.

So far you have several lists:

- Negative personality traits
- Unique characteristics
- Noticeable physical attributes
- Things you hate
- Things that worry you
- Things that frighten you

As I said before, all topics must be acted out with a specific attitude. To get the feel of this, write all of your material on little pieces of paper and put them in a bag. Get a portable tape recorder or a pen and paper. Find a private place where you can walk and talk to yourself or write without feeling uncomfortable. Pull out a topic from your grab bag of issues and start talking as fast as you can into your tape recorder or writing quickly, allowing yourself to really feel angry, worried, frightened, or proud. Exaggerate your feelings.

Are you angry about your *love life*? Go rant and rave into your tape recorder or write down all the stuff about your love life that angers you and why. Ask yourself, "Why does this anger me and what are some funny solutions?" Keep it loose. For instance:

❝I'm angry that I'm single. Why do all the princes I date end up being frogs? I'm angry that women

34

at thirty start thinking about having children and men at thirty start thinking about dating children. I'm angry at Florence Henderson. I don't know why I lie awake nights thinking about her, maybe because she is so normal. I'm angry that I'm not normal. That instead of having my two children and one husband, I have two cats and one dog. Is there something wrong with a woman who prefers the company of her dog to going on a date with a man? I don't know . . . maybe I'm bi-species. There should be a book called Women Who Love Dogs Too Much . . .**

Allow yourself to really act out your attitude. Get into it. Get intense. Get passionate. Don't try to be funny. Rant and rave about anything that comes to your mind about that topic. Don't think too much. When you run out of things to say, keep going by repeating, "I hate (your topic)" over and over. The good stuff usually happens when you run out of things to say. If you are *worried* about something, let it all hang out:

I'm worried about being thirtysomething . . . I'm just worried about getting old. Although I never thought I'd have to worry about being old because my name is Judy and I've never met an old person named Judy. Now that's true. Maybe something happens to girls with young names like Debby, Judy, and Susie. At a certain age they make you change it to Doris, Edna, or Myrtle. I'm worried. When does it happen? When is the day I'm old? I'm worried that one day I'm going to wake up and no matter how warm it is . . . I'll want to wear a coat. I'm worried that I'll get old and start putting jars of hard candy around the house. I'm worried that I'll have an uncontrollable desire to own a black vinyl handbag. I'm worried that one day I'll get into my car and the steering wheel will be too high. I'm worried ... etc.

For now, don't worry about how long or how funny your material is or isn't. Ranting and raving is a technique to get your raw material out of you and down on paper. Once that material is out, it can be sorted through and developed into stand-up using the formulas in the next chapter.

Contrasting Attitudes

An effective way to create material is to use an opposite attitude for your issue and talk about it with "mocking insincerity." There is nothing funny about "I'm a wild and crazy guy!" But when Steve Martin delivers those words with a strong attitude, he brings the house down. His attitude is that he's proud of being "wild and crazy!" And he delivers that information with exaggerated commitment.

David Letterman has made a career out of this technique of sarcastic mocking insincerity:

Oh, yes, we have such a big show tonight, an exciting show, you can just feel that something extra special is going to happen tonight.

In my classes, when students get stuck, I suggest that they tag on an unlikely attitude to their issue and talk about it using this technique of mocking insincerity. For instance, one student had being single on her "hate list." When she ranted and raved about how much she hated being single, it sounded as if she were whining and complaining. The material became more successful when she changed the attitude of hate to love and delivered it with this technique of mocking insincerity:

36

66Oh, I just love being single . . . I love it, love it, love it! It's just so much fun putting on a bracelet by yourself. And I have fascinating hobbies, like macrame and making a quilt out of used pot holders.99

Workshop #10

To get the feel of this attitude of mocking insincerity, try on the attitude of "love" to an item on your hate list. Rant and rave about how much you "love" the item in a tone of sarcastic mocking insincerity. Try talking about it the way you would imagine David Letterman would.

Another way to create contrasting or atypical attitudes is to add the attitude of "I'm proud" to items on your Negative Personality Traits list. Most people are *ashamed* of being a loser, but when you put on the atypical attitude of "I'm proud I'm a loser," you open up the comedy potential.

> **❝I'm proud I'm a loser ... it's something I'm good at. Hey, at least I'm dependable. If you need someone to fail, you can count on me.❞**

Here handicapped comic Gene Mitchener turns around a difficult topic:

> **❝I'm proud to be handicapped. If it weren't for me you'd be spending all day looking for a place to park.❞**

To practice this technique of having a contrasting attitude, add the attitude of "I'm proud" to your negative personality traits and/or to your unique characteristics. For instance:

I'm *Proud* of ___being a loner___

BECAUSE: ___I save on phone calls___

_____

_____

I'm *Proud* of ___being self-obsessed___
BECAUSE: ___I don't have to feign___
___interest in anybody else.___

I'm *Proud* of ___being screwed up___
BECAUSE: ___I get a scholarship to___
___therapy.___

I'm *Proud* of ___being a procrastinator___
BECAUSE: ___it saves me from being___
___a workaholic.___

Now you do it.

Take from the lists you made in Workshops #3 and 4 and insert the interesting responses here. Use both your negative personality traits, and your unique characteristics. Remember, no one else is going to see what you write and there are no right or wrong answers.

1. I'm proud of _____

BECAUSE: _____

_____

_____

2. I'm proud of _____

BECAUSE: _____

_____

_____

3. I'm proud of _____

BECAUSE: _____

_____

_____

4. I'm proud of _____

BECAUSE: _____

_____

_____

5. I'm proud of _____

BECAUSE: _____

_____

_____

Now try the ranting and raving exercise using the attitude of "I'm proud" with your topics. Imagine that you are talking to someone. Practice talking about your subject matter as if you are defending yourself to that person. You don't have to use the words "I'm proud." You can simply feel it. For instance, "I'm proud to be a nerd!" becomes "Okay, I'm a nerd . . ." And then defend yourself by going on to point out the advantages of being a nerd as did my student Steve Guentner:

> **❝I'm not ashamed. Nerds have a lot of good qualities. We are good for the economy. Who else buys all of those calculators, those white socks, glasses, shirt pocket protectors, plaid shirts, slide rules, computers, Star Trek videos, sci-fi books, and pays their parking tickets on time? Nerds! Nerds perform valuable services. Who runs for president? Nerds! Who will give you a ride to the airport at three in the morning? Nerds!❞**

Mix and Match

Try your hand at mixing and matching more of your issues to unusual attitudes. If you are a guy, *"adoring fat women"* is much more interesting and likable than *"hating fat girls."* If you're a gal, and an issue on your outer self is your *thighs*, for instance, try an unlikely attitude of, *love.*

❝I love my fat thighs. They keep me warm in the winter and if ever I get stranded in the Arctic Circle, they can keep many people warm. I love them. Men love women with fat thighs. Yes, they do. It gives them something to hold on to . . .❞

Very often my students will have typical responses on their hate list, such as "I hate standing in lines" or "I hate getting tickets." So what else is new? That will probably lead to a comedy dead end. But now switch it around so "I *love* getting tickets" and watch the comedy potential open up:

❝I love getting tickets. I guess I just like getting attention from men with guns. It makes me feel noticed. I spend all day getting dolled up and then go out and speed. And you know that rush you get when you see that red light in your rearview mirror? My heart goes into my throat and I throttle it. It's better than sex . . .❞

For practice, try your hand at ranting and raving about the following topics with these atypical attitudes:

1. "I *hate* sex."

2. "I'm *frightened* of paper clips."

3. "I *worry* about futons."

Now try yapping into your tape recorder using atypical attitudes with *your* topics. If *hating frozen vegetables* doesn't work for you, then try out another attitude. Try "I'm frightened about frozen vegetables," or "I'm worried, I'm frightened . . ." Get into the feeling. Keep talking. If nothing comes out, keep repeating your attitude. "I'm angry . . . I'm angry . . ." Get caught up in the passion of the moment. If you find yourself talking about something totally different from what you intended, that's okay. Let your spirit guide you. Flow with it. Don't try to be funny. Just be real and keep going. Really commit to the attitude and the words will come. If they don't, go on to another topic.

If you are having a problem getting this raw material up and out, don't worry. Writer's block happens to the best of us. Writer's block is the unwillingness of the unconscious to become conscious. I have learned to accept that there are just some times when it is impossible for me to create. The good news is that these periods always end. So don't push yourself. Be gentle. Writing stand-up is a process where you take one step at a time.

Chances are, amid your babblings there is some funny stuff.

1. Listen repeatedly to your audio tape and note which pieces sound as if they might be funny. Or maybe something you said will give you an idea for a totally different piece. Remember, don't tell stories. Each piece must consist of an attitude attached to a topic.

2. Work with a comedy buddy. Creating a support system while going through this workbook is highly recommended. In my classes it is mandatory for my students to work ten minutes each morning on their acts by themselves and to get together at least once a week with a comedy buddy. Having someone to react to your material will help you learn what is funny and will encourage you to develop more material. Additionally, just having someone to look at while you deliver your material is a crucial step toward talking in front of an audience.

3. Try out your material on office workers, friends, or on your mailman. Warning: Never let people know they are being used as comedy guinea pigs. Never preface it with "Do you think this is funny?" because they won't. Sneak your material into the conversation. The best possible place is at a party or a bar where people don't know you.
    Student Jennifer Heath tried out material at the Laundromat:

> **❝I worry about lint. Where does it come from? I wash my clothes over and over again and there is always lint, but my clothes don't get any smaller.**

43

***And why is it whatever color the clothes you wash,
the lint is always gray?***"

4. If someone laughs, jot down verbatim what you said so you'll remember it exactly the way it got the laugh. And congratulations. You've got the first piece of your act.

5. If no one laughs at anything, keep trying different material or get different friends. Whatever you do, don't give up.

Remember that when audiences see a comic do five minutes on Johnny Carson, what they don't see is all the material the comic had to throw out. Sometimes there might be one tiny shred of an idea in some of your rantings and ravings that you can use elsewhere. Comic Jerry Seinfeld says that a lot of his material comes to him out of routines that went in the toilet. It takes about one hour of babbling for every three minutes of material—if you're lucky.

Summary

By this point you have:

▶ Made lists of topics.
▶ Developed attitudes for your topics.
▶ Developed contrasting attitudes to your topics.
▶ Taped ranting and ravings.
▶ Worked with a comedy buddy.
▶ Tried material out on friends or strangers.
▶ Written down material that people laughed at.

Hold on to all your written and recorded material. In the next chapter you will learn comedy formulas for transforming this raw material into killer comedy routines.

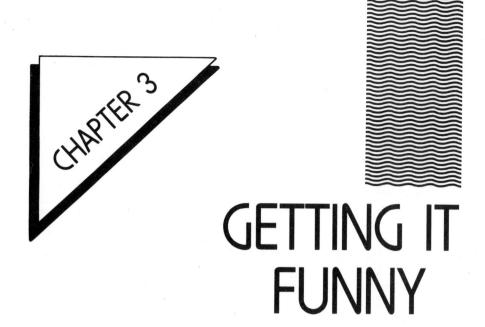

CHAPTER 3

GETTING IT FUNNY

The Formulas

So far you've taped some rantings and ravings and tried out some material. Most likely, some of your material got a laugh and some of your material was met with stone cold silence. You've also probably found that material that got a laugh when first tried didn't get a laugh when tried again. Do not fret. In this chapter you are going to shape and craft those rantings and ravings into professional comedy material using specific stand-up formulas.

You may be muttering under your breath. "Why didn't she give me these formulas right at the start and be done with it?" Good question.

I have found that material based only on formulas sounds contrived, without soul, and is not very funny. It lacks passion. And passion must come first. Passion provides the locomotion, the inspiration to carry you through an act.

45

Passion reveals your essence—it tells who you really are. But passion and talent are not enough. You must be able to make your ideas understandable and get them across to an audience.

Keeping this in mind, you are now ready to learn the formulas that will help you shape and structure ideas so audiences will understand exactly what you're trying to communicate.

I can't tell you for sure what an audience will laugh at, but I can say with certainty that an audience will not laugh at something they don't understand. Remember, most people sitting in a nightclub are drinking. While you're onstage with material that makes perfect sense to you, your mother, and your grocer, the question becomes: Is it clear to some horny guy, with two margaritas under his belt, whose only concern is getting laid?

Setup/Punch

All stand-up material must be organized into the setup/punch format. If your material isn't organized like this, you're not doing a stand-up. You might be telling a funny story, giving a poetry reading, delivering a speech, but it's not stand-up. Stand-up comedy is a very specific form of entertainment, consisting of a collection of setups and punches.

The "punch" is where the audience laughs. The "setup" is the one or so lines leading to the punch.

SETUP:
66*My mother is a typical Jewish mother. She was once on jury duty. They sent her home . . .*99

PUNCH:
66*She insisted* she *was guilty.*99

—Cathy Ladman

46

The setup is the unfunny part of a joke. It is the informative part of the joke that introduces the subject matter.

> **SETUP: (INFORMATION)**
> **"At my gym they have free weights . . ."**
>
> **PUNCH: (ECCENTRIC REACTION)**
> **"So I took them home."**

—Steve Smith

The setup creates anticipation. A punch delivers the laugh.

> **SETUP:**
> **"I'm into Jewish bondage . . ."**
>
> **PUNCH:**
> **". . . that's having your money tied up in an IRA account."**

—Noodles Levenstein

Even within a one-liner there is a setup and a punch.

> **SETUP:**
> **"I used to be a virgin, but I gave it up . . ."**
>
> **PUNCH:**
> **". . . there was no money in it."**

—Marsha Warfield

> **SETUP:**
> **"If blind people wear sunglasses . . ."**
>
> **PUNCH:**
> **". . . why don't deaf people wear earmuffs?"**

—Spanky

SETUP:
❝I'm a great lover . . .❞

PUNCH:
❝. . . I bet.❞

—Emo Philips

A good setup seduces the audience into listening to you. A good punch forces them to react. Here Rita Rudner sets up the punch by asking the audience a question, drawing them in:

SETUP: (QUESTION)
❝Why are women wearing perfumes that smell like flowers?❞

Then the punch is her offbeat reaction to the setup:

❝Men don't like flowers. I've been wearing a great scent. It's called 'New Car Interior.' ❞

Emo Philips gets the audience's attention by using a setup that shocks:

SETUP:
❝Probably the toughest time in anyone's life is when you have to murder a loved one because they're the devil . . . ❞

PUNCH:
❝. . . Other than that, it's been a good day.❞

Rita Rudner

48

And most important, the punch contrasts the setup with the unexpected.

SETUP:
❝I'm a quadrasexual.❞

PUNCH:
❝That means I'll do anything with anyone for a quarter.❞

—**Ed Bluestone**

Emo Philips

A punch without a setup is like sex without foreplay. Imagine wanting to kiss someone. An amateur lover rushes in without preparing the "kissee" for what's coming. A more confident lover "sets up" the situation by first, perhaps, touching the neck. Then taking off their glasses. Slowly moving toward the intended and then . . . the kiss.

You might have noticed that the above jokes do not contain specific attitudes such as *"I hate"* or *"I'm proud"* and so on. When refining material into the setup/punch format, most professional comics will act out the attitude rather than explicitly saying it. For instance, Rudner's attitude on the above piece could be *"I hate* women who wear perfumes that smell like flowers." The attitude of Bluestone's joke might be, *"I'm proud* of being a quadrasexual." The attitude is then communicated in the way the comic expresses the material.

Workshop #14

Tape a comic off the TV. Type out and analyze two minutes of his or her material. Answer the following questions:

1. What are the punchlines?

2. What are the setups?

3. Count the punchlines.

4. On the average, how many lines did it take to set up each punch?

5. Could you identify the comic's attitude on each setup?

Finding Your Punchlines

The first step in organizing your act is to identify what your laugh lines are—your punches. Scary, huh? Many students get discouraged here because they don't think they've said anything funny.

I repeat: You are not trying to be "funny." You have rantings and ravings about issues that you feel passionately about. To Woody Allen, there is nothing funny about his fear of dying.

> **❝I don't mind death, I just don't want to be there when it happens.❞**

To my student Nancy Wilson, there was nothing funny about her bouts with alcoholism.

50

SETUP: (INFORMATION)
I would drink because I wasn't married . . .

PUNCH: (EXAGGERATION)
. . . and then I would drink because I was married.

SETUP: (INFORMATION)
Then I would drink because I couldn't find my kids . . .

PUNCH: (EXAGGERATION)
. . . and then I would drink because I found them.

SETUP: (INFORMATION)
When I quit drinking I realized that I had identical twins. I didn't even know that . . .

PUNCH: (EXAGGERATION)
I thought that I was seeing double the whole time.

It is funny to watch someone so involved with her struggles and her issues. At this point, you are not necessarily capable of analyzing your material. In order to discover your punchlines, you need to be willing to try out your material on others. Remember, don't let them know you are trying out material. Just start talking to your hairdresser:

SETUP: (INFORMATION)
I just hate my hair. I was out with my boyfriend looking like some pre-Raphaelite dream . . .

PUNCH: (EXAGGERATION)
. . . I woke up the next morning looking like Don King.

—Student Mary Edith Burrell

51

Or to your pharmacist:

SETUP: (INFORMATION)
"I hate flavored douches . . ."

PUNCH: (EXAGGERATED REACTION)
"If I was meant to smell like a strawberry, I would have been born in a basket with a green thing growing out of my head."

—Student Jennifer Heath

Keep a tape recorder in your pocket and take it everywhere. And I do mean *everywhere*. Even in the middle of making love, comics have been known to say *"Wait a minute, I've got to get that down."*

Listen to your tape. Where anyone laughed, that's your punchline. You may have lost a lover, but you've got a piece of material.

Remember: Stand-up takes guts.

Workshop #15

PUNCHLINES

Listen to your tape and type out, double spaced, at least three pages of your rantings and ravings. Underline all the punchlines, the places where you expect that people will laugh. Then, read on . . .

Crafting Your Act into Setup/Punch Format

❝I didn't realize this was going to be such hard work. I thought comedy was supposed to be fun.❞

This is the stage in my class where students want to drop out.

Too bad comedy writing isn't the free-for-all it appeared to be on the old *Dick Van Dyke* TV show. Sally, Rob, and Buddy gave the impression that comedy writers goof around laughing at each other with pearls of wit rolling off their tongues. Anyone who has ever been around real comedy writers knows that sometimes searching for the right setup about underwear takes on the intensity and seriousness of strategic arms negotiations. Some material will pop out fully formed like a colt, and some will be like an epic poem or a sculpture that you just keep tinkering away with for weeks, months, or even years.

I do promise you that once you master the techniques in this chapter, the fun does come. The fun comes when you perform material that is so well thought out that the audience is in the palm of your hand. So hang in here and let's work on your act.

Setups

The most common problem of my students' beginning material is that they have long setups. The best setup is a short setup. My scientific survey reveals that the attention span of a drinking audience is one to four lines. The faster you can get to the punch, the stronger your act. This does not mean that you talk about each topic for only five lines. You can do thirty minutes on your dog as long as your routine is organized into a collection of short setup/punches.

Here is an example of student Harry Redlich's too-long setup:

❝I just don't understand this obsession with celebrity legends of the fifties and sixties. Like Elvis, people are upset that he died. Or Janis Joplin died so young. I know it's tragic, but I think a lot of these legends are better off having died young, because . . .❞

PUNCH:
❝. . . I personally would not like to see Janis Joplin as the celebrity contestant on Super Password.❞

Redlich starts out with a false setup since the punch has nothing to do with Elvis or celebrity obsession. In order to set up a punch, I encourage my students to really look at what they are trying to say and what point they want to make. Redlich is actually trying to communicate the way Hollywood desecrates its legends. Examine how the setup now becomes the "general theme" and the punch becomes the "specific example."

SETUP: (REVISED)
❝Nowadays it's hard staying a superstar. I'm glad a lot of legends died young . . .❞

PUNCH:
❝I mean, do you really want to see Janis Joplin on Super Password?❞

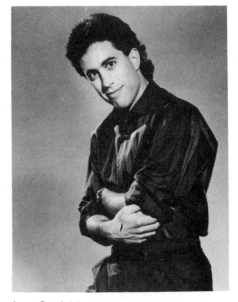

Jerry Seinfeld

You can have more than one punch. A lot of times a comic will have one setup and then three punches. Jerry Seinfeld is a master of this. He does a setup and then a punch and you laugh. He does another punch and

54

you laugh, and just when you think that there is nothing more to say, he adds another punch. (Take note of the escalating absurdity of Seinfeld's punchlines.)

> **SETUP: (REALISTIC INFORMATION)**
> **"I'm from Long Island. My parents just moved to Florida this past year."**
>
> **PUNCH: (FABRICATION)**
> **"They didn't want to move to Florida, but they're in their sixties, and that's the law."**
>
> **PUNCH: (MORE ABSURDITY)**
> **"There's leisure police that come and get you when you turn sixty."**
>
> **PUNCH: (EVEN MORE PREPOSTEROUS)**
> **"They have golf carts with sirens, 'Okay, Pop, get the clubs right in the back. Drop the snow shovel right there, drop it!'"**

The best setup is also one that tells the truth. Take a look at this student's joke:

> **SETUP: (UNTRUE INFORMATION)**
> **"I just lost 107 pounds. How did I do it?"**
>
> **PUNCH:**
> **". . . I just woke up one day and tossed my girlfriend out."**

This student then went on to a piece about being a male model. Even though he told us "No, *this* is true!" once we realized that we were conned by his first joke, that in fact he didn't really lose any weight, we no longer were willing to go along with him on his next joke. Sure, you may get a laugh with a joke like this, but you've also lost your credibility. Now, no matter how hard you try, the audience is going to be thinking that all of your setups are bogus. Establish your credibility by having truthful, honest, uncomplicated setups. Then get wild on the punches.

Workshop #16

CONDENSING YOUR SETUPS

Remember, every setup leads to a punch. If something is not a punch, then it has to be part of the setup. If it isn't, then cut it. Stand-up is similar to haiku poetry—there are no extra words. Every syllable is weighed, judged, and has to be exactly right. Look at student Eric Dickey's revised piece:

> ~~I love women. I especially like women who are really in shape. I joined an aerobics class and met this great-looking woman there. But~~ "Women *are* dangerous. I'm dating this aerobics instructor and these aerobics instructors, they look good. They're really in shape. We got into a fight and then this aerobics mama kicked my butt. But that's okay. I learned how to defend myself . . ."

> **PUNCH:**
> ". . . I turned off the music."

Remember that setups need to be true. Sometimes just switching around a few words will give a setup authenticity, just as with student George Chase's piece:

> **SETUP: (INAUTHENTIC)**
> "I hate road signs. They are everywhere telling me what to do: 'stop,' 'yield,' 'merge.' My mother recently took a job at the highway department and I think that she went a little crazy with it . . ."

> **PUNCH:**
> "'Call your sister,' 'change your underwear,' 'get married.'"

56

This is a good premise, but the setup has an untruth in it. His mother doesn't work for the highway department. This can be easily rectified by changing "My mother recently took a job at the highway department" to "I think, *what if* my mother got a job at the highway department . . ."

Now you try it. You have typed out three pages of material and have underlined the punchlines. Look over your material and:

▶ Delete all redundant words or ideas.
▶ Condense the setup for each piece.
▶ Rewrite each setup to be informational and true.

Contrasting the Setup with the Punch

A powerful way to create stand-up material is to have the setup contrast the punch. The setup guides the audience down a straight road, and the punch is a sharp left turn when they least expect it.

For example:

There you are with someone you want to kiss and you are confidently "setting up" the kiss, slowly moving toward him or her and then you . . . sneeze. You won't get laid, but you will get a laugh—and to most comics, that's better. A good setup manipulates the audience to anticipate one thing and then presents the unexpected. Humor is created by going against what is expected.

One way to contrast the setup with the punch is to have a sharply different attitude on the punch. Take a look at a very simple typical MC joke:

SETUP: (FRIENDLY)
❝You look like a great crowd tonight . . .❞

PUNCH: (HOSTILE)
❝. . . except for you.❞

The setup is delivered simply and honestly with the attitude of "I love being here . . ." implied. Then the punch contrasts the setup with the attitude of hostility, such as in Bob Saget's opener:

SETUP: (FRIENDLY/MOCKING INSINCERITY)
You're a great crowd. I love you.

PUNCH: (HOSTILE)
. . . I just want to take a Jacuzzi with you and throw in a toaster.

Here Jay Leno delivers the setup with a neutral, informational attitude, then says the punch with sarcasm:

SETUP: (INFORMATION)
In McDonald's they had some promotional giveaway and their sign reads, 'Offer available to McDonald's customers only.'

PUNCH: (SARCASTIC)
Now there's an exclusive group.

Think of the setup as being the logical, informational part of the joke and the punch as an unexpected twist or an extreme exaggeration. Look at this almost joke:

SETUP: (INFORMATION)
My boyfriend is such an egomaniac . . .

PUNCH: (INFORMATION)
He likes himself more than he likes me!

This is not very funny because the punch is the expected conclusion of this setup. But exaggerating the boyfriend's behavior makes the material funny.

PUNCH: (REVISED PUNCH)
How many men do you know shout out their own name when they make love?

Here Ellen DeGeneres sets up this joke talking about "deer heads":

SETUP: **(REALISTIC INFORMATION)**
❝You ask people why they have deer heads on the wall. They always say, 'Because it's such a beautiful animal.'❞

Then in the punch she SWITCHES to her "mother":

❝. . . I think my mother's attractive, but I have photographs of her.❞

SETUP: **(INFORMATION)**
❝My girlfriend thinks she's impressing me because she lifts weights . . .❞

PUNCH: **(SWITCH)**
❝. . . I tell her, 'if you want to impress me, pick up this check.'❞

—**Student Eric Dickey**

Here Eric contrasts a heavy object with a light object and at the same time expresses his point of view.

Here is an example of a joke where the setup provides sane, rational information and the punch contrasts it by being preposterous.

SETUP: **(REALISTIC)**
❝I went to a conference for bulimics and anorexics. It was a nightmare . . .❞

PUNCH: **(PREPOSTEROUS)**
❝. . . The bulimics ate the anorexics.❞

—**Monica Piper**

In all of the above jokes, the setups are sane, informational, and plausible. Audiences are hooked emotionally by the information presented in the setup.

SETUP: (SANE)
"I played with my grandfather a lot when I was a kid . . ."

We all have played with our grandfathers or know others who have. Once you've established a mutual reality between you and the audience, then you can get wild on the punch.

PUNCH: (INSANE)
". . . He was dead, but my parents had him cremated and put his ashes in my Etch-a-Sketch."

—**Alan Harvey**

Don't forget about attitude. Remember, each setup must contain an attitude. You can have many different attitudes in an act, but each setup/punch must have one specific attitude. The attitude need not be expressed in exact words of "I love . . . I hate . . ." but can be acted out. The way you say certain words will be enough to indicate your feelings.

For instance, Paul Provenza's attitude is he *hates* people who smoke cigars.

SETUP: (NORMAL)
"You know what bugs me? People who smoke cigars in restaurants . . ."

PUNCH: (LOONY)
"That's why I always carry a water pistol filled with gasoline."

Marsha Warfield *hates* skinny women:

SETUP: (INFORMATION)
"I hate skinny women, especially when they say things like 'Sometimes I forget to eat.'"

PUNCH: (HOSTILE REACTION)

60

66Now, I've forgotten my mother's maiden name and my keys, but you've got to be a special kind of stupid to forget to eat.99

Notice, in the above examples, the comics verbally tell you that their attitude is "I hate." Here is material from Roseanne Barr where the attitude is not verbally spoken, but acted out in voice, facial expression, and body language. What's funny is her contrary attitude. Read this joke as if she's *proud* of being a mother.

66The way I look at it, if the kids are still alive when my husband comes home from work, then I've done my job.99

—Roseanne Barr

Workshop #17

CONTRASTING SETUP/PUNCH

So far you have:

▶ Typed out several pages of your rantings and ravings.
▶ Underlined the punchlines.
▶ Condensed the setups.

Now, look at each setup/punch and answer the following questions:

1. Is each setup plausible, informational, and simple?

2. Does each punch contrast the setup by following one of these formulas:

SETUP	PUNCH
Information	Exaggeration
General theme	Specific example
Sane	Insane
Realistic	Fantasy
Adult's view	Child's view
Friendly	Hostile
Fact	Fiction

3. Does each piece contain an attitude? What is it? (Remember, you don't have to say the attitude in words, you can show it in your voice, facial expression, and body language. But you need to know what your attitude is on each piece. Remember, attitudes can change from piece to piece. You can go right from "I hate . . ." to "I love . . ." without any transitions.)

Workshop #18

USING SARCASM WITH OUTER-SELF ITEMS

In Chapter 2 you wrote down items that were physically obvious about yourself. (See Workshop #5, Outer Self, on pp. 28–31.) Saying what is contrary to the obvious is a very reliable way to make people laugh. For example, here are some sarcastic remarks that have worked:

A very hefty student got a huge laugh by opening his act with

❝Hello, my name is Al Barlaan, and yes, I am a Filipino sex god!❞

Another student, Ruth Reyerson, was *blond* and *overweight*. She came onstage and said,

"I know what you are thinking . . . Barbie."

When the laughter died down she went on:

"I am like Barbie, blond hair, blue eyes, except one thing. Barbie doesn't EAT!"

Student Beverly Jackson, a *gorgeous stacked blond* woman, opened with

"I know what you men are thinking . . . NASA scientist! Men look at me and all think the same thing. 'You are so . . . smart!'"

In all of these examples the setup is your physical appearance and the punch is your sarcastic reaction. Because the setup is unspoken, your physical appearance trait needs to be very obvious.

On page 30, you've selected two physical characteristics that stand out (i.e., fat, short, macho, etc.). Copy them below and write several of their opposites. Be as sarcastic as possible. If you draw a blank, use a thesaurus.

For example:

Quality 1. _____Skinny_____

Opposites:

_____macho man, a hunk of burning_____

_____love_____

_____

Quality 2. _____Fat_____

Opposites:

_____anorexic_____

_____

_____

Now you try it with your outer-self traits:
(NOTE: If you do not have any outstanding traits, and most of my students don't, simply move on to the next workshop.)

Quality 1. _____

Opposites:

_____

_____

_____

Quality 2. _____

Opposites:

_____

_____

_____

Being sarcastic about your physical attributes can serve as a great opener. Try out a few lines and see if any of the above strikes a funny chord in you. If it does, keep it in mind for your opener.

Six Additional Comedy Formulas

Every piece of material needs to have a setup, a punch, and an attitude. These six additional comedy formulas are optional. They are tools that will assist you in bringing clarity and hilarity to your material.

The six additional tools are:

64

- Comparisons
- Similes
- Observations
- Mimicking
- List making
- Callbacks

Comparisons

Comparing one subject against another is a simple and very effective way of organizing your material. For instance, if one of your issues is your parents, then compare their generation to yours.

> SETUP: **(FATHER'S GENERATION)**
> **"My father had three jobs and went to school at night . . ."**
>
> PUNCH: **(YOUR GENERATION)**
> **". . . If I go to the cleaners and the bank in the same day . . . I need a nap."**
>
> —Larry Miller

Russian-born comic Yakov Smirnoff compares Russia to the United States:

> SETUP: **(AMERICAN COMEDIANS)**
> **"American comedians can say anything they want . . ."**
>
> PUNCH: **(RUSSIAN COMEDIANS)**
> **"In Russia you've got to be very selective about what jokes you say. If you say, 'Take my wife, please,' when you get home, she's gone."**

Here Lotus Weinstock compares her beliefs now to her beliefs in the past:

65

SETUP: (THEN)
❝I once wanted to save the world . . .❞

PUNCH: (NOW)
❝. . . now I just want to leave the room with some dignity.❞

Here Bill Maher compares his religions:

SETUP: (INFORMATION)
❝My mother is Jewish, my father Catholic. I was brought up Catholic—with a Jewish mind.❞

PUNCH: (EXAGGERATED COMPARISON)
❝When I went to confession, I always brought a lawyer with me: 'Bless me, Father, for I have sinned and I think you know my lawyer, Mr. Cohen.'❞

Once again, notice that in all these jokes, each punch is an exaggeration, a twist, or a change of direction from the setup. The setup is serious and logical, and the punch shows the audience you're kidding. The setup establishes the collective reality and the punch communicates your distinctive view of the world.

Workshop #19

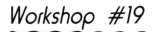

COMPARISONS

In this workshop you are going to write comparisons using some of the subjects you've listed in the workshops in Chapter 2. Look over your "I hate," "I worry about," and "I'm frightened about" lists and see if any of the subjects you've listed would lend itself to this formula. For example, if you had "politics" on one of your lists, compare opposing sides of an issue or philosophy:

SETUP: (LIBERALS)
"Liberals feel unworthy of their possessions . . ."

PUNCH: (CONSERVATIVES)
". . . Conservatives feel they deserve everything they've stolen."

—Mort Sahl

Look over other workshops in Chapter 2. If on your unique characteristics lists you had that you are a mix of religions or races, then compare them:

SETUP:
"My daughter is half Black and half Jewish . . ."

PUNCH:
". . . This means that if this were World War II, she would have to go into hiding and clean the house."

—Student Roseanne Katon

Now you do it. Look over all the Chapter 2 workshops and see which topics would lend themselves to this formula and fill in the blanks:

1. Item from list:_____
   One side:

   _____

   _____

   Other side:

   _____

   _____

2. Item from list:_____
   One side:

   _____

   _____

   Other side:

   _____

   _____

3. Item from list:_____
   One side:

   _____

   _____

   Other side:

   _____

   _____

4. Item from list:_____
   One side:

   _____

   _____

   Other side:

   _____

   _____

5. Item from list:_____
   One side:

   _____

   _____

Other side:

_____

_____

If you draw a blank, here are some additional topics you can use comparisons with:

▶ Compare your hometown to where you now live.
▶ Compare your fears now to the fears you had growing up.
▶ Compare your parents' generation to yours.
▶ Compare your dog's life to yours.
▶ Compare the advantages and disadvantages of being married.
▶ Compare your sex life to your grandmother's.

Similes

> **❝Sex is like air . . .**
> **. . . you don't miss it until you don't have it.❞**

A simile is where one object is compared to another. In comedy similes are very powerful tools because they create pictures. Comics compare what they are talking about to a common reference in pop culture or to an experience we've all had. Similes are usually introduced with "it's like . . ."

Similes can be used in a setup:

> **❝There's this guy sitting next to me . . . looks like a squid in stretch pants . . . So you know, I'm ready to spawn . . . so then he starts puffin' on a cigar the size of God's ego . . . And I said, 'Excuse me, but if I wanted to shorten my life, I'd date ya!'❞**

—Judy Tenuta

69

Judy Tenuta

Or similes can be used as the punch:

"Princess Di, she did all right for herself, didn't she? That Charles, he's like a Visa Gold Card with ears."

—**Carol Montgomery**

Those are examples of good similes where the comic creates an extreme, absurd picture using common references. Here are some examples of some bad similes.

SETUP: (INFORMATION)
"In bathing suits those Chippendale dancers look like they have . . ."

PUNCH: (UNFUNNY PUNCH)
". . . a large package."

70

A good simile can really spruce up a line:

SETUP: (INFORMATION)
"In bathing suits those Chippendale dancers look like they have . . ."

PUNCH: (REVISED PUNCH)
". . . a bag of marbles in Vaseline."

The more outrageous the comparison, the funnier the material can be. Think in terms of creating a picture that takes the audience on a mini-LSD flashback.

Carol Leifer

SETUP:
"Sex when you're married is like going to a 7-Eleven . . ."

PUNCH:
". . . There's not much variety, but at three in the morning, it's always there."

—Carol Leifer

SETUP: (REALISTIC INFORMATION)
"I put my clothes in the cleaners and then don't have the money to get them out again . . ."

PUNCH: (WILD EXAGGERATION)
". . . It's like they're in jail waiting on me to spring 'em . . . I have to go in there every so often and say, 'Can I just see the pants?'"

—Paula Poundstone

71

Workshop #20

Try your hand at creating visual pictures using Similes. For example:

> **SETUP:** *You're staring at me . . .*
> **PUNCH:** *like a* _lava lamp_ .
>
> —John Mulroony

> **SETUP:** *The waitress was so slow.*
> **PUNCH:** *She was like* _a snail on Valium_

Now you try it. Remember it's just a practice exercise. Jot down anything that comes to your mind. There are no right or wrong answers.

1. **SETUP:** *Chicago is so hot:*
   PUNCH:
   _____

2. **SETUP:** *My mother is so fat, she's like:*
   PUNCH:
   _____

3. **SETUP:** *My room is so messy, it's like:*
   PUNCH:
   _____

4. **SETUP:** *Good sex with Dr. Ruth, that's like:*
   PUNCH:
   _____

5. SETUP: *She was staring at me like:*
PUNCH:

Here are some of the similes that some comics have used with the preceding setups.

1. SETUP: *Chicago is so hot:*
PUNCH: *it's like someone's sitting on your chest licking your face.*

—Student Ellen Totleben

2. SETUP: *My mother is so fat she's like:*
PUNCH: *a float in the Macy's Thanksgiving Day parade. Shelley Winters and Orson Welles in the same dress.*

—Student Carrie Williams

3. SETUP: *My room is so messy, it's like:*
PUNCH: *the city dump on a good day.*

—Student Carrie Williams

4. SETUP: *Good sex with Dr. Ruth, that's like:*
PUNCH: *good wine with cottage cheese.*

—George Wallace

5. SETUP: *She was staring at me like:*
PUNCH: *a Mongoloid watching a magic act.*

—David Spade

Look through your written material. See if in your act there are any places for similes. If you describe anyone ("My brother is so fat . . ."), create a picture using a simile.

Everyday Observations

    66Ever wonder why there's a permanent-press selection on an iron?99

In the dictionary, the definition of an observation is "Close examination, especially of natural phenomena." Observations are where the comic tries to make sense out of a non-sensical world.

> **"Have you ever noticed that your garbage weighs more than your groceries?"**

It is the comic's job to observe the world he or she lives in and comment upon it. Comedy observations are specific observations viewed through your unique perspective about even the most ordinary elements of our lives. Notice how the following observations are all commenting on the absurdities found in everyday life:

> **"Have you ever noticed that mice don't have shoulders?"**
>
> —George Carlin

> **"Why is it that in 7-11 stores, they've got $10,000 worth of cameras watching 20 cents worth of Twinkies?"**
>
> —Jay Leno

> **"What is it about American fathers as they grow older that makes them dress like flags from other countries?"**
>
> —Cary Odes

> **"Did you ever notice when you blow in a dog's face he gets mad at you, but when you take him in a car, he sticks his head out the window?"**
>
> —Steve Bluestein

Observations can be short one-liners, but it is preferable to use the observation as the setup and your unbridled reaction to the observation as the punch. Using this technique, one observation can be extended to create an entire routine, as is the case with Jerry Seinfeld's inventive routine on cotton balls:

SETUP: (OBSERVATION)
"Ladies, what is the deal on cotton balls?"

PUNCH: (REACTION)
" . . . I have no cotton balls, I'm getting along just fine. I've never had one, never bought one, never needed one. I've never been in a situation where I thought to myself, 'I could use a cotton ball right now . . .'"

SETUP: (OBSERVATION)
" . . . Women need millions of cotton balls every single day."

PUNCH: (SIMILE)
"They buy these bags like peatmoss bags, and two days later they're all out . . . "

SETUP: (OBSERVATION)
" . . . The only place I ever see them is at the bottom of your little wastebasket . . ."

PUNCH: (REACTION)
"There's always two or three that look like they've been through some horrible experience . . ."

SETUP: (OBSERVATION)
" . . . I once went out with a girl, she left a ziplock baggy of cotton balls over my house . . ."

PUNCH: (SIMILE)
" . . . I took them out and put them on the kitchen floor like little tumbleweeds. I thought maybe the cockroaches would see it, figure that this is a dead town, 'let's move on.'"

SETUP: (OBSERVATION)

66. . . *Or when I go to the doctor, before he gives me the shot he puts the alcohol on me with a cotton ball, so I give him one of mine, just trying to get rid of it. Then he gives me the prescription . . .*99

PUNCH: (REACTION)

66. . . *I take it home, open up the bottle, there's another cotton ball in there. You can't get out of this rat race.*99

Workshop #21

Turning Everyday Life into Comedy Material

I have found that observational material is impossible to simply sit down and write. Observations are fragments of data that flow through your thoughts while you are involved in everyday living. Carry around a notebook and note these observations as they occur. Then try them out on people with the setup "Have you ever noticed that . . ."

Practice writing observations about these topics:

Observation about *shopping*:

Have you ever noticed that:

_____

Observation about your *pet*:

Have you ever noticed that:

_____

Observations about your *body*:

Have you ever noticed that:

Mimicking

❝. . . and now let me introduce you to my alter ego.❞

Mimicking does not mean being Rich Little, where you do impressions of celebrities. This means to mimic, to "act out" the people you talk about. Become them. Mimic their voices, their body language. Remember, stand-up is visually boring. In most comedy clubs all an audience gets to look at is a black curtain, a bright white light, and you. Since clubs look as if they were designed by Kafka, the more voices, facial expression, and body movement you can bring to an act, the more visually exciting your act becomes.

People love transformations. Instead of talking about your mom in the third person, talk about her as if you *are* her. Act her out. Mimic her manner, posture, and voice. It doesn't have to be exactly the way she talks. Unless she's a movie star, nobody's going to know what she sounds like. Student Howard Gluss had on his "hate list" that he "hated the way his mother got out of bed." He extended that into a hysterical routine by acting this out.

You don't have to stick with mimicking just people. If you talk about God, as my student Loretta Colla did, be God:

❝I wonder if God is chubby, his son is anorexic . . . Could you imagine Him at an Overeaters Anonymous meeting: (IN A DEEP VOICE-OVER) 'Hi, my name is God, and I'm an overeater and overachiever.' 'Hi, God!'❞

Comic Monica Piper does a chunk in which she pretends to be her dog screening her dates:

> **So you got a job? Oh, yeah, how long? Eighty-six to eighty-eight? Okay, that's fourteen years, that's good. You're not one of those guys who just pretends to throw a ball, are ya? I hate that. She didn't give you that line about you're the only one, huh? Wish I had a Milk Bone for every guy she's dragged back here. (SNIFFING) Oh, I see you still got yours. She made me get rid of mine.**

Communicating with your voice and your body is powerful technique that shows imagination.

Workshop #22

MIMICKING

The Sybil Exercise: Becoming Someone Else

Review your rantings and ravings:

▶ Who are the people you mention?
▶ Act out a dialog with that person.
▶ Become them, physically and verbally:
  How do they act when they are mad, when they are in love?
  How do they walk, eat?
  What habits do they have that you can imitate?

List Making
Creating Lists That Make People Laugh

Lists make good punchlines. There are different ways you can use lists to make people laugh. The first way is with the "List of Three." The comedy formula goes like this: the first two have something in common (setup) and the last one is the unexpected (punch).

For instance:

SETUP: (ORDINARY)
"I like to think of myself as a woman of European influence: (1) makeup by Germaine Monteil (2) nails by Fabergé ..."

PUNCH: (UNEXPECTED)
"... (3) body by Häagen-Dazs."

—Sheryl Bernstein

On a list of three, the setup includes the first two items on the list. They are rational and logical. The punch is the third list item, which is the change in direction.

SETUP: (RATIONAL)
"Being an Arab, I have the same interests as you. When I go to buy a car I look for all the same things: (1) color, (2) style ..."

PUNCH: (UNEXPECTED)
(3) "... how many hostages can fit in the trunk."

—Student Amy Rahal

79

Here is an example from one of my student's beginning material:

> SETUP: (INFORMATION)
> **"I can't understand why my wife left me: (1)
> Maybe it was that I left clothes on the floor; (2)
> Maybe it was because I left the toilet seat up."**
>
> PUNCH: (NOT FUNNY)
> **"(3) Or maybe it was because I read for hours in
> the bathroom."**

The problem with this piece is that the third item does not contrast the first two. Since the first two items are mundane, to make this work, the last item needs to be significant. Thus:

> PUNCH: (REVISED PUNCH)
> **"(3) Or maybe it was the stewardess."**

Look over your act and see if there are any punchlines that can be broken down into a list of three.

Callbacks

A callback is when you make a reference, later in your act, to something you said earlier.

Ellen DeGeneres uses callbacks in her act. Early in her act she does a chunk about her grandmother:

SETUP: (INFORMATION)
&&Dogs hate it when you blow in their face. I'll tell you who really hates that— my grandmother . . .&&

PUNCH: (EXAGGERATION)
&& . . . Which is odd, because when we're driving she really loves to hang her head out the window.&&

Later in her act DeGeneres makes a callback to her grandmother.

Ellen DeGeneres

SETUP: (INFORMATION/MIMICKING)
&&I think everybody has a philosophical side to them. I grew up that way because of my grandmother. At a very young age she said to me, 'Life is like a blender. You have so many different speeds, you have mix, blend, stir, puree, and you never use them all. In life you have so many different abilities and you never use them all.&&

PUNCH: (CALLBACK)
&&I said, 'Grandma—' and then I just blow in her face . . . I don't really like her.&&

Callbacks are popular with an audience, because they help the comic develop a special intimacy with the audience. Your mother is doing a callback when every time you get together she brings up the night you made her burned pancakes. Or when every time you and your cousin get together you "call back" how Grandma hid her money in the cookie jar.

81

≈≈≈≈≈≈≈≈≈≈≈≈≈≈≈≈≈≈≈≈≈≈≈≈≈≈≈≈≈≈

Look through your material and see if there is any subject matter, emotion, or phrase that you can call back.

If you use callbacks, remember, the original joke needs to get a laugh and stand on its own. If you can work a few in, you'll find that audiences really appreciate them.

A final note:

You don't have to incorporate all of these tools into your act. I find that most students excel in one technique or another. You might find that you naturally make lists, or most of your material is observational, or you speak in pictures.

Work over your written material and rantings and ravings by sculpting it and expanding it using these tools:

COMPARISONS
▶ Do you have issues where you can ponder two sides?

SIMILES
▶ Look through your act for anything you mention—such as the house you grew up in, your boss, *anything*—and picture it and describe it, using a simile. Compare it to something very visual and understandable. Add as many similes as possible.

OBSERVATIONS
▶ Keep your eyes open for observing the mundane absurdities of life.

MIMICKING
▶ If you mention any person, or animal, or even inanimate objects, practice becoming them instead of talking *about* them. Play around with becoming other people. Your act should contain a host of characters from your life. Act them out. You don't have to be a great actor or "feel" anything. Do a caricature of them. Have fun and tape-record what comes out of your mouth.

LIST MAKING
▶ Three is the magic number in comedy.

CALLBACKS
▶ Make a reference to something you mentioned earlier in your act.

Summary:

By this point you have

▶ Written out a draft of your act.
▶ Arranged your material into setup/punch format.
▶ Deleted all unnecessary words.
▶ Crafted your act using one or more of these techniques:
Comparisons
Similes
Observations
Mimicking
List making
Callbacks

Congratulations are in order if you have completed all the workshops to this point. Relax, the hard part is over, and the rest is smoother sailing. In the next chapter you will learn various comedy styles from some of the biggest names in comedy.

CHAPTER 4

GETTING IT STYLED

Creating Your Own Style

❝Not another rubber chicken!❞

Until now, we have focused on creating stand-up from your personal issues: finding your issues, or issues that reflect the world around you, putting them into the setup/punch format, and communicating them *verbally* to an audience. Purists believe that this is the only true form of stand-up. There are, however, many successful comics who employ other styles of comedy, including

- ▶ props
- ▶ political humor
- ▶ impressions
- ▶ characters
- ▶ music

Props

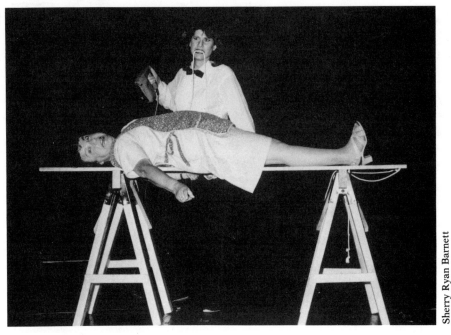

Sherry Ryan Barnett

Judy Carter Sawing Grandma in Half

I started out as a magician. At the beginning I was petrified to talk to an audience, so I hid behind my magic props.
Tearing up a newspaper, having something "to do," helped
reduce my fear, but the trick was what got the applause,
not me. As my confidence grew I began to create magic
tricks that were expressions of my issues, tricks that were
actually metaphors for what was going on inside of me.
Being a compulsive dieter, I created the "Levitating Celery
Stalk," which I would eat as it floated. As an expression of
my defiance, I performed a death-defying "Escape from My
Grandmother's Girdle." And during my angry period, as
my finale, I would perform the "Sawing a Man in Half"
with a Black and Decker Skill saw. As the years passed,
however, I felt the need to express more complex feelings,
feelings that could not be expressed in magic tricks. Consequently, I began to talk more and do less magic. Then

one night I went totally "propless." This was not an act of courage, but rather it was the result of my arriving at the club and my suitcase arriving in New Jersey.

A lot of very successful comedians use props. Gallagher has made a career out of smashing watermelons with his "sledge-a-matic." Bruce Mahler uses a raw chicken as a puppet. Wild man Charlie Fleischer plays abstract musical instruments, and Gary Mule Deer carries a trash can full of props onstage, including: a rubber chicken, a typewriter, snorkel and fins, a

Gallagher

giant lobster bib, giant fly swatters, a toy horse, a rifle, lots of toy frogs, a hangman's noose, a stuffed dog, Dorito chips (he plays guitar with these), real avocados, and Siamese quarter-pounder hamburgers joined together at the bun. And that's just for his opening five minutes.

Props can enhance your act, but if used improperly they can upstage the very thing you want the audience to focus on: you. *You* need to get the laugh, not the prop. Some beginning comics use props to hide behind, as if to say "Don't look at me, look at this gadget." If you decide to use props, remember that all the rules of stand-up still apply. It is not enough to hold up some goofy item and say, "Isn't this stupid." You need to have an attitude about what you are presenting. The gadget has to have something to do with *you* and your views of life.

Political Humor

If you are interested in political humor, the newspaper is a great source of material. Wherever the magnifying glass of the media decides to descend, there will always be a joke. The problem is that writing political material in this fast-paced world can be an exercise in futility; your best laugh can vanish as headlines change. Someone can be in the news every day for a month and two weeks later his or her name is not even recognizable. Do you remember the name of Gerald Ford's running mate?

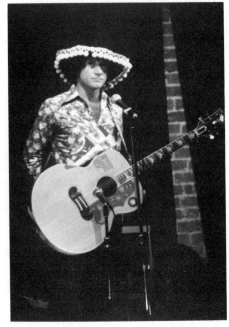

Gary Mule Deer

When doing perishable material, it is necessary to find a place where you can perform weekly, if not daily. Political comic Will Durst works practically every night of the week, changing his act nightly.

> 66This is the same Justice Department that suspects the Teamsters are linked to the mob. Suspects. They're also inclined to believe that fire is hot, but they're not sure.99
>
> **—Will Durst**

Durst feels that if something happens and he doesn't deal with it, that day, onstage, he is bogus as a topical-social comic.

88

Mark Russell

Other distinguished political comics include *Saturday Night Live*'s Dennis Miller, who does the news satire spot, and political satirist and pianist Mark Russell, who has his own show at the Russell Hotel in Washington, D.C., as well as on National Public Television.

Besides writing topical material, most political satirists have a core thirty minutes of solid material that can survive the test of time and where all the rules of setup/punch still apply:

SETUP: (INFORMATIONAL)
"Charles Manson appeared at his latest parole hearing with a swastika carved into his forehead . . ."

PUNCH: (SARCASTIC RESPONSE)
". . . what better way to show the board you're putting your act together?"

—Dennis Miller

When doing political humor, remember that no matter how funny a joke is, in order to laugh, the audience needs to agree with your political point of view. For instance:

SETUP: (OBSERVATION)
". . . I don't understand these 'Right-to-Lifers.' Have you noticed that they are the same people who are for the death penalty? Now figure that?"

89

PUNCH: (EXAGGERATION)
(MIMICKING THEM)❝*. . . 'save the fetus, wait until you're sure it's a human being, then electrocute that bastard to death!'*❞

That joke of mine killed at a Pro-Choice benefit and got booed off the stage at a Baptist banquet. This doesn't mean that you cater your material to the sentiments of the crowd. On the contrary, getting booed didn't stop me from using that abortion joke. I find that disturbing material might not create laughter, but it does wake them up. Mark Russell also believes in taking risks: ". . . when you are known as a satirist, they expect not to agree with you. They want that red meat."

Russell, who calls himself an "equal opportunity offender," believes that it's okay to upset an audience, as long as you hit on both sides of an issue. If you are performing for a specific group, such as the National Organization of Women, you can get away with a one-sided slant to your material:

SETUP: (INFORMATION)
❝*My mother is against abortion for another reason . . .*❞

PUNCH: (CONTRAST)
❝*. . . she doesn't feel it's fair to kill the fetus and let the father live.*❞

—John DeBillis

To establish credibility, a political comic needs to find balance in his point of view. Russell writes material the

Aaron Rapport

Dennis Miller

same way legislation is written: he compromises, he takes a little from this side, a little from that side.

Johnny Carson is a master of balanced sentiment. If he hits on the Democrats, he balances it by hitting on the Republicans. An audience needs to feel a sense of fair play and Carson delivers it. However, you will never find Carson doing hard-hitting jokes about sensitive issues such as abortion, race issues, and so on. When performing political material for television, it is often necessary to play it safe by sticking to material that is in tune with national opinion, such as:

SETUP: (INFORMATION)
"Weight lifters are now taking steroids and male hormones . . ."

PUNCH: (EXAGGERATION)
". . . One guy had so much male hormone in him, he had to be classified as an East German woman."

—Carl Wolfson

That joke will work on television because it pokes fun at a country that is currently emotionally neutral. If that joke was poking fun at Israel, for instance, it would have a harder time getting past the network censors.

Also, a political act needs to be balanced with material that is about *you*. If you are going to slash and attack the president's imperfections, give your own shortcomings equal time. A little self-deprecating humor makes you seem fallible to the audience and makes them feel more comfortable. Politicians use this technique because they know that poking fun at their flaws makes them appear more likable, and electable.

I discourage newcomers to stand-up from doing political humor. It is a lot easier to get laughs with material based on personal issues. When you are doing material about yourself, nobody is going to question your credibility. But when you're doing political humor, it isn't enough to have a strong attitude. Unless they are Walter Cronkite, stand-ups who comment on others need to establish their qualifications by having distinctively clever and skillfully crafted material.

TIPS AND POINTERS ON DOING POLITICAL HUMOR

- Read the paper daily.
- Get in the habit of writing a few lines every day.
- Balance your point of view.
- Have some material that is self-deprecating.
- Stockpile material that will stand the test of time.
- Never open with your new stuff. Open with your sure-fire, all-purpose lines that you know will prime the pump and get them laughing, and then ease into the new stuff.
- Arrange all material into the setup/punch format.
- If you are performing out of town, ask to be sent news clippings ahead of time, so you know what the local issues are. Mark Russell finds three or four extremely obvious things that are going on locally—items that the townspeople are excited about, such as potholes, traffic, the sheriff's peccadillos, and so forth.
- Know what you are talking about.

Impressions

Impressionists such as Rich Little, Fred Travalena, and Marilyn Michaels get their applause by transforming themselves, voice, looks, and body language, into celebrities who are instantly recognizable. Since celebrities come and go, these pros have a stable of at least seventy-five different impressions and are constantly learning new voices. Most impressionists will flawlessly duplicate a celebrity's voice and physicality and put them into unusual situations, such as, "What if Mr. Rogers were President?" Or "What if John Wayne had a conversation with Dr. Ruth?"

92

Movie parodies are very popular with impressionists. Michaels acts out the whole *Wizard of Oz* in three minutes and *"Gone With the Wind"* in two minutes, playing all the parts. Fred Travalena does a tribute to *Superman* where Lois Lane is Dr. Ruth, Jim Nabors is Jimmy Olson, Jack Nicholson is Clark Kent, and Superman turns out to be Elvis Presley.

Fred Travalena

Nate Cutler

Impressionists also imitate singers. Newcomer Valery Pappas does Cher, Liza Minnelli, and a flawless impression of Phoebe Snow singing "The Poetry Man." Pappas creates her impressions from listening to a song over and over again until she can re-create every breath, every nuance, and then she exaggerates it. Pappas says: "Impressionists need to accentuate the star's quirky qualities. When I do Liza Minnelli, I exaggerate the way she pushes and sells a song. If Liza sells it 50 percent, I have to sell it 100 percent."

There is also a hip breed of "new wave" impressionists such as $100,000 *Star Search* winner Mark McCollum, who skips the usual star caricatures in favor of imitating cartoon characters singing rock music. His act includes Yosemite Sam leading the Silver Bullet Band, a foghorn Leghorn born to rap, and Porky Pig, complete with reverb, belting out a version of U2's "Pride in the Name of Love."

If you have a talent for singing or speaking impressions, do the people who are most identifiable. You can throw in some obscure ones for fun, but doing impressions is a business, and like anything else, you have to do something that people can relate to. Travalina suggests that newcomers go for the top box-office people of the day, and "try to find your own five or six that will be your specialty. It might be discouraging for a newcomer who sees the impressionists who have visibility doing fifty or one hundred voices and think, 'What am I going to do?' There are always four or five that none of them are doing yet and those are the ones you go for. That's how you get noticed."

You also don't need to have a talent for mimicking voices to do impressions. There are comics who incorporate impressions of inanimate objects in their acts. Bill Kirchenbauer imitates inanimate objects by doing a hysterical impression of a noisy garbage truck at six in the morning as well as imitating a stick of gum being chewed by convulsing his body and ending up on the bottom of a chair.

You can get a feel for these kinds of impressions by practicing becoming such things as

- a parking meter
- a dog in an old age home
- a cheap pair of sunglasses talking to a pair of Ray-Bans

Once you get an impression down, the most important element becomes commitment. Totally commit to the impression by jumping into it with all your being.

Characters

Doing characters is the same as doing impressions, except that the person you're imitating is not a celebrity, but rather a stereotypic character we recognize from everyday life: a nerdy linoleum salesman, a spacey Valley Girl, an obnoxious guy in a singles bar. We all recognize Lily Tomlin's Ernestine, the surly telephone operator, and Whoopi Goldberg's Fontaine, the reformed junkie.

94

Many performers who do characters deviate from the standard setup/punch format. Tomlin performs her characters as if she were doing a scene from a play. As in a theater, an imaginary wall comes between her and the audience. The character in most cases doesn't talk to the audience as in stand-up, but rather talks to another imaginary character. Because of the theatrical nature of this, most people who do characters perform in theatrical

Lily Tomlin

Photofest

settings, rather than stand-up clubs.

When you are doing a one-woman show, as Tomlin does, you have the luxury of doing long character pieces where you have the time to carve dramatic moments. For one HBO special Whoopi Goldberg stayed in her Fontaine character for the entire hour. However, in a comedy club, the owner is not interested in dramatic art. He's interested in keeping his customers laughing. For that reason, most stand-up comics who do characters keep them short and weave them into their routines. Robin Williams is a master at this. For a "Comic Relief '88" three-minute segment discussing everything from Contra-gate to the Gulf of Hormuz, Williams hopped from one persona and voice to another, including a talk-show host, a tele-evangelist, a Mafia don, Ollie North, Humphrey Bogart, a zonked-out hippie, George Wallace, and an Iranian.

Using Setup/Punch

When doing characters, the setup/punch formula still applies. The setup usually includes information about the character, and the punch is the acting out of the character. Going directly from character to character without any setups will sometimes confuse an audience as to who is speaking. When comic Joey Camen introduces his racist character, "Clifford Fletcher," he sets up his character with:

❝I'm *against racism, but I met this guy* . . .❞

With this setup, the audience realizes that it's not Camen being the racist, but his redneck character. This introduction creates a context for the character to come alive. During the setup you connect with the audience, which is expected in a comedy club, and on the punch you act out the character, cutting off from the audience.

Creating a Character

You can find characters from observing the people you know, such as a memorable teacher, a family member, or the woman behind the counter at the dry cleaners'. Marsha Meyers, former member of the improvisation group War Babies and an improvisation teacher, suggests that characters can evolve from a thought, an observation, or a physical idea such as ". . . this guy is just like a light bulb."

You could do everything a light bulb would do and make up a character, a very electric, eccentric kind of character.

When creating a character:

▶ Label in your own mind what category your character falls into (i.e., baglady, biker, librarian . . .).
▶ Ask yourself what mannerisms are typical of the character you picked. For example, if your character is a librar-

ian, typical mannerisms might be that she is quiet, neat, and so on.

- ▶ Give your character an exaggeration of what mannerisms we already expect. Give him or her a lot of eccentric qualities. For example, not only does the librarian like quiet, but she gets migraines from even a pin dropping.
- ▶ Find quirky mannerisms and phrases that you can call back. For example, we all recognize the Valley Girl's "Oh, for sure!" Or Ernestine's snorty laugh.
- ▶ Give the character a point of view. Hook up your character's mannerisms with an issue. For instance, what if a biker comes into the library? What is the librarian's opinion of the biker and how would it change her behavior? You need to know how your character feels about many different issues, and it is important to be specific.

Whom does he or she vote for?
What is his or her religion? etc.
How does he or she behave in different situations?
Where does he or she live?
Whom is he or she speaking to?

Cynthia Szigeti, who teaches improvisation at L.A.'s Groundlings Improvisational School, birthplace of Pee-Wee Herman, Laraine Newman, and *Saturday Night Live*'s Phil Hartman, helps her students create characters by doing what she calls a "'Ruminating Exercise'":

- ▶ Sit in a chair and do your character by talking in character as fast as possible, without thinking, without pausing.
- ▶ Say everything you know about the character. If you run out, just keep going. After five minutes you will most likely run out of material.

According to Szigeti, when *you* run out of material, that's when the *character* starts to talk and that's when the good stuff comes out. Sometimes it feels as if you are "transchanneling" that person.

Song parodies, where a comic puts new lyrics to a recognizable tune, are a great way to make people laugh. Singer/composer/comedian Dale Gonyea, a young Victor Borge, would get big laughs from changing

"You must remember this, a kiss is still a kiss,"

to:

"You must remember this, a quiche is still a quiche."

And in his hands "Downtown" became "Groundround."

Song parodies, however, are professionaly limiting because you can never own the songs, so you can't ever do them on TV. Later in his career Gonyea found that he needed to come up with totally original tunes as well as lyrics. Here is an excerpt from his original song "Name Dropping":

"Is Shelley Long or Short? Was John Gielgud Good all day? What did Ernest Heming Weigh? Is Glenn Close? Is Jamie Farr? Did Tommie Tune his own guitar? And what did Stevie Wonder?"

One student, Jessie Goldberg, found that singing a song was the best way to express his "tenderness" to his ex-wife in his song, "All the Best to You":

"I hope you get fat, and get wrinkles on your face. And you lose all your hair and your teeth fall out of place. And I hope that you fail in everything you do. Otherwise all the best to you."

Dale Gonyea

If you have a musical talent, incorporate it into your act. Judy Tenuta's parents bought her an accordion and lessons from a door-to-door salesman when she was a child; now she uses it in her act, hitting the keys for emphasis:

"He said, 'Judy, Judy, I must possess you'—ta da da—he had an accordion, too."

And Tenuta sings off-kilter songs, such as a Country & Western tribute to the pope:

"I just want a cowboy in a long white silky dress."

Charlie Fleischer plays abstract musical instruments of his own invention and ends his act by playing *Beethoven's Fifth* . . . on a harmonica.

99

So here is a chance to finally make those French horn lessons pay off. Get it out of the closet and see if it can fit into your act.

Finding Your Schtick

Sooner or later my students automatically gravitate to their karmic schtick. It's not as if they make an intellectual choice about whether they want to use props or sing in their act. It seems to evolve naturally. Almost as if they couldn't help themselves. One student would pick up props on his way to class. By the time he got to class he would have a paper bag jammed full of odds and ends he couldn't wait to show us. Another student just had to comment on things she read in the paper, while another student, no matter how hard she resisted, kept going into characters.

Your style is usually formed in childhood and you can't escape it. As a child, Charlie Fleischer was good at art, so in his act he gives voices to his foam rubber sculptures. Archery was the only thing Gary Mule Deer got an "A" in at college. This became his show stopper as he uses his guitar like a bow and arrow to shoot a lighted cigarette out of a rubber chicken's mouth. Mark Russell started playing piano as

Charlie Fleischer

a kid living in Washington, D.C., so it was a natural for him to go on to play piano in a hotel across the street from the Senate and talk about what's going on in Capitol Hill. Victoria Jackson made a smash first appearance on the *Tonight Show*, doing material along with gymnastic feats she learned as a child. Instead of trying to escape your childhood, embrace it and put it into your act.

If you are not sure at this point what stuff you want to put in your act, don't worry. Your style will be revealed to you. It is a discovery of what you already are—of what you are cut out to do. This process of discovery can happen overnight, or, more likely, it can take months or years.

Summary

Don't be too quick to label and limit yourself. Most comics keep it simple, using the standard setup/punch format. However, don't fight your natural tendencies. If you get an urge to play the tuba, do birdcalls, sing a song, or iron clothes, do it.

Be patient, be true to yourself, follow your natural inclinations, and your God-given talents will reveal themselves to you.

CHAPTER 5

GETTING IT READY

The Opening

> **❝Do you love me yet?❞**
>
> —Mark Miller

Your opening is the most important part of your act. Within ten seconds an audience will decide whether or not they like you. If you create a bad first impression, you'll spend the rest of your act on damage control.

A good opening connects you with the audience. A good opening is grounded in reality. Here are some pointers in choosing your opening piece:

▶ Comment on something that is truly noticeable about yourself, such as a big nose, wild hair, and so on. Try opening your act with one of the items from the outer-self workshop.

"*I'm worried that my hair is going to get bigger than I am and take me places I don't want to go . . .*"

—Student Jennifer Heath

▶ Open with something that reflects your persona. A good opening defines who you are and lets the audience know what to expect. One of my students' acts was about her bar life. She started off with

"*Oh, a bar stool . . . I feel right at home.*"

If you are going to do magic tricks, start off with a trick. If you are going to be angry through most of your act, start off with being angry. For instance, Judy Tenuta opens her act screeching.

"*Hello, pigs!*"

Tenuta's ballsy opening sets up the audience for her brand of hostile, irreverent humor.

▶ If you can't find anything obvious about yourself, open with something that is obvious about the audience. A comic to a small crowd:

"*Did you all come in the same car?*"

When I found myself performing for an all-white audience, I opened with

"*Hello, my, aren't we all Caucasian.*"

▶ Open with a topic that you and the audience have in common, such as the city you live in, the traffic getting there, the food in the club, and so on.

When Robin Williams performed at the Metropolitan Opera House, he opened his act by commenting on the enormous chandeliers the audience had just watched rise up to the ceiling:

&&I would like to thank Imelda Marcos for her earrings. I wonder if Pavarotti is over at the Improv going 'Two Jews walked into a bar . . .'&&

&&Hello, Santa Fe, I like your town. The police here, their uniforms look like the Maytag man. They pull you over, you say, 'What, is my refrigerator broke down?'&&

—**Paul Rodriguez**

▶ Start your act with something currently going on in your life, something that just happened (or you can pretend just happened). For instance, if you are doing a routine about traffic, say it happened on your way to the club tonight.

Greg Gorman

Paul Rodriguez

&&On the way here I saw a sign for an exit on the Hollywood freeway for 'The Braille Institute — Next Right.' Now, who is this sign for? Creates a terrible traffic jam. There were blues singers, dogs, and canes all over the road.&&

—**Arsenio Hall**

▶ DON'T start with Hitler. It puts people in a bad mood. Save controversial issues for later, when the audience is with you.
▶ DON'T start with "Hey, how are you all doing?" There are so many original ways to start an act, why start with a cliché?

- DON'T start with "Hey, is this thing on?" Or ... "It's so bright up here." Or ... "Boy, am I nervous." Dwelling on your fears in your opening will only increase them as you go on. This makes everyone in the room nervous.
- DON'T open with material that will give the audience a false impression of who you are. One of my students opened with a very angry, tough attitude that got her a good laugh. However, she lost the audience because the bulk of her material wasn't angry but rather nice, polite observations about being a mother. So, don't lead the audience on. Open with something that you can sustain for the rest of your act.
- DON'T open your act with sexual material. You don't want the audience to climax in your first ten seconds and fall asleep for the rest of your set.

Above all, know what your attitude is. Focusing on how you feel about what you are talking about will help you get over stage fright and move you through this difficult part of your act.

Workshop #25

THE OPENING

Look through your material and select the best possible opening material:

- Material about your appearance
- Material that reflects your persona
- Material about the audience
- Material about a common current topic, or
- Material about something very current in your life

Sketch your opening material here.

_____

_____

_____

_____

_____

_____

About Segues

Don't concern yourself with transitions. TV time is so precious that a comic needs to move from thought to thought without wasting any time with stupid segues like

"And speaking about bananas, I was in the market the other day and . . ."

In America, we are so sophisticated about stand-up that an audience recognizes when a comic is doing a segue and it sounds artificial. Letterman and Carson make fun of themselves when they do segues. Segues have become jokes themselves. As comic Barry Sobel says,

"Silly audience, segues are for kids."

In real life, people jump from topic to topic as thoughts occur to them. A woman can be talking about her sick dog and in midsentence remind herself to go pick up her dry cleaning. Suddenly changing topics is what makes a comic "off-the-wall." Think of what happens when a ball bounces off a wall: It heads in one direction and then suddenly heads in another direction. Student Patty Lousie Iacobello goes from talking about being "a Catholic slut" to talking about "Hey, I hang out with the homeless," and suddenly says "Okay . . . now I'd like to sing a song."

On a TV spot, wild comic Bobcat Goldthwait performed his monolog on a bed of "hot coals" with a raw steak strapped to his ankle:

Bobcat Goldthwait

❝Two guys walk into a bar . . . aiiee!

After the hotfoot bit, Bobcat flashed a grin and without any segue continued:

❝God told me he'd give me eight million dollars if I'd kill Oral Roberts.❞

You will find certain topics will naturally lead to others. However, if they don't, don't push it. End one chunk. Stop . . . take a breath, and start a new topic with energy and enthusiasm.

The Set List

Now that you have your opening, the middle of your material needs to be organized into a set list. A set list is a list of code words of your act. Just like musicians make a list of the songs they are going to sing, comics make a list of the chunks of materials they plan to deliver: "First I'm going to talk about *dating*, then I'm going to talk about *getting old . . .*"

The set list is a comic's personal, cryptic way of providing the one word or phrase that, when looked at, gives an immediate memory code.

Most comics organize their material by subject matter. When you rehearse your material, you will find that certain topics naturally flow into other topics. I suggest starting with your least personal topics and ending with the most personal. Remember, though, that all of your material needs to be about you.

Here is an old set list of my act for a fifteen-minute show:

Dating
Afraid of sleeping alone
Computer dating
Dog
Getting old
Gym
Cinderella
Relationships

I start off with a dating chunk because many of the people in the audience are on dates and my lack of success on dates is a natural lead-in to my piece about sleeping alone:

66. . . as soon as I turn off the lights my house becomes a Stephen King novel. I think there is a man under the bed, a man in the closet, a man behind the door. I mean, where was he prom night when I needed him? . . .99

I then do a piece about my unsuccessful computer date:

66... he had a real nice Wang and he was user-friendly with it, but I need a guy with a hard disk drive, none of this floppy business ...99

Logically this takes me to worrying about my relationships with my dog:

66maybe I'm bi-species. I'm reading a book ... Women Who Love Dogs Too Much ...99

And from there, I travel to worrying about being old:

66... one day I'm going to wake up and no matter how hot it is, I'm going to want to wear a coat ...99

Then I do a gym piece about how I'm fighting old age, but:

66These gyms are all coed, you have to wear a diaphragm to get into the Jacuzzi. One girl got pregnant on the thigh machine.99

At this point I feel that the audience knows me better, and I get more personal as I talk about my longing for a good relationship and my disappointments:

66Cinderella lied to us. There should be a Betty Ford Center where they deprogram you by putting you on an electric chair. Play 'Some Day My Prince Will Come' and hit you and go, 'Nobody's coming ... Nobody's coming ... Nobody's coming ...'99

110

Tips on Using the Set List

> ▶ Arrange your act in terms of escalating intimacy.

Going in front of an audience is like going on a first date. They don't know you, so don't scare them away by starting off with a routine about your pubic hair. Many comics prefer to arrange their acts in order of escalating intimacy. Start with safe topics, such as job stuff, dating, food, and so on. Then as you and the audience get to know each other, move on to more personal topics like relationships and sex.

> ▶ Don't take your set list onstage.

Unless comics are trying out new material, they rarely take their set lists onstage. One student was so worried about forgetting her act that she wrote her set list on her hand. The only problem was that she sweated and then spent most of her act trying to read her palm. An audience that pays a cover and two-drink minimum would like to think that the comic has made the effort to memorize their act. It would be like watching a sitcom with the actors holding their scripts. Just in case, I always write my set list a few hours before I go on, choosing which material I want to do that night and where to put the new stuff.

> ▶ Use the set list as a memorization aid.

Usually just the act of writing out the set list helps me to remember my act and gives me a general idea of the order of the material because it forces me to visualize my pieces. Writing down the code words of my act sends a picture to my brain of the entire piece.

Arranging material according to its logical emotional flow makes memorizing the order almost unnecessary. You can see from my set list how every subject connects emotionally to the one before it. My set list is designed from the way that my brain "worries." It is very natural for me to go from worrying about not dating, to worrying about sleeping alone. The code words of the set list then act as memory triggers for what I already instinctively know.

▶ You don't have to be perfect.

I have never followed my set list to the letter. There are always things that pop unexpectedly out of my mouth and things I edit as I perform. The set list is a suggested route, but don't let yourself get chained to it. The shortest way from Los Angeles to San Francisco is up Interstate 5. But be a traveler who is willing to get off the main route and take side trips. Even though you know where you are going and you've mapped out the best way to get there, take the opportunity to explore the back roads. When you get lost, you know you can always get back on the main route and hit your destination.

Workshop #26

〰〰〰〰〰〰〰〰〰〰〰〰〰〰〰〰〰〰〰〰〰〰〰〰〰〰〰〰

YOUR SET LIST

Limiting yourself to one word or phrase, write down the topics in your act:

First Draft:

_____   _____

_____   _____

_____   _____

_____   _____

_____   _____

_____   _____

Now rearrange your material going from the least intimate to the most intimate. Don't force your pieces to connect with each other unless they naturally do. Remember, you *can* jump from topic to topic.

Second Draft:

_____   _____

_____   _____

_____   _____

_____   _____

_____   _____

_____   _____

Now to get the set list in your head, get comfortable, close your eyes, and imagine an audience in front of you. Without looking at any notes, start talking your act and let the order of your material come naturally into being.

Write your Final Draft Set List here:

_____   _____

_____   _____

_____   _____

_____   _____

_____   _____

_____   _____

The Closing

66Leave them laughing . . .99

   You will need to modify your set list so that the material you know will kill is at the end of your set. And if you are near the end of your set and you get a big laugh, get off the stage. Some comics get a big laugh near the end of their set, then try to top it and end with a thud. Leave them wanting more. Instead of getting to everything on your set list, if you get a laugh near the end of your act, say "Thank you, good night," and get the hell out of there.

Workshop #27

What material do you think is going to get the biggest laugh? Write it down here:

_____

_____

_____

_____

_____

_____

_____

_____

Since it's difficult to know exactly how long your act is going to be and which pieces will get the biggest reactions, it's best to be ready for two different endings, one earlier than the other. In this case, when your time is up, you can end on a laugh and not have to rush material trying to get to the big laugh before your time is up.

Earlier Possible Ending:

How to Rehearse Your Act

66Hey, Mom, listen to this one.99

Many comics do not rehearse their acts. Although they write their material down, they wait until they are in front of an audience to say it out loud.

Jerry Seinfeld feels that there is absolutely no need for rehearsal, that you have to learn to shape it to the audience and there's nothing you can do by yourself. According to Seinfeld, "A good comedy act is not a monolog, it's a dialog and the audience has a part, and you have to balance the two together."

My suggestion for beginners is to memorize your act by acting it out with attitude and feeling in front of your comedy buddy, not in front of a mirror.

A performer's biggest fear is that he or she is going to forget the act. Consequently, out of this fear, comics overmemorize their material and become, Robo-comic! No matter what happens onstage they deliver their act as planned. The waitress has dropped a tray of drinks, the customers are having a food fight, and the microphone has gone out, still the performer continues as if nothing has happened. Being perfect might get you an "A" in algebra, but being perfect has nothing to do with being funny. Sometimes the best part of a comic's act is when he forgets it. People love to watch other people in danger. Why do you think people pay to watch tightrope walkers? It is the possibility that they will fall that keeps us captivated. A good tightrope walker will pretend to lose her balance to make her act exciting.

Memorize your material, but always be willing to let go of it so you can deal with what is going on in the moment. Remember:

DON'T try material out on relatives. You wouldn't practice a striptease act on your librarian. Don't practice stand-up on your mother.

DO test material with your comedy buddy or by sneaking it into a conversation, but never let anyone know that you are testing out material. Material that bombs in a kitchen might kill in a club.

DON'T rehearse your material without first getting in touch with your attitude and picturing what you are saying. If you don't do this, your material will sound like a collection of lifeless words. People don't respond simply to words; they respond to the feelings and pictures behind the words. Imagining is a very powerful tool. It forces you to relive what you are talking about. The first time you tell a story you naturally picture it as you remember it. The second time you tell the story you will probably be more focused on trying to get a reaction and less in touch with your *own* feelings. You will stay more focused on your feelings or attitude if you visualize what you are talking about. This will keep your material spontaneous and alive.

DON'T overrehearse. Know your material, but don't set it in concrete, because you will have to modify your act depending on the audience. You are not performing in a vacuum. Things that are beyond your control will happen. In real life people in the audience will say things to you. Waitresses will drop glasses. You need to be willing to open up your act, maybe drop some of your planned material and respond to the immediate circumstance.

I learned this the hard way. I was invited to perform at a camp for handicapped children. I was nervous about performing for children. As comic-magician Tom Mullica says: "Performing for children is like walking through Lion Safari Country with a meat suit on."

Since I didn't have any material appropriate for children, I decided to do mostly magic tricks. I rehearsed and rehearsed. I got to the camp, very prepared, only to find that it was a camp for *blind* children. So much for my magic tricks. I got onstage and told the audience that I was standing there stark naked and talked about how cold it was. Well, what would you have done?

Stand-up, like ballroom dancing, is an interactive, personal form of entertainment. Who the audience is always affects your act. Performing in front of an audience your own age is different from performing in front of an audience your parents' age. The act of one of my students was based on her being a lesbian. Her act went over great at the Gay Pride Festival, but would she go over in front of a straight crowd? Not knowing how the audience would react to her, she had to keep herself flexible. After she revealed she was a lesbian, a woman in the front row let out a

"Eww!" She used the straight woman's negative reaction to improvise additional material.

> **❝You might want to consider the advantages of being a lesbian: You don't have to worry about the toilet seat being up, you don't have to worry about disease, and . . . you never have to sleep in the wet spot.❞**

It was this flexibility that made her go over so well. And get a dinner date.

So . . . know your material, but be willing to have it change.

Workshop #28

Memorize your act by acting it out several times.

- ▸ Practice your material in chunks.
- ▸ Act out your material using a strong attitude.
- ▸ Visualize what you are talking about.
- ▸ Practice your act as if you are performing for:
    a group of loving friends.
    a convention of New York cab drivers.
    a group of dentists.

If you find yourself having problems with memorizing certain chunks, ask yourself:

1. What is your attitude for the chunk?

2. Can you visualize what you are talking about?

3. Is your setup simple or too complicated?

Material that is good rolls off your tongue. If your material is getting all twisted up, toss it. The material might be awkward because of:

- ▶ A language problem—your choice of words is formal and stiff.
- ▶ An attitude mismatch—try on a new attitude and go back to ranting and raving about the issue with a different attitude as outlined in Chapter 2.
- ▶ It's redundant—edit down your setups.
- ▶ Lack of commitment—you are simply bored with the topic. Toss it and find issues that interest you.

Timing/Delivery

"Timing is everything . . ."

—George Burns

Timing is so difficult to teach—it's something you have to feel, like jazz. There have been times onstage when my timing was so good, I was so in sync with the universe, I could do no wrong. And there were times when my timing was so off that no matter how hard I tried, I couldn't get my act into the groove. There is a comedy groove; when you become more experienced, you'll know when you've hit it, and you'll be able to slide into it more and more often. Until then, here are some technical clues to help you with timing and delivery.

Emotional Tags

The emotional tag is what you improvise after the punch. It is *your* spontaneous, genuine response to what you've just said, and it creates a feeling of intimacy between comic and audience. It can be as simple as:

"Yup!" "That's right!" "I know . . . I know."

Just as a pitcher has a follow-through after the ball leaves his hand, a comic has a follow-through after the punch leaves his or her mouth. An emotional tag is a carry-through of your attitude. You have your setup, then your punch, and then your emotional tag. It's what you do while people are laughing (or not laughing).

How you feel at the end of each punch will change, so the emotional tag will always be different—it is never permanently set. It is unique for just that moment. Leave room for the emotional tag, but don't rehearse it. Don't try to be funny, just react. "Yeah . . . that's my mother!" or just a "Yup" will do the job fine. You can even just make a face. The idea is not to plan these emotional tags but to leave room for them to happen.

After the emotional tag, don't forget to breathe. I know it sounds stupid to remind you of this, but you'd be surprised. It's setup, punch, emotional tag, and then take a breath. Don't run all your material together. It's all right, even necessary, to have moments of quiet in your act. I've seen some great jokes not get a reaction because the comic didn't leave even a moment for the audience to react. Very often the emotional tag is what gets the laugh. It honks to them.

Workshop #29

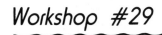

EMOTIONAL TAGS

Emotional tags cannot be rehearsed. They are the spontaneous, genuine portions of your act that are made up at the moment. But get a feel of what they are like by acting out one piece and then connecting to yourself after the punch.

A tag can be on how you feel about what you said: "Boy, that was a stupid idea." Or it can be just a sound: "Uh huh." Or just nod your head. David Letterman uses this technique. After a joke that doesn't get a response he says,

❝Hey, these are the jokes, folks!❞

Get used to leaving that space to add thoughts after the punch, taking a breath and creating a moment. This is what will create your rhythm and make your act more like a real conversation with give and take.

Summary

By this point you have:

▶ Written out your opening.
▶ Drafted out a set list.
▶ Decided on your closing.
▶ Rehearsed your act.

All the work you've done leads you to one place: performing in front of a real audience. The next chapter will take you by the hand through the performing experience.

CHAPTER 6

GETTING IT UP
... ONSTAGE

"Dying is easy, comedy is hard."

—Edmund Kean, nineteenth-century actor

Sure, performing is scary. But you wouldn't spend a month building a boat and then never put it in the water. Now it's time to do your act in front of an audience and see if it floats.

Even if you are not considering a career in stand-up, it is still imperative that you try out your act in a comedy club or at an amateur night. You can't truly understand the principles of making people laugh unless you perform in a place where people go to laugh. Once you've performed in a stand-up club, interjecting humor in a speech, a toast, or a sales pitch will be a piece of cake. (See Chapter 9.)

By now you have a set list and three to twenty minutes of material. In this chapter I will give you exercises to reduce your fears, as well as tips from some of the biggest names in

comedy to guide you through the performing experience. But first you need to find a place to perform.

Getting a Gig

Practically every city has a comedy club that sets aside one night a week for amateur showcases. (See Appendix for a list of comedy clubs.) Very often hotels, bars, schools, or organizations will have talent nights where amateurs are given anywhere from three to twenty minutes of stage time. Make a few phone calls and find a place where you can sign up to perform five to ten minutes of stand-up.

Don't be too eager to perform at the top comedy clubs. It's best to start off at a not-so-known club until you've developed your talent. See Chapter 8 for additional places to perform.

Two Hours to Showtime

"What Do I Wear?"

Wear what feels comfortable. Avoid making big statements with your clothes. If your clothes are funnier than you are . . . you've got a problem.

Women: Don't dress sexy, unless that suits your persona (à la Mae West). Avoid tight clinging dresses, cleavage, and so on. Sex and comedy generally do not mix. Don't take my word for it: the next time you are making love, try telling a joke and see what happens:

66Hey, Fred, that looks like a penis . . . only smaller.99

Dress comfortably and attractively. Accentuate your brain and not your body.

Thirty Minutes to Showtime

Get Information

Check in with the person in charge and find out how much stage time you have. Whether you are an amateur or a pro, you will always be asked to bring your act in under a certain amount of time.

Amateur nights in comedy clubs give comics anywhere from three minutes to fifteen minutes. Find out if the club has a way of signaling you when your time is up. Whether it is a red light that goes on in the back of the room or the MC shining a flashlight in your eyes, get off the stage when your time is up if you want to be invited back.

Twenty Minutes to Showtime

Check Out the Audience

- ▶ How old are they?
- ▶ How drunk?
- ▶ What is the audience's predominant race or gender?
- ▶ Is there a large group from one organization?

By looking at them, or by asking, you will get an idea what type of an audience they are and what material you might add or cut. Just as I didn't do magic tricks for a blind audience, you wouldn't go over big by doing that "clitoris piece" for a group of Mormon librarians.

Checking out the audience might also inspire some last-minute specialty material. I once opened for a jazz artist who had a hard time finding opening acts because his audiences had the reputation of "coming down from coke by eating Jews." To ignore that I was the only Caucasian in the room would be a missed opportunity. I ended up adding material about how "I had a dream too!" and "I'm not a racist. I have a black cat named Kunte Kitty." And so on. It ended up to be a wonderful night. Prince was in the audience and later invited me to open for him.

Warning: You can run a risk by creating last-minute specialty material. I once opened with an improvised comment about the Jewish New Year, which was the next day. Since the audience wasn't Jewish and didn't care about anything Jewish, they continued eating their pork rinds and ignored me for the rest of my act. Don't open with new material. Throw it in between chunks that you are sure of.

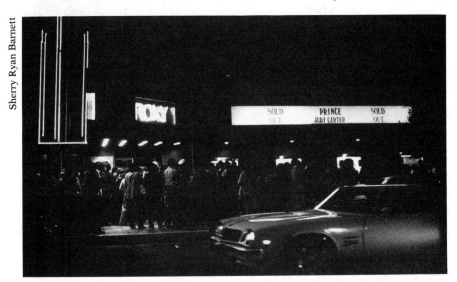

Sherry Ryan Barnett

126

Fifteen Minutes to Showtime

❝Oh, they love him . . . they'll hate me . . .❞

Check out the comics. When performing in a comedy club, some performers find watching other comics too distracting and try to arrive at the club just a few minutes before they go on. Others arrive early to watch the comics on before them. Getting wrapped up in someone else's act can distract you from focusing on your act, but sometimes it's helpful to know what the previous comic did in case his or her material is similar to yours. One night I wondered why my material on dating wasn't working, not knowing the comic before me had done fifteen minutes on dating.

Geri Jewell

When you start performing a lot, in some cases the person before you might actually have done your material.

Sometimes the person you follow will provide you with a better opening. Lotus Weinstock had to follow Geri Jewell, a comedian with cerebral palsy who got a two-minute standing ovation. Lotus then opened with.

❝What a gimmick.❞

So watch the comic before you, but don't let him or her unduly influence you.

127

Ten Minutes to Showtime

Drugs and Alcohol

Just say no. I can always tell when someone onstage is high. They get sloppy. They repeat things. They get dull. They get frantic. Don't push away your feelings. Allow yourself to feel fear. It's not going to kill you. Know that your level of fear has nothing to do with how funny you will be. Experiencing fear is uncomfortable, but it's not going to kill you and it will vanish when you step onstage.

Five Minutes to Showtime

I'm nauseous.

Relax. In a club, you get bombarded with stress. Needy comics will want to try out jokes on you. Waitresses will bump into you. Your spot might be changed. All of your fears will escalate as each minute passes. Chances are you won't have a dressing room with a Jacuzzi, so find some niche where you can be alone and connect with yourself. Get quiet, close your eyes, and listen to your heart. It takes a few minutes until you will be able to hear it. This exercise will calm your nerves and center you. At this point, don't spend your time practicing your act. Have faith that you know it. Brains tend to shut down under stress. Comic Paula Poundstone sometimes gets so scared before she goes on that she can't remember her act, but it always comes back as soon as she hits the stage. Spend these few minutes connecting with yourself and breathing.

128

Thirty Seconds to Showtime

Your Performance

The MC is now introducing you ... Remember, you are going onstage to communicate, to reveal yourself to the audience, not to make them laugh. Do you remember running home from school because you couldn't wait to tell your mother or friend something? This is the kind of energy you need, this urgency to communicate, to propel you onstage. If your only intent in going onstage is to make the audience laugh, you will be giving your power away. It has been my experience that anytime I expect something to happen, I'm setting myself up for disappointment.

Also, don't forget to turn your tape recorder on. *Always tape-record your performances.* Listening to the tape the next day will help you to further evaluate your material and performance when you get to the exercises in Chapter 7.

Your Time Onstage

❝Boy ... it's so dark out there. I can't see anything.❞

You're up on the stage. You feel a bright light on you. You can't see anything but the first three rows. There is a microphone in front of you. First adjust the microphone to your level without making a big deal out of it. Don't rush right into your act. Take a moment to breathe. You need to adjust to being onstage and the audience needs to adjust to you too.

Take a moment to let them look at you. Find a warm face in the audience to connect with. Say "Hi" warmly and openly. Wait for a response. Make this person your friend. During your act check back with your "friend." Do your emotional tags directly to him or her. This connection with someone in the first three rows will create a likability that will carry to the very last row.

❝Oh, my God . . . they're laughing!❞

When the audience laughs, don't just rush on to your next piece, but stop and acknowledge them. Listen to them. Let yourself receive them. Think of the audience as a child whose response needs to be acknowledged. An audience will stop laughing if they don't feel you are enjoying their response. Most of the time we don't laugh out loud at television shows because there is no one to hear us. Laughter needs to be appreciated and received. Employing this philosophy, after a so-so laugh I do a bit where I take out my wallet and give money to the big laughers in the audience. Boy, does it encourage them. So when you get a laugh, stop talking and take it in. You've done all the work. Now enjoy it.

❝Has this ever happened to you?❞

When you ask an audience a question, leave room for them to respond. Take your time and don't rush your material together. Leave room for your emotional tags. Remember, "the funny" is often what happens in between the jokes.

Microphone Technique

❝Testing, 1, 2, 3 . . . is this thing on?❞

Get to the club early so you can familiarize yourself with the microphone. Since some people have trouble dealing with objects of that shape, here are some tips in dealing with the microphone.

▶ Never perform stand-up without one. The microphone gives you control over an audience. When you battle with hecklers, you may not be wittier, but at least you will be louder.

▶ Don't play with the mike stand. When you come onstage, adjust the stand so the microphone is just under your mouth. You don't want the microphone blocking your face. Adjust it approximately three inches from your mouth, and once you adjust it, leave it alone. It is annoying to see a nervous neophyte hanging on to the stand for dear life, adjusting and readjusting it. As your mother would say, leave it alone.

▶ Don't say first thing, "Is this thing on?" People will tell you if it isn't.

▶ If you move around in your act, using one hand, take the microphone out of the stand and, with your other hand, move the stand behind you. In off time, practice doing this with some grace. Stands are ugly. Get them out of the way so you don't spend your set tripping over them.

▶ Don't yell into the microphone. If you are going to yell during your act, move the microphone away from your face.

▶ Don't break the microphone. You'll never get asked back again.

Bombing

❝Oh, my God . . . I'm in hell.❞

Picture being onstage. You deliver your material. No response. They stare at you. Someone coughs. You deliver another piece and once again . . . nothing. You start to sweat. You know . . . you are bombing.

I imagine that all readers have been picturing this as they read every page. This fear of bombing is the biggest deterrent to creative accomplishment in any career. Many comics are so frightened of this happening that they will almost never try out new or chancy material. Bombing is a part of the creative process. I have never met a successful comic, writer, singer, or salesperson who hasn't bombed. It goes along with the territory. To be good you need to take risks, and that will increase your chances of bombing. But bombing will help you to realize what doesn't work and your act can only get better.

Misconceptions About Bombing

66I'll never work again . . .99

Jay Leno did. Sam Kinison did. When comic Jerry Seinfeld first started out, he bombed every other show and was satisfied with that, because every performance is a lesson. Everyone who is worth their salt bombs. Accept that when starting out you will bomb at least 50 percent of the time. As you perform more and more, this percentage will decrease, but there is no guarantee against bombing.

The late, marvelously eccentric Andy Kaufman continually bombed. Before he was a star, he opened for Sonny and Cher and part of his act was taking a nap onstage. He was booed off the stage, but he kept with his vision until the rest of us caught on.

Sam Kinison revealed in a *Rolling Stone* interview that he bombed in his audition for Rodney Dangerfield's cable special: "I came in on a Friday night. Full house. They were ready to laugh at anything . . . except me. I did eight minutes and emptied the room."

Margaret Smith tells how when she first began her deadpan style and got no reaction from the audience, the MC said after she left the stage. "Margaret Smith, ladies and gentlemen, fresh out of Bellevue."

❝I bombed. They hate me! I don't deserve to live.❞

Remember, it's your material that bombs, not you. Separate your act from your worth as a human being. You will create a lot of misery for yourself if you judge your self-worth by how an audience responds to your act. Bombing means that something in your *act* didn't work. It doesn't mean that *you* didn't work. Bombing means that there is a problem, a challenge. Your job is to discover and work at finding a solution. Deal with your act as a separate, objective part of your life. Not *as* your life.

❝Bombing kills.❞

Bombing doesn't feel great, but it won't kill you. When you lose that connection with the audience, it does feel like you just broke up with someone, but at least you don't have to split up the furniture.

❝My material sucks.❞

Know that *you can't please everyone.* Your material might be great but not right for a particular audience. Your material might be hip, but your audience might be from Omaha. Furthermore, you will not be able to tell how you did until you listen to your tape. Many times, because of the acoustics in the room and the mood you are in, you may not be able to hear the audience laugh.

What to Do When You Bomb

One of the biggest reasons comics bomb is that they are not connected with themselves. They go on automatic pilot, phony, and the audience stops listening early in

re strategies to handle bombing:

ATEGY #1: Commit to your act and go on as
d.

Just keep plugging along until the audience catches up with you. This approach takes confidence and comes only after having a lot of stage experience. It takes guts to commit to your vision when no one else in the room does. But this is what makes the great ones great.

▶ STRATEGY #2: Admit that you know you are bombing.

When you really feel like your act is flopping into the toilet, admit it. *"Oh, my God ... I've just taken a trip to hell!"*

If you are really overwhelmed with a panic attack, the worst thing is to pretend everything is fine. Have you seen comics start to die and pretend it's not happening? They speed up their acts. They smile even more. They think they are faking it. All of this artificial behavior will make an audience feel more and more uncomfortable. When an audience sees someone struggling but pretending to be cool, it makes it hard for them to laugh. They will sense your pain.

The best way to relieve their and your suffering is to "call" the situation. To stop your act and speak what is really going on in your mind. Speaking the subtext of the situation is a relief. It's joyous. It's funny.

Letterman and Carson make a whole routine out of bombing.

> **66. . . Is there a revolver in the house? Hey, I'm going to keep plugging ahead.99**
>
> **—Johnny Carson**

134

(AFTER A JOKE THAT DIDN'T WORK) *66Boy, Paul, I'm not feeling well tonight. Maybe I'm ovulating.99*

—David Letterman

One of my students started bombing because she was freaked out by her husband being in the audience. Using the calling it technique, she stopped her act and said, "My husband is here and I'm worried that if I'm not funny, he'll divorce me." Once she included the audience in on her reality, she got a big laugh.

One night I was playing to a group of beer-drinking college students. I was dishing it out, but they weren't buying. I had to stay onstage for twenty minutes. I disconnected from myself. I sped up. They started talking. I talked louder. So did they. I was so disconnected that a part of me was hearing meaningless words come out of my mouth and watching my gesticulating hands. Then something peculiar happened. I was doing a piece about how I'm not myself on dates. I started it "You know I'm not myself ..." And instead of saying "... on a date." What came out of my mouth was "I'm not myself ... right now." The truth was so powerful that I then started rambling.

> *66Oh, I'm insecure. Boy, it's hard to be funny when you're retaining water, and we might invade Central America, and you're sitting here with a date, and I haven't had sex in six months. With only five more points on my SATs I could have been a CPA. Does anyone have a Kleenex?99*

They gave me napkins, I blew my nose, and went on with my act with their full attention and ended up with a standing ovation. My connecting with myself was the catalyst to connecting with them.

If something is on your mind that is that big, share it. Stop your act. Take a breath. Let out your thoughts. When a joke bombs, you can ask the audience if they have a better punchline.

Another reason you might find yourself out of touch with the audience is that you said something that made them feel uncomfortable. In this case, comment on what you think is going on in the minds of certain people in the audience. It's you imitating the inner voice of someone in the audience.

"Oh, Harry, he just said the 'F' word. Oh, make him stop!"

▶ STRATEGY #3: Walk off the stage.

In the end, if all else fails . . . get off the stage. Early in my career I was opening at the Sahara-Tahoe for Loggins and Messina's farewell tour. It was the last night of their tour and the place was so packed that they had to delay the show for one hour. Delaying a rock concert is the worst thing you can do for the opening act, because a lot of the fans have timed their drugs to come on for the headliner. When *I* went out, they were peaking and they were pissed. My opening included me playing the accordion. They wanted me dead. I was being a trouper, and tried to continue my act using all the techniques mentioned in this chapter. It was when I started playing my parody of "Lady of Spain" that they started throwing shot glasses. I ducked and tried to continue playing when suddenly, a drug-crazed guy leapt out of the audience, put a tablecloth over my head, and set it on fire. At this point, a security guard lifted me up and my accordion and carried me offstage while I shouted, "Put me down, I know I can get them."

Remember, it's not a failure to *walk* offstage. Sometimes I have stayed onstage in front of an abusive audience, trying to get love and understanding and ending up going in

137

the gutter. "Okay, let's talk about dicks . . ." Sometimes I did get them, but more often I walked offstage without laughs and, more important, without my dignity.

WARNING: Be careful about becoming hostile.

Very often when comics get frightened, they feel they have to protect themselves by being hostile. Student Linda Adelman is a perfect example of how fear can turn a perfectly nice person into an attacking bitch:

She started a piece:

> **❝I took my mother to a spa, you know, a fat farm . . .❞**

And then, trying to connect with a friendly woman in the first row:

> **❝Have you ever been to a spa? No? Well you should!❞**

This got her a nervous laugh but lost her her likability. If you feel the impulse to attack the audience, squelch it. You might get a laugh, but as many agents and TV producers will tell you, likability is one of the most important qualities needed for a successful career.

Workshop #30

BOMBING

This exercise is going to sound weird. After you have some stage experience under your belt, try going onstage with the intent to bomb. This will take away your fear. Go on in an off time, and do it, get it over with. Know it isn't so awful. Practice calling the situation—commenting on what others are thinking.

Johnny Carson's entire act depends on bombing, so after a lame joke he can make comments such as:

> **❝Well, I liked that one.❞**
> **❝Hey, folks, some of them are bad news and I can't help it.❞**

Carson looks forward to bombing so he can be funny. Letterman does the same thing.

> **(AFTER A BAD JOKE) ❝Oh, help me please. Someone come down from another planet and rescue me.❞**

When you ski, you have to practice how to fall right. When you are a comic you need to practice recovering techniques or you'll never get back up.

Don't be so frightened of bombing that you perform your act as if you are on a jungle gym, grabbing on to each joke as if you will fall and die if you stop. The excitement is the swing between the rungs— The uh-oh, you might miss it. The oh no, you have to go back. Swing with it.

Hecklers

> **❝You suck! Next! Boring!❞**

A heckler is someone who wants attention. It's like someone who's standing on the ledge of a building. The difference with a heckler is that you *want* them to jump. Most comics have a couple of choice lines for hecklers who are out to disrupt their act.

Diane Ford

❝It's kind of silly to heckle. You've spent big money to see the show and you're ruining it for yourself. It's like going to the ballet and trying to trip the dancers.❞

—Jimmy Brogan

Sometimes you need to be very strong:

❝Sir . . . why don't you put a condom over your head? You're acting like a dick, you might as well dress like one.❞

—Diane Ford

❝You bucket of lust. You make me want to have my tubes tied.❞

—Judy Tenuta

After a while battling with a drunk can get very tedious. Most comics will work out a signal with the club owner on when to boot out a drunk who is disrupting the show. But if the club owner is also drunk and the audience has taken over your show, get off the stage, go home, take a bath, and try it again tomorrow night.

Dialoguing with the Audience

There are different schools of thought about opening the door for "dialoguing" or "improvising" with audience members. The late, old-time comedian Phil Foster advised new comics never to let the audience talk. He said that as soon as you open yourself up for dialog, you risk losing control. When you ask the audience for a response, you are causing *them* to think instead of just following *your* line of thought. However, some comics, such as Jimmy Brogan, invite the audience

Jimmy Brogan

into a dialog and work their material into conversations.

66So where are you folks from?99

Although improvising material out of talking to an audience hasn't found a place on television, it definitely has a place in the clubs. However, I have found that students who depend on this method are usually acting out of laziness. They don't want to go through the homework of constructing solid stand-up material. Unless you are a brilliant improviser, such as Robin Williams or Jimmy Brogan, don't depend on the audience to give you your act.

Summary

So far you have:

▶ Picked out your clothes.
▶ Familiarized yourself with the microphone.
▶ Performed your act for an audience.
▶ Taped your performance.

No matter how your performance went, the next chapter will help you improve it.

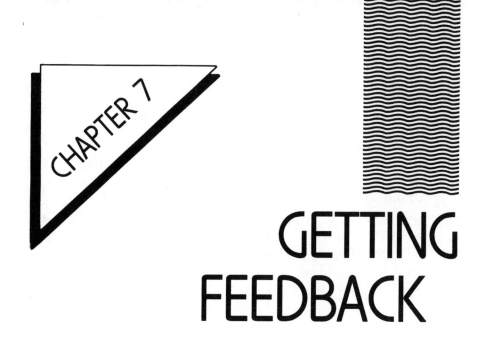

CHAPTER 7

GETTING FEEDBACK

The Morning After

❝Is it time to quit my day job yet?❞

You have performed and taped your act and now it's time to evaluate your performance. When a piece doesn't work, it can be one of four things:

1. Your material sucked.

2. Your performance/delivery sucked.

3. The audience sucked.

4. All of the above.

Don't worry, whatever went wrong . . . it can be fixed. And this chapter will show you how.

Judging Yourself

Be Kind

You've heard of "treat others the way you'd like to be treated." Most of us judge ourselves so critically that if we treated others the way we treat ourselves, we'd end up running Joan Crawford Child Care Centers. In order to objectively evaluate our performance, we have to learn kinder, more productive ways of judging ourselves.

Thinking in terms of "I killed. I was great" or "I bombed. I was awful" is very limited. There is a whole world in between "good" and "bad." Every time you perform you have an opportunity to learn. So, instead of "I sucked, let's get loaded" try: "This *piece* didn't work, let's fix it." The first attitude leads to a dead end, the second to progress.

Detach from Your Act

Remember, you are judging your *act* and not your self-worth. When you're onstage, you're not always the best judge. In order to objectively examine your act, you need to detach from it, actually pretend that someone else did it. When I listen to my tape, even after a good show, I start hearing things I can't stand, things that have nothing to do with my act. Such as "I hate my voice, it sounds like a chipmunk." Most people hate the sound of their own voice even though we don't usually complain about another person's voice. So after you perform, let it be. Don't make changes on your way home. Even wait a few days before you listen to your tape.

Getting Feedback from Others

There is never a shortage of people who want to give advice. Beginners are so needing of attention and feedback that many times they change their material based on the comments of an idiot. One thing that has always amazed me about comedy is that everyone thinks they're an expert. I wouldn't have the gall to tell my plumber how to do his work, but after I appeared on TV he was chock-full of suggestions for me. *Everybody* thinks that they're funny. Generally, I listen only to a few trusted people. And when I do, I simply listen, and then if the next morning I'm excited about making a change, only then do I do it. Be careful about taking advice from other people.

Have Patience

It takes time to be good. Jim McCawley tells comics to give it a good seven years. It took Charlie Fleischer eight years before he got his big break doing the voice of cartoon character Roger Rabbit. Now when people ask Fleischer if they should stick with it, he tells them: "Get out of the business, don't even try."

Fleischer figures that if he can talk someone out of it, that's good, because if you are meant to do it, no one can talk you out of it. Lots of people will try to tell you how impossible it is to do a stand-up. That it's no way to make a living or support a family. But most comics do stand-up not as a whim, but because they *have* to do it.

Success comes to the ones who persist. If you are dedicated, if you believe in yourself and you really want to do stand-up, you will survive. All of the overnight successes have usually been slaving away at their act for years and *then* they happened overnight.

Listen to the tape of your performance and write down everything the audience laughed at. Write it down exactly the way you said it. Leave these pieces alone.

As you listen to your tape, you will find material that didn't work. Don't throw anything out yet. Making a chunk work takes time and effort. In his routine on the stages of drunkenness, it took comic Larry Miller an entire year before he found the right words to express

Larry Miller

how it feels when the sun hits you when you've been drinking. He pored over this image, trying to find the right simile. He first tried:

> **❝. . . that sun is like a police lineup.❞**

Then he tried

> **❝. . . it's like a nightwatchman's flashlight.❞**

But Miller also wanted to illustrate what that sun symbolizes in terms of the morning-after pangs of guilt and the rush of reality. And the simile he came up with is . . .

❝that sun is like God's flashlight.❞

When you can paint a picture like that, put the commas in the right place and find the right chewy words, you are creating a rich moment that you and the audience will relish.

By following the instructions in this workshop, your out-of-order chunk might be repairable.

Answer these questions:

1. What was your *attitude*? Was it strong? Clear?

2. Did you have a short, understandable *setup*?

3. Was there a sharp contrast between the setup and *punch*?

4. Was the material *authentic* (i.e., are you a gorgeous woman making jokes about how ugly you are)?

	OKAY	*NOT OKAY*
Attitude	☐	☐
Setup	☐	☐
Punch	☐	☐
Authenticity	☐	☐

For those items you checked "NOT OKAY," here is a second checklist to help you diagnose *exactly* what went wrong:

☐ Try on a different attitude (see Chapter 2).

☐ Condense the setup for each piece by deleting all redundant words.

☐ Rewrite each setup to be informational and plausible.

☐ Have the punch contrast the setup.

☐ Do your words create strong visual images?

☐ Can you add any similes?

☐ If you mention someone, try mimicking them.

☐ If you have a "list," does the third item contrast the first two items?

☐ Is there a subject you can call back?

Workshop #32

Very often great material doesn't work because of a flawed performance. I find that material that kills one night can lay dead as a duck the very next night. When this happens to me, the cause is usually that I am out of sync with myself and with the audience. If you've decided the material was okay but it got no laugh (and it did get a laugh somewhere else), look at the performance by answering these questions:

IN GENERAL

YES NO

☐   ☐   Did you take time to relax and center yourself before going on?

☐   ☐   Did you feel connected to the audience?

☐   ☐   Did things change at a certain point? When? What happened?

YOUR OPENING

YES NO

☐   ☐   Did a problem occur during your first thirty seconds onstage (i.e., tripped over the mike, etc.)?

☐   ☐   Did you come onstage with the need to communicate something?

148

YOUR OPENING

YES   NO

☐   ☐   Were you clear on your attitude for the first piece?

☐   ☐   Did you take your time before you spoke?

☐   ☐   Did you make a connection with someone in the audience?

☐   ☐   Was the subject matter on your first piece a turn-off?

☐   ☐   Were you hostile to the audience? Why? Were you nervous?

☐   ☐   Did you take your time with your delivery?

☐   ☐   Did you find a "new friend" to connect with?

TIMING

YES   NO

☐   ☐   Did you "force" your material at the audience, or did you "talk" to them?

☐   ☐   Did you have an eagerness to communicate ideas, or were you trying to make them laugh?

☐   ☐   Did you take time setting up your jokes?

☐   ☐   If the audience wasn't with you, did you speed up or did you stop and talk to them?

☐   ☐   Did you stop and acknowledge the audience when they laughed?

☐   ☐   Did you add emotional tags after each punch?

☐   ☐   Did you leave room between jokes?

☐   ☐   Did you "call it" if things weren't working?

≋≋≋≋≋≋≋≋≋≋≋≋≋≋≋≋≋≋≋≋≋≋

AUDIENCE OR ENVIRONMENTAL CONDITIONS

If your act bombed and you can find nothing wrong with the material or your delivery, then the problem might not rest with you but with the audience, or with circumstances beyond your control. If this is the case, ask yourself: What did you know about the audience?

YES NO

☐ ☐ Was your material right for the audience? Or did you do material that the audience couldn't relate to?

☐ ☐ Did you use certain words that could have offended them?

A phrase that is acceptable in New York or L.A. might be unacceptable or not understood in the Sun Belt. When I was opening for Jim Nabors in Kansas, I said in a setup, "You know what really pisses me off?" The audience reacted very negatively. I had no idea that "pissed off" was an offensive term in Kansas. In Disney World, after opening night, I was presented with a list of forty-nine words I couldn't say. For instance: "For my next *trick* ..." And I was doing a magic show!

YES NO

☐ ☐ Did the comic preceding you do similar material?

If the three comics before you were obsessed with dating, the audience could have gotten tired of the topic.

YES NO

☐ ☐ Was there a disruption in the room?

Before or during your act things can happen that will affect your act. For instance, once during my act, a man started choking on his food. He had the attention of the entire audience. Instead of trying to compete with this, I stopped the show until the man coughed up something. Then afterward I said, "Boy . . . I didn't realize that that was such a killer joke."

Another time Steve Martin unexpectedly showed up at the Comedy Store and I had to follow him. Half the audience had left, and I opened with "I'd like to thank Steve Martin for opening for me. I'm not worried about having to follow him. At least I have tits."

When a major event happens before or during your act, it is difficult to evaluate the specifics of your act. All you can do is to roll with it. Go with it. Ski it. Surf it. You get the idea?

Getting Back on the Horse

Even if you got knocked down in your first time onstage, it's important to get back in the ring. Whatever your problem is, it can be solved. It's ludicrous to think you're going to be really brilliant after a couple of times onstage. It's a process. A process that takes a sincere commitment. I've had students who've been really wonderful the first night, and then they get smug and stale. I've seen others who struggle with their inner demons right up to and after performance time and have gone on to much success.

Success doesn't happen according to your tight time schedule. Perhaps there is a Goddess of Comedy who decides when our time in the spotlight comes. Know you will have good nights and you will have bad nights, and you can learn from both. So keep creating, performing, and evaluating your material, because luck happens to people of action.

Summary

In this chapter you have:

- ▸ Written down verbatim the pieces that worked.
- ▸ Rewritten material that didn't work.
- ▸ Evaluated your performance.

It is most important to keep performing, to get as much "ring time" as possible. It can be difficult to find places to perform when just starting out, so the next chapter is filled with suggestions on how to find work.

CHAPTER 8

GETTING RICH

How to Make Money as a Stand-Up Comic

Stand-up is big business. Besides the obvious markets such as comedy clubs and television where well-known comics make their living, there are also countless places to work where comics whose names you wouldn't recognize make a very good living.

The Catch-22 of getting jobs is that in order to work you need to be good but in order to be good, you need work. With that in mind, I've included in this chapter places you can perform while you are developing your act, strategies to create work, and places to perform where you'll get paid, including

- ▶ comedy clubs
- ▶ colleges
- ▶ industrials
- ▶ cruise ships

- hotels
- television

Also included are tips from leaders in the industry on:

- how to get work
- how to get an agent
- performing on television
- how to get on sitcoms

Places to Perform When Starting Out

One of my first gigs was performing at a Holiday Inn restaurant that had a revolving stage. The problem was that by the time I got to my punchlines, the stage had revolved to a totally different group of people. Not only didn't they laugh, but they had no idea what I was talking about. I've also performed at Boy Scout dinners, weddings, amateur night at the Elks Club, and Teddy Roosevelt National Park in Medora, North Dakota, where I followed Mr. Doodles and his Dancing Poodles. My act was clean—the stage wasn't.

When starting out, comics perform wherever they can. Jay Leno worked at a strip club where the customers made it a custom to flick their lighted cigarettes at the comic. Judy Tenuta worked in a dive where, as she was being introduced, a rat ran across the stage and the owner blew it away with a .357 Magnum.

Amateur Nights

Many comedy clubs and hotels have amateur talent nights where neophyte comics perform anywhere from three to twenty minutes. In larger cities where the competition is fierce, it's sometimes difficult to get spots at the popular

154

clubs. Here are some unconventional strategies that some of my students have tried, with varying degrees of success, to get spots:

- ▶ Call up a club and ask if the club owner can give you a specific time slot because you have a large family who is coming to see you. Since clubs make their money off a cover charge and two-drink minimum, very often the person who brings in the most people are the ones who get asked back. It sometimes helps to be Catholic.
- ▶ Call up pretending to be your manager. Say that your client is an actor appearing in a soon-to-be-released film and you want to arrange for him or her to try out three minutes of stand-up.

With regard to amateur nights, show up early, have patience, and know that things can only get better.

In the beginning of your career you will most likely not be performing under the most ideal situations. In comedy clubs, the choice spots are usually reserved for the pros, and the up and coming are relegated to the graveyard shift. Very often you will be performing at 1 A.M. for three drunks and one couple whose passion for each other interests them more than you. Under these circumstances, you do have to make adjustments. Budd Friedman, owner of the Improv in L.A., suggests to comics who go on before small late-night audiences that they "talk *to* them." This means that, when performing for just a few people, it can be to your advantage to toss aside your set material, talk directly to the customers, and improvise. One cold night in Cleveland, I was forced to go on for only two people. This was a problem, especially because my act called for bringing one of them up on the stage. I didn't do my planned act. I got offstage, sat down at their table, had a couple of drinks, and told a couple of jokes. After the "show" we all went to their house for breakfast.

When working late nights, there is a tendency to work dirty. I suggest not giving in to the inclination to do "dick jokes" and keep your objective on developing material for television.

Create Your Own Events

Instead of waiting for someone to employ you, you can provide work for yourself by creating your own events.

▶ One student advertised in the paper that he writes and arranges roasts.
▶ Another student with business savvy cut a deal with a local hotel arranging his own amateur night. He brought in the talent, emceed, and even reaped profits.
▶ Actor/comic Taylor Negron, co-star of the film *Punchline*, started by performing on the sidewalks of Venice Beach.
▶ At the beginning of her career, comedian Carrie Snow, who calls herself "the full-figure comedian, the eighteen-hour gal, Elvis's love child, and garage sale hostess," rented herself out as wisecracking party guest "guaranteed to liven up any party."

At this point in your career, the trick is to get as much stage experience as you can.

Get stage time by

▶ performing weekly at amateur nights.
▶ creating a fund raiser starring yourself.
▶ volunteering as entertainment for any cause.

Classes

Classes are great because you don't feel so alone. My students find that my class gives them direction and a supportive environment to develop their acts and the confidence to go out and tackle the difficult world of comedy. My students get a videotape of their showcase, which many have parlayed into jobs. Student Nancy Wilson, a forty-four-year-old housewife, got a booking after showing a tape from the class showcase. From there she sent her tape to several clubs and got booked at The Comedy Haven in Palm Springs as well as Bob Zany's club in Fresno. When Wilson later moved her family to Minneapolis, she auditioned at the Funny Bone and was booked as opener-emcee and also chosen as one of the local comics to audition for *Star Search*.

To find out about a class in your area, ask your local comedy club to recommend one. Sometimes universities will have comedy classes as a part of their adult extension program. When you find a class, ask if you can sit in on a session before signing up. It's important to find a class that is right for you.

How to Get Work

Get Your Act on Video

Get a video of yourself performing *in front of an audience* rather than performing for your living-room furniture. Video tips:

- ▶ Your tape should be no longer than twenty minutes and stay away from filler, such as "Where are you from?"
- ▶ Put your best stuff first. Jan Smith, owner of Igby's, says, "An act has to be able to grab me and get my attention within five minutes."
- ▶ Don't edit the tape. The club owner wants to see exactly how you work with an audience without any special video effects.

Get Pictures

You also need an eight by ten glossy black-and-white picture of yourself. Don't get fancy on this. Just a simple head shot on a white background. Club owners tell me that they get these weird pictures with the comic in a long shot. A club owner wants a face shot, because the newspapers are more likely to print that for publicity than a weird wacky kind of picture. Remember, your picture doesn't have to be funny . . . you do.

Meet Comics

Watch comics on TV, know who's happening. Hang around comedy clubs and get to know the comics who are working. Most comics are very bored on the road and like to talk shop. A personal relationship with a working comic is a good way to get your foot in the door. Comics can recommend you to club owners and even take you on the road as their opening act. I have helped many of my students get work by recommending them as opening acts when I headline.

Read Trade Magazines

Besides the two main rags of showbiz, *Daily Variety* and *The Hollywood Reporter*, there are comedy magazines that give you up-to-date information about what's going on in the world of comedy. (See Appendix for a listing of comedy magazines.)

Agents and Managers

A common illusion among newcomers to stand-up is that getting an agent is the key to getting work. When I started out in stand-up, I thought that an agent would get me work, protect me from bad gigs, and guide my career. When the only thing my first agent did for me was to take 10 percent of the gigs I got myself, I changed agents. In my first five years I must have changed agents six times. Slowly I came to realize that switching agents is like rearranging the deck chairs on the *Titanic*. It doesn't help.

There are many different types of agents, depending on where you are in your career. If you are a star, chances are you are signed with one of the large corporate agencies, such as the William Morris Agency, the Agency of the Performing Arts, ICM, and others that handle only top-name performers and deal in television packaging, movies, and concerts. For those of you who are almost stars, there are an assortment of agencies, some that cover all media, and others that specialize in booking comedy clubs, hotels, colleges, industrials, or cruise ships. (See Appendix for a list of agents who handle comics.)

An agent usually does not help you form your act. An agent is supposed to get you jobs, negotiate your contracts, and take 10 percent for their services. On the other hand, a personal manager is not legally allowed to solicit work, but is involved with every aspect of a comic's career, making sure that the various areas are working together effectively toward a predetermined goal. Very often a manager will assist a performer in finding an agent, help a performer develop an act, make career decisions, and take anywhere from 15 to 20 percent of a performer's salary. (See Appendix for a list of personal managers.)

Most reputable agents and managers do not take on a performer until he or she is making money. If you sign with an agent or manager early in your career, chances are you will be paying a commission on jobs that you've found yourself. When you're starting out, it is not necessary to have an agent or a manager to work because most comedy clubs prefer to book directly through the comic.

When just starting stand-up, your focus shouldn't be on

finding an agent or a manager, but rather on developing your act. An agent doesn't make you a hot commodity, you do. You are the one who has to go out there night after night and deliver the goods. If an agent gets you work and you bomb, you won't be on his or her client list too long.

How to Get an Agent

The way to get an agent is to get work. Once you start getting work and making money, most smaller agencies will be more than happy to sign you and take 10 percent of your salary.

What do the big guys look for? Marty Klein, president of the Agency of the Performing Arts and the agent who discovered Steve Martin, says that he's "interested in somebody that has their own identity, their own look, their own style, their own sense about themselves."

Klein will never sign any comic after watching them only once. He will watch a comic over and over again, looking each time to see how the audience reacts. He needs to be certain that if he sells a comic to someone, nine times out of ten the comic will deliver the goods.

Confidence, consistency, and determination make an artist very desirable to an agent. When I began, after working my act around town for a year, I decided that I wanted to work Playboy Clubs, which at the time were the major source of employment for comics. I tried calling Irvin Arthur, the agent who booked the clubs. When my calls were not returned, I went uninvited to his office and waited five hours until he finally saw me. By that weekend, I was working my first paid job at a Playboy Club in L.A., and Arthur later signed me as a client. It takes this kind of unrelenting belief in yourself to survive in the world of comedy.

Agents and managers regularly go to comedy clubs looking for new talent. When you are at the point where you are killing nightly, don't worry ... your phone will start ringing.

The Money-Making Gigs

Comedy Clubs

The best place to start a comedy career is at your local comedy club. In practically every city, including Tuscaloosa, Alabama, there's a successful comedy club. (See Appendix for a list of comedy clubs.)

Usually these clubs book three acts a week. In most clubs, the opener gets ten to twenty minutes; the middle gets twenty to thirty minutes; and the closer gets thirty-five to sixty minutes.

Most clubs have at least one night a week as a workshop night for newcomers, and very often the opening act is booked from those workshops. Silver Saundors Friedman, owner of the original Improvisation in New York, the birthplace of David Brenner, Bette Midler, Lily Tomlin, Andy Kaufman, Richard Lewis, and Elaine Boosler, has created a supportive home for comics. Once a month she holds an audition where comics are chosen from a lottery drawing. They do three to five minutes in front of a live audience, and if they succeed, Silver puts them into "the process." They are then welcome to come in any time to watch the show and also get to join the pool of comics who perform on Monday and Tuesday "Hang out nights." Silver isn't looking for someone who has a finished act, but rather someone who has "spontaneity, truth, and a reasonable idea of what funny is."

It is not necessary to have been on television to get booked into a comedy club, even as a headliner. Bob Fisher, owner of Pasadena's Ice House and booker for seven other clubs, would rather book a funny act that has never been on national TV than an average act that may have been on the *Tonight Show* seven times.

When you have at least twenty minutes of solid material on video, try to make a connection with the booker by phone or by letter before mailing your tape. Don't expect a lot to happen and don't expect to get your tape back. Club owners such as Fisher get, on the average, a hundred calls a day and sixty tapes a week. So if you don't get an immediate response, don't take it as a rejection.

Don't worry about trying to tailor your act to a specific club because each comedy club has a different style and format. What works at Caroline's in New York might be considered distasteful at the Ice House in Pasadena. Jan Smith, owner of Igby's, usually won't hire comics who use blue material, yet Mark Breslin, owner of Yuk Yuk's Komedy Kabaret and booker of fifteen clubs in Canada, looks for acts that are controversial and somewhat threatening to the status quo. Breslin prefers comics whose challenges create chaos, while Smith would prefer a comic who entertains and pleases. Whatever kind of act you have, you'll find a place to work.

When working clubs, there is a tendency to get down and dirty. It is hard to keep your act clean when the comic before you did a half hour of "dick" jokes. A beginning comic needs to have the foresight to remember that comedy clubs are a steppingstone to television. A lot of comics have gotten stuck on the comedy club circuit because they saw the clubs as an end in themselves and developed material that worked exclusively on the club level.

Warning!!!!

Stay far away from performing at the top comedy clubs until you have really developed your talent. Producers and directors are always in the audience in the major clubs in Los Angeles, and first impressions are everlasting. If you are from a small town, stay there until you are ready. Likewise, Chicago, Denver, Dallas, Philadelphia, are good comedy workshop towns where you can develop your talents in a safe place. Roseanne Barr spent four years developing her act in Denver and then she hit L.A. as a hot commodity. It's best to fall on your face for a couple of Elks in Syracuse and then hit L.A. or New York as a hot new kid.

Colleges

A comic who has sixty minutes of good clean material and has an act that appeals to college students can make up to $150,000 a year in the college market, even with no television exposure. Acts that appeal to college students include material on cafeteria food, fraternities, teachers, dorms, and so on. Items to keep away from are blue material, racist jokes, religious jokes, and other sensitive issues. This can differ from campus to campus. Material that would work at Harvard might be considered risky for a Mormon college in Utah.

College bookings are organized by the National Association for Campus Activities (NACA). Each year the NACA sponsors eleven regional conventions and one national convention that's held in February. At these conventions, comics showcase twenty minutes of their act before a group of 400 to 2,000 students who are directly responsible for booking you. At the showcase, all performers' prices are set and made available to the buyers before the convention. After the showcase the student buyers explorer the Exhibit Hall where, according to Edward Jackman, NACA's Comedy Entertainer of the Year, "Your act is sold like produce at a farmer's market." In the Exhibit Hall each agency maintains a booth with publicity, prices, and availability of the acts they represent. Very often a group of neighboring colleges will "co-op buy" a comic and organize a series of one-nighters. The more shows your agent books in the same general area during the same time period, the lower the comic's price. One convention can reap many dates. Comic Jackman's record is 60 dates at the Southeast regional and 132 at the National. At $1,000 to $1,500 a show, that's not too sloppy.

The best way to participate in the college market is to submit a twenty-minute video of your act to the NACA selection committee through a college agent. This videotape needs to kill. It needs to show how good you are, what you can do, and how well you appeal to the college audience, and it needs to do all of this in three minutes, because that's all they watch of each tape, *three minutes.*

It's not absolutely necessary to work with an agent to get college gigs. You can choose to be self-represented, although there is a significant amount of expense involved in maintaining a presence at the NACA conventions. Not only do you have the expense of airfare and hotel, but you have the added expense of developing quality promotional materials and maintaining a booth in the Exhibit Hall. According to the NACA, acts that have representation have a much better success rate than self-represented acts. College agents usually charge 20 percent. Charlie Steanham, president of the Blade Agency, a college agent for twenty-five years, finds some acts by referral, some from comics who contact him unsolicited, and some from performing at the NACA showcases.

Most college agents will ask you to submit current press materials (eight by ten glossy, resume, bio, clippings) and a video.

Don't get involved in the college market until you have an hour of clean material that appeals to college students. If you do manage to get a gig before you are ready and you don't deliver, word travels fast. Also, know that there is a tremendous amount of travel involved. When I worked col-

164

leges I would fly into Dallas, rent a car, and spend three weeks going from college to college doing one-nighters.

If you are interested in getting more information about the college market, call or write the NACA. (See Appendix for the address of the NACA and a list of college agents.)

Industrials

I've performed before groups ranging from a Lockheed management banquet to a convention of sex therapists. (And the strange thing is, the Lockheed group got wild with laughter while the sex therapists just watched.) Companies such as IBM, Northern Telecom, Aetna, and so on often hire comics to entertain at their meetings or conventions.

A comic in this field needs to have forty to sixty minutes of material that is wholesome in nature and that has a broad universal appeal. Most companies don't want to take a risk by hiring anybody too controversial. Agent Charlie Steanham says that it is more difficult to sell comedy in the industrial market, especially comedy without proven name value, because many meeting planners and corporate executives are fearful that the comedy will be offensive.

According to Steanham, "Comics without TV exposure can make $1,500 to $3,500 a night doing industrials, and if they've done *Star Search* and have gone to the finals, it's $3,500 to $4,000."

Cruise Ships

Certain agents book comics exclusively on cruise ships, although many ships prefer to book the comic directly. In order to be considered to work cruise ships, you need to have three different twenty-minute sets of squeaky clean, noncontroversial material. Imagine doing a show for your grandmother and you've got the picture what kind of acts these ships book.

You need to have three different sets because on a ship, the audience stays the same. The bad part is if you bomb you don't get to go home. You have to eat breakfast with the audience the next morning. When I worked a ship the only place where I could be alone was in the movie theater where they were showing *Jaws* going out and *The Poseidon Adventure* coming home.

The good part about working the ships is that you only work a few nights a week and the rest of the time you get the same privileges as the other passengers, and you get to travel and eat your way around the world.

If you have cruise ship material, Dannie Hammond of Sitmar Cruises suggests you send the cruise company a videotape with two totally different twenty-five-minute sets.

Hotels, Casinos, Concerts

Most of the big rooms in hotels and casinos are reserved for the stars of comedy, but it does happen that a newcomer opens for a headliner and ends up playing some of the bigger rooms. This happened to one of my students who showed her tape to a working comic and ended up going on the road with her, playing concert engagements.

Television

Television is very seductive. You get paid a lot of money and can become famous overnight. Yet just as fast as a comic can rise, so can they fall. The prevailing advice from producers and big name comics is: Don't do TV until you are ready. This means until you have

- been killing nightly in the clubs.
- at least forty-five minutes of clean material.
- broken down your act into four different six-minute chunks.

Television devours material. A singer can get away with doing the same song for twenty years and nobody gets upset. A comic tells the same joke a couple of times and producers start to say "I've heard it before."

The world of television has changed. Before, you had to have an act that would work on a couple of shows, such as Johnny Carson, and have a certain way of doing it that would fit into the show's style. But now there are so many ways of "making it" with late-night TV, cable comedy shows, local comedy shows, and syndicated comedy shows that TV comedy is no longer an elite club.

Everybody's going to get a break. Everybody's going to get the Carson bookers or the Letterman bookers to look at them . . . once. George Schlatter, creator/producer of TV's *Laugh-In* and the *Comedy Club*, says: "I'll look at everybody, but if I don't like them, it's tough for them to get me to look at them again. So don't blow it by showing me your act before you are ready."

Doing your act on television can be a very frightening experience if you've only worked clubs. Gone is the small smoke-filled room, the stand microphone, and the closeness of the audience. In most TV studios, the studio audience is far away from you, and sometimes there is no audience. I once had to perform my act to three cameras. I had to make believe that after each chunk I was hearing a roar of laughter, which they would dub in later.

Recently there have emerged producers and directors who are more sensitive to the needs of comedy. Shows such as Schlatter's *Comedy Club, Live at the Improv, Star Search*, and others tape their shows in a club setting with real customers.

Working in Front of a Camera

Doing an act for TV is very different from working a club. A comic needs to know how to relate to a TV camera. Here

167

are some camera technique tips from producer George Schlatter:

- ▸ Relate to the camera as just one member of the audience. Don't lock on the camera, but include it in as part of your audience. Divide your attention between talking to the camera and responding to the live people in the audience.
- ▸ Deliver the setups to the studio audience and the punchlines to the camera. If you run into the audience, forget about the camera. It is just there as a bystander.
- ▸ Slow down. Slowing down gives a comic an air of confidence. If the audience feels that you're hurrying or rushing, unless it's part of your act to rush, they become a little uncomfortable.
- ▸ Look like you've got the job. A lot of performers look like they're still auditioning for a job. Once you're on television, you've got the job. You've got to have a balance between being eager and being confident, although you don't want to be so confident that you look cocky.

Star Search

In between the *Gong Show* and the *Tonight Show*, there are many television shows that will give a newcomer a chance. TV's *Star Search* is one of those shows that will book a comic without an agent or union card.

Here are some tips from *Star Search*'s talent coordinator, Mary Downey:

- ▸ Be ready. Before submitting a tape or asking for an audition, a comic should have at least thirty minutes of strong, clean, original material. We want them to be able to win all three or four rounds, and when you start editing an act into two-minute chunks for our show, you lose material.
- ▸ A winning two-minute segment should have more than one theme and have as many laughs and one-liners as possible.
- ▸ Audition turn-offs. Unoriginal subject matter (everybody does K mart jokes), blue material, sloppy appearance or talking to the audience, because you can't on our show.

► Audition turn-ons: An unusual, imaginative hook, such as Darryl Sivade's puppets that sing cool jazz. A fresh personality or imaginative material. Likability, stage presence, professionalism, star potential, and, of course, funny.

If you would like to be considered for *Star Search*, send in a tape that's over five minutes long but less than thirty. They will look at all tapes, but to be safe, put your strongest stuff up front. *Star Search* has also booked comics sight unseen from audio tapes as well as from auditions across the country, even in small-town comedy clubs. They usually will take a club owner's suggestions, but if a comic has called, or sent a tape previously, they may ask the club owner to put up a specific comic. (See Appendix for *Star Search* address.)

How to Get Cast in TV and Film by Doing Stand-Up

Robin Williams, Richard Pryor, Michael Keaton, Roseanne Barr, and Paul Riser are all stand-ups who went on to acting careers in sitcoms and film. Kelly Goode, director of comedy series development for CBS, looks for "a comic whose act incorporates characters in it as opposed to just telling jokes." Casting directors and network casting executives all obsessively go to stand-up clubs to discover talent. Dennis Erdman, former director of casting for NBC, would call in comics he saw the night before to read for a part the very next day. In many cases Erdman was disappointed to find that a comic who had incredible power and presence standing alone onstage could be comatose when having to read a scene with another person in an office. Just because comics do well in stand-up doesn't mean that they will know what to do when they walk into a casting director's office and are handed a script to read. It then becomes necessary to learn how to translate that stand-up energy and fire into something that is viable within the context of a TV show.

Erdman's suggestions:

169

- ▶ Don't do your act in an office. Instead invite the director to come down and see your show the next time you are performing. Stand-up belongs onstage, in front of an audience, not in front of a desk.
- ▶ Take acting classes. Make sure that whatever it is about you that piques the interest of casting directors, either your personality or your delivery, can be maintained and sustained within the context of reading a scene or playing a role.
- ▶ Send postcards to casting directors to notify them where and when you are playing. Casting directors want to find new people. It's their job. They always want to be the one who discovers a new talent and so they are very responsive. If the casting director can't go, usually someone from the office will be sent.
- ▶ Don't rush your career. Know that ultimately there's a place for everyone.

Summary

To go on to make money in stand-up:

- ▶ Work as often as you can.
- ▶ Keep writing and improving your material.
- ▶ Get a good videotape.
- ▶ Don't showcase until you are ready.

Know that when you have forty-five minutes of good, solid material, you will get work. Until then, keep working on new material, hold in the reins on your desire to be seen, and when you are ready—let 'er rip.

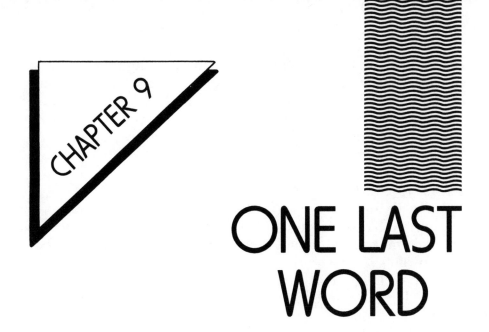

CHAPTER 9

ONE LAST WORD

Punching Up Your Life with Humor

For those of you who are not going on to pursue stand-up careers, you will find that the principles you've learned in this book and the self-confidence you've gained by performing will help you in every area of your life.

Humor is a powerful tool. Making a customer laugh can get a waitress a bigger tip. In business, a statement delivered with humor becomes a stronger statement. When you add humor to a speech to the stockholders, you may not be questioned as much because they're too busy laughing. People who are funny also give the appearance of being in charge, and this puts people at ease.

Dorothy Tubbs, my real estate agent, says, "Buying a home is a stressful situation and having a sense of humor tends to relax the buyer and relieve pressure."

For salespeople, humor relaxes customers and makes them

less critical, hostile, or aggressive. Lynda Montgomery, salesperson of the Family Fitness Center, says: "When trying to close a deal I use humor. A woman says, 'I better ask my husband.' I say, 'Have you asked him about being fat?' When they laugh, they're more likely to enroll because it makes them more comfortable."

For actors, the ability to make others laugh is often essential to getting ahead.

Agent Dyan Ullman says, "In a casting session when it's a matter of equal talent, the actor who gets the part is the one that makes you laugh. It seems like they are going to be fun on the set."

Director Leslie Hill says, "When you cast, you meet a lot of people, and the ones you remember are the ones who made you laugh."

Lee Garlington, actress, says, "When you make other people laugh, you relax them and then you stay more relaxed."

And we all know, having a sense of humor is critical to having a successful relationship, whether it's across the boardroom table or across the kitchen table. I know that having the ability to make fun of my negative personality traits has defused many a fight with my loved ones.

n Closing . . .

My greatest happiness has been when my act reflects the issues going on in my life at that exact moment. The worst part is when my life changes and my act remains the same. You've seen this happen—an aging comic still talking about how hot he is picking up girls. A svelte anorexic comic still doing a piece on how fat and unattractive she is. Or a "hip" comic still doing his "drugs are cool" chunk even though the pendulum of acceptance on drugs has swung the other way.

As you perform, you will find that material you've created that kills now might not work next year. One thing is for sure: Whatever is going on now will change. Your life will change and your act must change along with you. A year from now the things you've written on your "hate list" might seem tame. As you gain confidence, that chunk on "how shy you are" will become artificial. You get married and that great chunk on being single feels hollow and phony. And especially if you do material based on television or politics, killer material will have to be turned out to pasture overnight. I am not saying that everything you say onstage has to be true. But if you are in sync with yourself, old material will feel uncomfortable to you, and that will be communicated to the audience. Creating material is a constant process. Hopefully this book has taught you how the creative process works. Even if you don't continue with stand-up, I hope that you will continue to find the humor in life and communicate it to those around you. The ability to make people laugh is a gift that needs to be shared, especially with people working at the Department of Motor Vehicles.

I'm glad that I'm finished writing this book. I have found that there is nothing more unfunny than writing *about* comedy. This book has covered practically every aspect of creating and performing stand-up material. Now here is my final advice: When you go onstage, forget everything I've said. Forget about the formulas, forget about emotional tags, even forget about your act. When you step on that stage—*have fun*. And remember.

❝Fuck 'em if they can't take a joke.❞

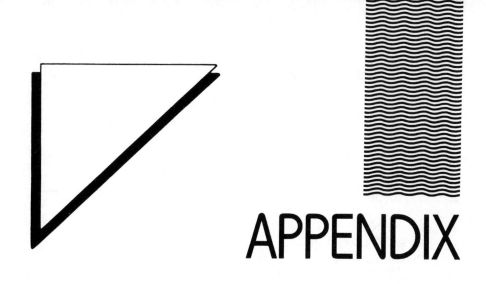

APPENDIX

Comedy Schools

Judy Carter's Stand-Up Comedy Workshop
239K Pacific Street
Santa Monica, CA 90405
(310) 396-8887
FAX (310) 450-9851

Comedy Magazines

Just for Laughs
22 Miller Avenue
Mill Valley, CA 94941
(415) 383-4746

Comedy U.S.A.
401 East 81st Street
New York, NY 10028
(212) 628-2850

For information regarding the college market, call or write the
NATIONAL ASSOCIATION FOR CAMPUS ACTIVITIES (NACA) at:

NACA
3700 Forest Drive, Suite 200
Columbia, SC 29204
(800) 845-2338

Comedy Clubs Nationwide

ALABAMA

The Comedy Club
430 Green Springs Hwy., #28
Homewood, AL
(205) 942-0008

The Comedy Club
1407-14 N. Memorial Pkwy.
Huntswood, AL
(205) 536-3329

The Mobile Comedy Lounge
2503 Government Blvd.
Mobile, AL
(205) 470-1555

ALASKA

Pierce Street Annex
701 East Tudor Road
Anchorage, AK
(907) 563-3568

ARIZONA

Coyote Comedy Club
2285 E. Butler Avenue
Flagstaff, AZ
(602) 773-0248

John Heinz' Comedy Cove
502 W. Camelback
Phoenix, AZ
(602) 265-3300

The Last Laugh
8041 N. Black Canyon Hwy.
Phoeniz, AZ
(602) 995-5653

Fun Seekers Comedy Club
4519 North Scottsdale Road
Scottsdale, AZ
(602) 451-9454

The Improvisation
930 E. University D1-201
Tempe, AZ
(602) 921-9877

Laff's Comedy Nightclub & Caffe
2900 E. Broadway
Tuscon, AZ
(602) 32-FUNNY

CALIFORNIA

Comedy Land
1717 SW Street
Anaheim, CA
(714) 957-2617

La Plaza Restaurant
2370 Buchanan Road
Antioch, CA
(415) 754-6556

The Improvisation
945 Birch Street, Suite A
Brea, CA
(714) 529-7878

The New Gallaghers
21340B Devonshire Street
Chatsworth, CA
(818) 709-9831

The Top Flight
303 Main Street
Chico, CA
(916) 342-5131

Laughs Unlimited
7630 Greenback Lane
Citrus Heights, CA
(916) 969-1076

Old Molloy's
1655 Old Mission Road
Colma, CA
(415) 755-1580

Tommy T's Comedy House
1655-B Willow Pass Road
Concord, CA
(415) 686-LAFF

The Graduate
805 Russel Blvd.
Davis, CA
(916) 758-4723

The Other Cafe
5800 Shellmound Street
Emeryville, CA
(415) 601-4888

L.A. Cabaret
17271 Ventura Blvd.
Encino, CA
(818) 501-3737

Comedy & Magic Club
1018 Hermosa Avenue
Hermosa Beach, CA
(213) 372-1193

The Improvisation
8162 Melrose Avenue
Hollywood, CA
(213) 651-2583

The Improvisation
4255 Campus Drive
Irvine, CA
(714) 854-5459

The Comedy Store
916 Pearl Street
La Jolla, CA
(619) 454-9176

Comedy Land
1129 North H Street
Lompoc, CA
(714) 957-2617

The Comedy Club
49 S. Pine & Ocean
Long Beach, CA
(213) 437-5326

The Fun House Comedy Club
4225 Crenshaw Blvd.
Los Angeles, CA
(213) 631-FFUN

Igby's
11637 Tennessee Place
Los Angeles, CA
(213) 477-3553

Fubars
1150 Arnold Drive
Martinez, CA
(415) 370-1222/1282

Sweetriver Saloon
510 Merced Mall
Merced, CA
(209) 383-5542

The Laff Stop
9365 Monte Vista
Montclair, CA
(714) 624-7867

Premiere Nite Club
1477 Plymouth Street
Mountain View, CA
(415) 961-4786

The Laff Stop
2122 SE Bristol
Newport Beach, CA
(714) 796-5700

Comedy Nite
2216 El Camino Real
Oceanside, CA
(619) 757-2177

Bob Zany's Comedy Outlet
Radisson Suite Hotel
2101 West Vineyard
Oxnard, CA
(805) 988-0130

The Improvisation
832 Garnet Avenue
Pacific Beach, CA
(619) 483-4522

The Ice House
24 North Mentor Avenue
Pasadena, CA
(818) 577-1894

Black Angus
3195 North Main
Pleasant Hill, CA
(510) 938-9900

Sunshine Saloon
1807 Santa Rita Road
Pleasanton, CA
(415) 846-6108

Sweetriver Saloon
1328 Stoneridge Mall
Pleasanton, CA
(415) 463-0209

Laughs Unlimited
1124 Firehouse Alley
Sacramento, CA
(916) 446-5905

Comedy Isle
998 W. Mission Drive
San Diego, CA
(619) 488-6872

Bay Area Theatresports
Asian American Theatre
403 Arguello
San Francisco, CA
(415) 824-8220

Cobbs Comedy Club
The Cannery
2801 Leavenworth
San Francisco, CA
(415) 928-4320/4445

El Rio
3158 Mission Street
San Francisco, CA
(415) 282-3325

The Holy City Zoo
408 Clement Street
San Francisco, CA
(415) 386-4242

The Improvisation
401 Mason Street
San Francisco, CA
(415) 441-7787

Josie's Juice Bar
3583 16th Street
San Francisco, CA
(415) 861-7933

The Punch Line
444 Battery Street
San Francisco, CA
(415) 474-3801

94th Aero Squadron
1160 Coleman Avenue
San Jose, CA
(408) 287-6150

The Last Laugh
29 North Pedro
San Jose, CA
(408) 287-LAFF

The Last Laugh
150 South First
San Jose, CA
(408) 287-5255

Tommy T's
150 West Juana
San Leandro, CA
(415) 351-LAFF

Bob Zany's Comedy Outlet
333 Madonna Road
San Luis Obispo, CA
(818) 761-2799

The Planet
Dunfey Hotel
1770 S. Amphlett Blvd.
San Mateo, CA
(415) 572-8400

Bellrose Cabaret Night
1415 5th Avenue
San Rafael, CA
(415) 454-6422

Bobby McGee's
Embassy Suites
101 McInnis Parkway
San Rafael, CA
(415) 479-1623

The Flatiron
724 B Street
San Rafael, CA
(415) 453-4318

Fourth Street Tavern
711 4th Street
San Rafael, CA
(415) 454-4044

New George's
842 4th Street
San Rafael, CA
(415) 457-4044

Tommy T's
2410 San Ramon Valley #230
San Ramon, CA
(415) 743-2830

The Crow's Nest
2218 East Cliff
Santa Cruz, CA
(408) 476-4560

Bob Zany's Comedy Outlet
The Broadway
510 S. Broadway
Santa Maria, CA

The Improvisation
321 Santa Monica Blvd.
Santa Monica, CA
(213) 394-8664

Daily Planet
120 5th Street
Santa Rosa, CA
(707) 578-1205

Studio Kafe
418 Mendocino Avenue
Santa Rosa, CA
(707) 523-1971

Sweetriver Saloon
248 Coddington Center
Santa Rosa, CA
(707) 523-0400

Comedy Land
The Sheraton
400 Alisal Road
Solvang, CA
(805) 688-8000

Cabaret Sauvignon
478 1st Street East
Sonoma, CA
(707) 996-3600

Breakaway Comedy & Dance
Hammer Ranch Center
Stockton, CA
(209) 957-2081

Rooster T. Feathers
157 W. El Camino Real
Sunnyvale, CA
(408) 736-0921

The Barn
14982 Red Hill Avenue
Tustin, CA
(714) 259-0115

Nitty Gritty Lounge
905 Lincoln Road East
Vallejo, CA
(707) 642-4413

'Laughs on Us'
Airtel Plaza Hotel
Sherman Way
Van Nuys, CA
(818) 997-7676

Bob Zany's Comedy Outlet
Shagnastys
210 West Center Street
Visalia, CA
(818) 761-2799

The Punch Line
1661 Bothello
Walnut Creek, CA
(415) 935-2002

Bob Zany's Comedy Outlet
3835 Thousand Oaks Blvd.
Westlake, CA
(818) 761-2799

Jeff Valdez Comedy Corner
1305 North Academy
Colorado Springs, CO
(719) 591-0707

Comedy Works
1226 15th Street
Denver, CO
(303) 595-3637

George McKelvey's Comedy Club
10015 East Hamden
Denver, CO
(303) 368-8900

Comedy Works
7 Olde Town Square #144
Fort Collins, CO 80524
(303) 221-5481

Wit's End
8861 Harvan Street
West Minster, CO
(303) 430-HAHA

CONNECTICUT

The Treehouse Cafe & Comedy
   Club
116 Newtown Road
Danbury, CT
(203) 794-1222

Billy Jack Cafe of Comedy
53 Welles Street
Glastonbury, CT
(203) 633-2638

The Last Laugh at Brown
   Thompson
942 Main Street
Hartford, CT
(203) 325-1600

The Treehouse Cafe & Comedy
   Club
Road 86 at Route 27
Mystic, CT
(203) 536-9126

The Treehouse Cafe & Comedy
   Club
354 Connecticut Avenue
Norwalk, CT
(203) 855-9910

Governor's Comedy Shop
56 West Park Place
Stamford, CT
(203) 324-3117

DELAWARE

Wilmington Comedy Cabaret
Greenery Restaurant
410 Market Street
Wilmington, DE
(302) 652-6873

FLORIDA

Haggerties
1745 NW 2nd Avenue
Boca Raton, FL
(407) 391-2344

Ron Bennington's Comedy Scene
401 U.S. 19 North
Clearwater, FL
(813) 787-6647

The Improvisation
3015 Grand Avenue #325
Coconut Grove, FL
(305) 441-8200

The Comic Strip
1432 North Federal Hwy.
Ft. Lauderdale, FL
(305) 565-8887

Governor's Comedy Shop
3001 E. Commercial Blvd.
Ft. Lauderdale, FL
(305) 776-JOKE

Bijou Comedy Club
15271-1 McGregor Blvd.
Ft. Myers, FL
(813) 481-6666

Comedy Cafe
16520 Tamiami Trail
Ft. Myers, FL
(813) 481-1151

P.J. Clark's
122 North Second Street
Ft. Pierce, FL
(407) 767-0657

Tropicz
6790 Old Dixie Hwy.
Holiday, FL
(407) 767-0657

The Comedy Zone
Ramada Inn Mandarin
I-295 & State Road 13
3130 Hartley Rd.
Jacksonville, FL
(904) 268-8080

The Punchline
911 Bay Meadows Road #101
Jacksonville, FL
(904) 641-4444

Uncle Funny's Comedy Club
Mark Twain's Playhouse
8700 SW 137 Avenue
Kendall, FL
(305) 388-1992

Coconuts Comedy Club
Holiday Inn
430 Duval Street
Key West, FL
(305) 296-2991

The Lone Star
3109 West Vine
Kissimmee, FL
(407) 767-0657

Coconuts Comedy Club
Quality Inn
US 98 North
Lakeland, FL
(813) 688-7972

The Chopping Block
117 West Main Street
Leesburg, FL
(407) 767-0657

The Side Door
Mile Marker 51 Overseas Hwy.
Marathon Key, FL
(407) 767-0657

Septembers Comedy Club
Bald Eagle Drive
Marco Island, FL
(813) 394-1070

Wiseguys Comedy Club
131 East Hibiscus
Melbourne, FL
(407) 767-0657

Coconuts Comedy Club
9090 Dadeland Blvd.
Miami, FL
(305) 670-0773

Coconuts Comedy Club
Peacock Plaza & Coconut Grove
Miami, FL
(305) 446-2582

Coconuts Comedy Club
Hojo's
16601 NW 2nd Avenue
Miami, FL
(305) 940-7371

Uncle Funny's Comedy Club
Holiday Inn
21485 NW 27th Avenue
Miami, FL
(305) 624-7266

Big Splash Seafood Emporium
3101 SW 34th Avenue
Ocala, FL
(407) 767-0657

Bonkerz Comedy Club
3621 West Silver Springs
Ocala, FL
(904) 732-2665

Bonkerz Comedy Club
5100 Adanson Street
Orlando, FL
(407) 629-2665

Coconuts Comedy Club
Comfort Inn
8421 S. Orange Blossom Tr.
Orlando, FL
(407) 857-5851

The Comedy Zone
At the Holiday Inn
6515 International Drive
Orlando, FL
(407) 351-3500

The Comedy Zone
Holiday Inn Winter Park
626 Lee Road
Orlando, FL
(407) 645-5600

Hilarities Comedy & Magic
    Theatre
2401 PGA Blvd.
Palm Beach Gardens, FL
(407) 624-0336

Coconuts Comedy Club
Holiday Inn U Mall
7200 Plantation Road
Pensacola, FL
(904) 474-0100

McCurdy's Comedy Club
7150 N. Tamiami Trail
Sarasota, FL
(813) 751-6887

Coconuts Comedy Club
6110 Gulf Blvd.
St. Petersburg Beach, FL
(813) 360-7935

Groucho's Comedy Club
HoJo's & U.S. 1
Stuart, FL
(407) 229-6288

Uptown
Vero Beach, FL
(407) 767-0657

Comedy Corner
2000 S. Dixie Highway
West Palm Beach, FL
(407) 833-1812

The Funny Bone
247 Buckhead Avenue
Atlanta, GA
(404) BONE-555

Punch Line
280 Hildebrand Drive
Atlanta, GA
(404) 252-LAFF

Punch Line Variety Club in
    Underground
151 Kenny's Alley
Atlanta, GA
(404) 252-LAFF

The Comedy Zone
The Macon Hilton
108 First Street
Macon, GA
(912) 746-1461

A Comic Cafe
1215 Powes Ferry Road
Marietta, GA
(404) 956-7827

The Comedy House Theatre
317 Eisenhower
Savannah, GA
(912) 356-1045

University Inn Comedy Club
1516 Pullman Road
Moscow, ID
(208) 882-0550

The Laugh Factory
4395 Fox Valley Center Drive
Aurora, IL
(708) 978-2800

The Wacko's Comedy Club
6312 West Roosevelt
Berwyn, IL
(312) 749-9225

R.G. Nostalgia
2300 Eames Street
Channahon, IL
(815) 467-2180

Comedy Sportz O'Chicago
1516 North Wells
Chicago, IL
(312) 527-2500

Control Tower
6339 South Central Avenue
Chicago, IL
(312) 735-1200

The Improvisation
504 North Wells Street
Chicago, IL
(312) 527-2500

Rusty's Comedy Club
1723 North Halstead
Chicago, IL
(312) 436-7333

Zanies Comedy Nite
Club
1548 North Wells
Street
Chicago, IL
(312) 337-4027

Gus's Comedy Club
1803 Ramada Blvd.
Collinsville, IL
(618) 346-GUSS

Who's On First
684 West North Avenue
Elmhurst, IL
(312) 833-3430

The Last Laff
3000 Warrenville Road
Lyle/Naperville, IL
(708) 505-1000

The Comedy Womb
8030 W. Ogden Avenue
(above Pines Rest.)
Lyons, IL
(312) 442-5755

Mr. Ed's Comedy Concerts
Prospect Theatre
18 South Main Street
Mt. Prospect, IL
(708) 698-2584

Zanies Comedy Nite Club
2200 South Elmhurst Road
Mt. Prospect, IL
(708) 228-6166

Funny Bone Comedy Club
1504 North Naper Blvd.
Naperville, IL

The Last Laff
Alligauers
2855 North Milwaukee Avenue
Northbrook, IL
(708) 823-LAFF

Bill Brady's Comedy Capers
Barrel of Laughs
10345 South Central Avenue
Oak Lawn, IL
(312) 499-2969

Jiminy Cricket's Comedy Club
137 North Third Lower Level
Quincy, IL
(217) 223-8705/(712) 276-3035

Laffs-R-Us
10712 North 2nd Street
Rockford, IL
(815) 633-2100

The Last Laff Comedy Nightclub
6350 North River Road
Rosemont, IL
(312) 823-5233

Zanies Pheasant Run
Pheasant Run Resort
North Avenue
St. Charles, IL
(708) 513-1761

The Funny Bone Comedy Club
1725 Algonquin Road
Shaumburg, IL
(312) 303-5700

On Broadway
210 Broadway
Springfield, IL
(217) 528-0210/(216) 276-3035

Roars North
The Grand Slam
1340 Grand Avenue
Waukegan, IL
(708) 662-0056

INDIANA

Finney Bones
4501 Washington Avenue
Evansville, IN
(812) 477-5233

Snickerz
5629 St. Joe Road
Fort Wayne, IN
(219) 486-0216

Broad Ripple Comedy Club
6281 N. College Avenue
Indianapolis, IN
(317) 255-4211

Crackers Comedy Club
8702 Keystone Crossing
Indianapolis, IN
(317) 846-2500

Indianapolis Comedy Connection
247 South Meridian Street
Indianapolis, IN
(317) 631-3536

The Last Laff
Radisson Star
I-65 U.S. 30
Merrillville, IN
(219) 769-6311

IOWA

Penquins
209 First Avenue SE
Cedar Rapids, IA
(712) 276-3035

The Funny Bone Comedy Club
2144 West Kimberly
Davenport, IA
(319) 386-HAHA

Pepperoni's Comedy Club
El Fredo's Pizza
523 West 19th
Sioux City, IA
(712) 258-0691

The Funny Bone
Cobblestone Market
8529 Hickman Road
Urbandale, IA
(515) 270-2100

KANSAS

Bushwackers Comedy Invasion
531 North Manhattan
Manhattan, KS
(913) 539-4321

Stanford's Comedy House
9045 Metcalf
Overland Park, KS
(913) 649-8288

Celebrations Comedy Club
549 South Rock Road
Wichita, KS
(316) 683-3166

KENTUCKY

The Funny Bone
600 West 3rd Street
Covington, KY
(606) 431-5653

Comedy On Broadway
146 North Broadway
Lexington, KY
(606) 254-5653

The Funny Farm
The Mid-City Mall
1250 Bardstown Road
Louisville, KY
(502) 452-6520

Legends Comedy Club
Hurstbourne Hotel
9700 Bluegrass Pkwy.
Louisville, KY
(502) 452-6520

LOUISIANA

The Funny Bone
4715 Bennington Avenue
Baton Rouge, LA
(504) 928-9996

Jodie's Comedy Shop
4000 Industrial Drive
Bossier City, LA
(318) 747-3000

MAINE

Laughing Lobster
Route One
Wells, Maine
(207) 646-6866

MARYLAND

Comedy Factory Outlet
Lombard & Light Street
Baltimore, MD
(301) LAFFTER

Slapstix
The Brokerage
34 Market Place
Baltimore, MD
(301) 659-7528

Comedy Connection of Greenbelt
6000 Greenbelt Road
Greenbelt, MD
(301) 345-0563

Quackers Comedy Club
100 South Washington
Havre de Grace, MD
(301) 939-2877

K & J's Comedy Cafe
4069 Pinefield Shopping Center
Waldorf, MD
(301) 870-7660

MASSACHUSETTS

The Comedy Celler/Play It Again
    Sam's
1314 Commonwealth Avenue
Allston, MA
(617) 426-6339

Dick Doherty's Comedy Vault
Remington's
124 Boylston
Boston, MA
(617) 267-6626

Nick's Comedy Shop
100 Warrenton Street
Boston, MA
(617) 482-0930

This End Up
The Encore
275 Tremont Street
Boston, MA
(617) 628-3325

Nick's Comedy Stop
Maui Restaurant
Route 28
Brockton, MA
(800) 441-JOKE

Catch A Rising Star
30 JFK Street
Harvard Square
Cambridge, MA
(617) 661-9887

Nick's Comedy Stop
Ducoa's Restaurant
Route 9
Framingham, MA
(800) 244-JOKE

Jay's
1220 North Street
Pittsfield, MA
(413) 585-8615

Nick's Comedy Stop
Kowloon Restaurant
Route 1
Saugus, MA
(617) 231-2500

The Laugh Connection
1125 Fallriver Avenue
Seekonk, MA
(508) 336-8254

Dick Doherty's Comedy Loft
Joseph II's Restaurant
Woburn, MA
(617) 935-1729

MICHIGAN

Joey's Comedy Club
Southfield Road
Allen Park, MI
(313) 382-7041

Mainstreet Comedy Showcase
314 East Liberty
Ann Arbor, MI
(313) 996-9080

Minges Creek
21 Minges Creek Place
Battle Creek, MI
(616) 979-4646

Joey's Comedy Club
Roxy
I-94 & Haggerty
Belleville, MI
(313) 699-1829

Chaplins West
16890 Telegraph Road
Detroit, MI
(313) 533-8867

Chaplins East
34244 Groesback Hwy.
Fraser, MI
(313) 792-1902

Russo's
11255 South Saginaw
Grand Blanc, MI
(313) 695-1671

Comedy Den
2845 Thornihill SE
Grand Rapids, MI
(616) 949-9322

The Historic Holly Hotel
100 Battle Alley
Holly, MI
(313) 634-3922

Comedy Down Under
100 West Michigan Avenue
Kalamazoo, MI
(616) 344-0081

Connxtions Comedy Club
2900 North E Street
Lansing, MI
(517) 482-1468

Joey's Comedy Club
Stoyans
36071 Plymouth Road
Livonia, MI
(313) 261-0555

Long Branch
595 North Lapeer Road
Oxford, MI
(313) 628-6500

The Fire Alarm
Hwy. 141 at Brietung Avenue
Quinnesec, MI
(906) 774-8686

Mark Ridley's Comedy Castle
269 East Fourth
Royal Oak, MI
(313) 542-9900

Mainstreet Comedy Showcase
Ramada
17201 Northline Road
Southgate, MI
(313) 284-7111

The Other Place Comedy Club
718 Garfield
Traverse City, MI
(616) 941-0988

The Looney Bin
1655 Glengary in the Wolverine
Walled Lake, MI
669-9374

MINNESOTA

Comedy Gallery at Grandma's
522 Lake Avenue South
Duluth, MN
(218) 727-3006

Strykers
107 Shady Oak Road
Hopkins, MN
(612) 938-4090

189

Totally Bonkers
2999 Hwy. 61
Maplewood, MN
(612) 482-0384

Comedy Gallery Riverplace
Riverplace
25 Main Street SE
Minneapolis, MN
(612) 331-JOKE

Stevie Ray's Comedy Theatre/
  Cabaret
1819 Nicollete Avenue
Minneapolis, MN
(612) 872-0305

Totally Bonkers
21900 Minnetonka Blvd.
Minnetonka, MN
(612) 474-1335

Totally Bonkers
Holiday Inn
Hwy. 55 & I-494
Plymouth, MN
(612) 559-1222

Comedy Gallery at Charlie's
102 6th Avenue South
St. Cloud, MN
(612) 252-4538

Comedy Gallery St. Paul
175 East 5th Street
St. Paul, MN
(612) 331-JOKE

Totally Bonkers
2814 Rice Street
St. Paul, MN
(612) 484-7215

Williams Uptown Minneapolis
2911 Hennepin Avenue
Uptown, MN
(612) 823-6271

MISSISSIPPI

The Comedy Zone
Royal D'Iberville Hotel
1980 West Beach Blvd.
Biloxi, MS

The Comedy Zone
The Lighthouse Restaurant
5 Dike Street
Madison, MS
(601) 856-8877

MISSOURI

Deja Vu's Comedy Night Live
701 Cherry Street
Columbia, MO
(314) 443-3216

Comedysportz
8th St. Cafe Theatre
323 West 8th Street
Kansas City, MO
(816) 842-ARGH

Stanford's Comedy House
543 Westport Road
Kansas City, MO
(816) 753-JOKE

The Comic Strip
Hwy. 54
Lake Ozark, MO
(314) 365-4041

Catch A Rising Star
250 St. Louis Union Station
St. Louis, MO
(314) 231-6900

The Funny Bone Comedy Club
940 Westport Plaza
St. Louis, MO
(314) 469-6692

The Funny Bone Comedy Club
19 Ronnie's Plaza
St. Louis, MO
(314) 469-6692

NEBRASKA

The Royal Grove Nightclub
304 West Cornhusker Hwy.
Lincoln, NE
(402) 477-2026

Spaghetti Works Comedy Club
228 North 12th Street
Lincoln, NE
(402) 475-0990

The Riverside Ballroom
Johnny Carson Blvd.
Norfolk, NE
(402) 371-9961

Noodles Comedy Club at
  Harrigans
514 South 11 Street
Omaha, NE
(402) 346-8024

The Funny Bone Comedy Club
705 North 114th Street
Omaha, NE
(402) 493-8036

NEVADA

Catch A Rising Star
3645 Las Vegas Blvd.
S. Las Vegas, NV
(702) 739-4397

The Comedy Stop
Tropicana
The Island of Las Vegas
3801 Las Vegas Blvd.
S. Las Vegas, NV
(702) 739-2222

The Improvisation
The Riviera
2901 Las Vegas Blvd.
S. Las Vegas, NV

Sandy Hackett's Comedy Club
2700 South Casino Drive
Laughlin, NV

Catch A Rising Star
Bally's
2500 East 2nd Street
Reno, NV
(702) 324-4544

Laff Trax at Caesars
Caesars
Stateline, NV
(702) 588-3515

NEW JERSEY

The Comedy Stop
Tropicana Hotel
Boardwalk
Atlantic City, NJ
(609) 822-7353

Wally's Backstage Cafe
87 South Washington Avenue
Bergenfield, NJ
(201) 387-1373

Cherry Hill Comedy Cabaret
Hyatt
Cuthbert Blvd.
Cherry Hill, NJ
(609) 665-6581

Casual Times
1085 Central Avenue
Clark, NJ
(718) 896-4001

Bananas Comedy Club
Holiday Inn
2117 Route 4 E.
Fort Lee, NJ
(201) 947-7444

Main Street USA Comedy
    Cafe
146 Main Street
Hackensack, NJ
(201) 488-5888

Mount Laurel Comedy
    Cabaret
Viscount
Route 73 & NJ Turnpike
Mt. Laurel, NJ
(609) 866-JOKE

Rascals South
1500 Hwy. 35 S.
Ocean Township, NJ
(201) 517-0002

Mitchell's Comedy Cafe
5 West Broad Street
Palmyra, NJ
(609) 829-3161

The Clubhouse
116 Watching Avenue
Plainfield, NJ
(718) 896-4001

Catch A Rising Star
Hyatt Regency Princeton
Princeton, NJ
(609) 987-1234

Jokers Comedy Club
304 Route 22 West
Springfield, NJ
(201) 376-9400

Rascals
425 Pleasant Valley Way
West Orange, NJ
(201) 736-2726

NEW MEXICO

Laffs Comedy Night Club
3100-A Juan Tabo Blvd.
Albuquerque, NM
(505) 296-JOKE

Pyramid Comedy Club
Holiday Inn
5151 S.F. Road
Albuquerque, NM
(505) 821-3333

Las Cruces Comedy Club
Hilton Hotel
705 South Telshor Blvd.
Los Cruces, NM
(505) 522-4300

Sante Fe Comedy Cantina
3011 Cerrillos
Santa Fe, NM
(505) 438-3939

Jimmy's Comedy Alley
47-29 Bell Blvd.
Bayside, NY
(718) 631-5055

Comedy Loft
Route 6 & 202
Brewster, NY
(914) 279-7999

Pips
2005 Emmons Avenue
Brooklyn, NY
(718) 646-9433

Toppers
1736 Shore Parkway
Brooklyn, NY
(718) 946-7400

Garvins of Huntington
47 Green Street
Huntington, Long Island, NY
(516) 673-1195

Konkoma Komedy
262 Portion Road
Lake Ronkonkoma, NY
(516) 467-6969

Governors Comedy Shop
90 Division Avenue A
Levittown, NY
(516) 731-3358

Between The Ribs
180 West Park Avenue
Long Beach, NY
(516) 431-7427

Chuckles
159 Jericho Turnpike
Mineola, NY
(516) 746-2770

Comedy Loft
260 Route 59
Nanuet, NY
(914) 623-6500

Boston Comedy Club
82 West 3rd Street
New York, NY
(212) 477-1000

Catch A Rising Star
1487 First Avenue
New York, NY
(212) 794-1906

Comic Sense
55 Grand Street
New York, NY
(212) 219-3054

The Comic Strip
1568 Second Avenue
New York, NY
(212) 861-9386

Dangerfields
1118 First Avenue
New York, NY
(212) 593-1650

Duplex
61 Christopher Street
New York, NY
(212) 255-5438

Gladys'
988 Second Avenue
New York, NY
(212) 888-2122

The Original Improvisation
358 West 44th Street
New York, NY
(212) 765-8268

Stand-Up New York
236 West 78th Street
New York, NY
(212) 595-0850

Steve McGraw's
158 West 72nd Street
New York, NY
(212) 362-2590

West End Comedy Club
2911 Broadway
New York, NY
(212) 662-6262

Boomers
1509 Main Street
Port Jefferson, NY
(516) 473-9226

Bananas Comedy Club
Route 9 & Sharon Drive
Poughkeepsie, NY
(914) 471-5002

The Comedy Dugout
9726 63rd Road
Regal Park, Queens, NY
(718) 268-2400

The Funny Bone Comedy Club
149 State Street
Rochester, NY
(716) 325-2663

Hiccups
150 Andrews Place
Rochester, NY
(716) 325-4088

East End Comedy
91 Hill Street
Southhampton, NY
(516) 283-5800

Grandpa's Comedy Club
106 New Drop Plaza
Staten Island, NY
(718) 667-HAHA

Wise Guys
117 Bruce Street
Syracuse, NY
(315) 475-0866

NORTH CAROLINA

The Comedy Zone
5317 East Independence Blvd.
Charlotte, NC
(704) 568-HAHA

Old Heidelberg Village Comedy
   Club
115 North Duke Street
Durham, NC
(919) 682-2337

The Comedy Zone
Kagneys
944 Bragg Blvd.
Fayetteville, NC
(919) 275-0811

The Comedy Zone
Ramada
830 West Market Street
Greensboro, NC
(919) 333-1034

Charlie Goodnights
861 West Morgan Street
Raleigh, NC
(919) 833-8356

The Comedy Zone
Ramada
420 High Street
Winston-Salem, NC
(919) 723-7911

OHIO

Hilarities
1546 State Road
Cayahoga Falls, OH
(216) 923-4700

Hilarities
1230 West 6th Street
Cleveland, OH
(216) 781-7735

The Improvisation
2000 Sycamore #1
Cleveland, OH
(216) 696-4677

It's Comedy Comedy Club
5100 Pearl Road
Cleveland, OH
(216) 661-5233

The Comedy Club
Ramada Inn N.
1213 Dublin-Granville Road
Columbus, OH
(614) 431-0663

The Funny Bone
6312 Busch Blvd.
Columbus, OH
(614) 431-1471

Jokers Comedy Club
8900 Kingsridge Road
Dayton, OH
(513) 433-LAFF

Wiley's Comedy Club
101 Pine Street
Dayton, OH
(513) 224-JOKE

Munchees
E. Liverpool Motor Lodge
2340 Dresden
East Liverpool, OH
(614) 764-0867

Winners
5445 Beaver Crest Road
Lorraine, OH
(216) 932-2535

The Funny Bone Comedy Club
8140 Market Place
Montgomery, OH
(513) 984-LAFF

Craig's Comedy Club
Best Western
Newark, OH
(216) 932-2535

Funny Farm Comedy Club
Holiday Inn
1375 State Route 55
Troy, OH
(513) 335-0021

Funny Farm Comedy Club
Holiday Inn Petroplex
1620 Motor Inn Drive
Youngstown, OH
(216) 759-HAHA

Jester's Comedy Club
Howard Johnson's
4055 Belmont Avenue
Youngstown, OH
(216) 757-8173

OKLAHOMA

Jokers Comedy Club
5929 North May
Oklahoma City, OK
(405) 840-JOKE

Laff's Comedy Warehouse
310 East Sheridan-Bricktown
Oklahoma City, OK
(405) 23-LAFFS

OREGON

The Last Laugh
426 NW 6th Avenue
Portland, OR
(503) 29-LAUGH

PENNSYLVANIA

Uriah's Comedy Club
101 Bellwood
Altoona, PA
(216) 932-2535

Days Inn
138 Pittsburgh Street
Butler, PA
(216) 932-2535

Bucks County Comedy Cabaret
625 North Main Street
Doylestown, PA
(215) 345-JOKE

King of Prussia Comedy Cabaret
Route 202 South & Warner Road
King of Prussia, PA
(215) 265-2030

Johnny B's
Days Inn
Meadville, PA
(216) 932-2535

Funny Bone East
Radisson Hotel
Monroeville, PA
(412) 856-7888

The Bank Street Comedy Club
31 Bank Street
Philadelphia, PA
(215) BANKST1

The Comedy Works
126 Chestnut Street
Philadelphia, PA
(215) WACKY-97

The Funny Bone Comedy Club
221 South Street/Abbot Square
Philadelphia, PA
(215) 440-9670

The Funny Bone Comedy Club
Station Square
Pittsburgh, PA
(412) 281-3130

RHODE ISLAND

Comedy Kuckoo Nest
1450 Elmwood Avenue
Cranston, RI
(401) 467-8851

Cartoons
105 Chases Lane
Middletown, RI
(401) 849-8666

Windsors Comedy Club
1144 Ocean Road
Narragansit, RI
(401) 467-3276

Coconuts Comedy Club
Newport Harbor
49 Americas Cup Avenue
Newport, RI
(401) 847-9000

SOUTH CAROLINA

The Comedy Zone
2934 West Montague Avenue
Charleston, SC
(803) 744-8281

The Punch Line
628 Harden St.
Columbia, SC
(803) 779-5233

The Punch Line
115 Pelham Road
Greenville, SC
(803) 235-5233

Embers Pub Comedy Club
906 Montague Avenue
Greenwood, SC
(803) 223-7970

Coconuts Comedy Club
15 Heritage Plaza
Hilton Head, SC
(803) 686-6887

The Old Post Office
16 Pope Avenue
Hilton Island, SC
(912) 356-1045

The Comedy Zone
1000 Beach Club Drive
Myrtle Beach, SC
(803) 449-5000

SOUTH DAKOTA

Filly's Comedy Shoppe
Hilton Inn
445 Mt. Rushmore Road
Rapid City, SD
(605) 348-8300/
    (712) 276-3035

The Comedy Catch
3224 Brainard Road
Chattanooga, TN
(615) 622-2233

The Comedy Zone
Justins
453 East Main Street
Kingsport, TN
(615) 378-3800

The Comedy Zone
Holiday Inn
1315 Kirby Road
Knoxville, TN
(615) 584-3911

Zanies Comedy Showplace
2025 8th Avenue
Nashville, TN
(615) 269-0221

The Improvisation
4980 Beltline Road
Addison, TX
(214) 404-8501

The Comedy Corporation
770 Road to 6 Flags East #110
Arlington, TX
(817) 792-3700

The Velveeta Room
317 East 6th Street
Austin, TX
(512) 469-9116

Good Humor Comedy Club
Brownsville, TX
(713) 444-4312

The High Tide Comedy Club
900 Shoreline Blvd.
Corpus Christi, TX
(512) 877-1600

The Improvisation
9810 North Central
Dallas, TX
(214) 750-5866

The Comic Strip
Park at Alto Mesa
6633 North Mesa
El Paso, TX
(915) 581-8877

The Comic Strip East
Airport Hilton
2027 Airway Blvd.
El Paso, TX
(915) 778-0445

El Paso Comedy Club
900 Sunland Park Drive
El Paso, TX
(915) 833-2900

The Comedy Place
4709 Dowling
Houston, TX
(713) 523-0550

Comedy Showcase
12547 Gulf Freeway
Houston, TX
(713) 481-1188

Waterworks Comedy Club
101 Mill Street
Waco, TX
(817) 756-2181

UTAH

The Comedy Circuit
10 North Main
Midvale, UT
(801) 561-7777

VIRGINIA

The Comedy Zone
2799 Jefferson Davis Hwy.
Arlington, VA
(703) 418-1234

Garvins Comedy Club
333 Waterside Drive
Norfolk, VA
(804) 627-6600

Comedy Club
Matt's British Pub
109 South 12th Street
Richmond, VA
(804) 643-JOKE

Thoroughgood Inn Comedy Club
Independence Blvd.
Virginia Beach, VA
(804) 499-2500

WASHINGTON

Comedy Penthouse
Bailey's Bar
821 Bellevue Way
Bellevue, WA
(206) 455-2445

El Camino Restaurant & Comedy
610 North Callow
Bremerton, WA
(206) 479-4487

The Comedy Underground
Swannies
222 South Main
Seattle, WA
(206) 628-0303

The Improvisation
1426 18th Avenue
Seattle, WA
(206) 628-5000

C.J. Shenanigan's
3017 Ruston Way
Tacoma, WA
(206) 752-8811

WASHINGTON, D.C.

Comedy Cafe
1520 K Street NW
Washington, DC
(202) 638-JOKE

Garvin's Comedy Club
13th L Street NW
Washington, DC
(202) 726-6337/(202) 783-2442

WEST VIRGINIA

The Comedy Zone
1000 Washington Street
Charleston, WV
(304) 343-4661

High Street Comedy Club
116 High Street
Morgantown, WV
(216) 932-2535

Park Central Comedy Club
318 West College
Appleton, WI
(414) 738-5601

Funny Business Comedy Club
122 State Street
Madison, WI
(608) 256-0099

Toons Comedy Club
3841 East Washington
Madison, WI
(608) 244-2481

Sir Laughs A Lot Comedy Castle
201 North Mayfair Road
Wauwatosa, WI
(414) 377-0574

Comedy Organizations

Comic Relief
2049 Century Park East, Suite 4250
Los Angeles, CA 90067
(213) 201-9210

Comedy Crusade Against Diabetes
1660 Duke Street
Alexandria, VA 22314
(800) 232-3472 X 288

MS Day for Darlene
Multiple Sclerosis
600 South Federal
Chicago, IL 60605
(312) 922-8000

NACCO (National Association of
  Comedy Club Owners)
P.O. Box 519
Longport, NJ 08403
(609) 822-7353

PCA (Professional Comedians
  Association)
410 West 42nd Street, 3rd floor
New York, NY 10036
(212) 643-5233

Agents Who Handle Comics

Admire Presentations, Inc.
170 West 76th Street, Suite 101
New York, NY 10023
(212) 580-4128

APA (Agency for the Performing
  Arts)
888 Seventh Avenue
New York, NY 10023
(212) 582-1500

9000 Sunset Blvd., 12th floor
Los Angeles, CA 90069
(213) 273-0744

Ambassador Artists
P.O. Box 50358
Nashville, TN 37205
(615) 352-2500

Arne Brav Associates
1143 Arno Road
Franklin, TN 37064
(615) 791-1213

Banner Artists Int'l
1650 Broadway, Suite 508
New York, NY 10019
(212) 581-6900

Bernie Young Agency
6006 Greenbelt Road, Suite 285
Greenbelt, MD 20770
(301) 937-2600

Bill Feggan Attractions
131 North 2nd Street
Raton, NM 87740
(505) 445-5528

Blade Agency, The
P.O. Box 1556
Gainesville, FL 32602
(904) 372-8158

Buddy Lee Attractions
38 Music Square East
  Suite 300
Nashville, TN 37203
(615) 244-4336

Celebrity International
1020 16th Avenue South
Nashville, TN 37212
(615) 259-3400

Coconuts Comedy Productions
12016 Lagoon Lane
Treasure Island, FL 33706
(813) 360-7935

Comedy Connection
3004 Semmes Avenue
Richmond, VA 23225
(804) 232-3181

Comedy Line Productions
2378 Colvin Ext. #4
Tonawanda, NY 14150
(716) 822-4356

Comedy West
1206 Mill Creek Blvd., C-201
Mill Creek, WA 98012
(206) 485-4674

CAA (Creative Artists Agency)
1888 Century Park East
Suite 1400
Los Angeles, CA 90067
(213) 277-4545

Creative Booking Service
5009 Monroe Road, Suite 103
Charlotte, NC 28205
(704) 532-1980

Creative Talent Consultants
333 North Broadway, Suite 3011
Jericho, NY 11753
(516) 433-6588

Lil Cumber Attractions
6515 Sunset Blvd., Suite 300A
Hollywood, CA 90028
(213) 469-1919

Dana Pennington Associates
8721 Santa Monica Blvd.
West Hollywood, CA 90069
(213) 850-1909

DCA Productions
437 W. 44th Street
New York, NY 10036
(212) 245-2063

DMR Booking Agency
The Galleries of Syracuse, Suite 250
Syracuse, NY 13202
(315) 475-2500

Eastcoast Entertainment (ATL)
1780 Century Circle
Atlanta, GA 30345
(404) 634-0016

Entertainment Connection, The
401 Pennsylvania Parkway,
   Suite 104
Indianapolis, IN 46280
(317) 575-5777

Entertainment United
64 Division Avenue
Levittown, NY 11756
(516) 735-5550

Fireball Entertainment
P.O. Box 1769
New York, NY 10025
(212) 666-6881

Fleming/Tamulevich and Associates
733-735 North Main Street
Ann Arbor, MI 48114
(313) 995-9066

Funny Bone on Tour
734 Westport Plaza, Suite 275
St. Louis, MO 63146
(817) 265-2277

Funny Business Agency (Canada)
1280 Bay Street
Toronto Ontario
Canada, M5R3LI

Funny Business Agency
4519 Cascade Road
Grand Rapids, MI 49506
(616) 949-7387

G.G. Greg Agency
1288 East 168th Street
Cleveland, OH 44110
(216) 692-1193

Gary Grant Talent Associates
P.O. Box 928
Port Washington, NY 11050
(516) 744-9547

Gersh Agency
P.O. Box 5617
Beverly Hills, CA 90210
(213) 274-6611

Gilchrist Agency, The
310 Madison Avenue, Suite 1003
New York, NY 10017
(212) 692-9166

Greater Talent Network
150 Fifth Avenue, Suite 1002
New York, NY 10011
(212) 645-4200

Hollander-Lustig Entertainment
321 North Lake Blvd., Suite 103
North Palm Beach, FL 33408
(407) 863-5800

ICM (International Creative
  Management)
40 West 57th Street
New York, NY 10019
(212) 556-5600

8899 Beverly Blvd.
Los Angeles, CA 90048
(213) 550-4000

In-Tune Talent
1800 North Highland Avenue
Hollywood, CA 90028
(213) 465-9135

Irvin Arthur Associates
9363 Wilshire Blvd., Suite 212
Beverly Hills, CA 90210
(213) 278-5934

Jackman & Taussig
1815 Butler Avenue, Suite 120
Los Angeles, CA 90025
(213) 478-6641

Joey Edmonds Agency, The
2669 North Building
Chicago, IL 60614
(312) 871-1444

Just for Laughs Agency
22 Miller Avenue
Mill Valley, CA 94941
(415) 383-4746

Knapp Comedy Promotions
P.O. Box 838
Highland Park, IL 60035
(708) 433-8669

William Morris Agency
1350 Avenue of the Americas
New York, NY 10019
(212) 586-5100

151 El Camino Drive
Beverly Hills, CA 90212
(213) 274-7451

N.Y. Entertainment
221 West 57th Street
New York, NY 10019
(212) 586-1000

Omnipop
223 Jericho Turnpike, Suite 200
Mineola, NY 11501-1606
(516) 248-4019

10700 Ventura Blvd., Suite C
Studio City, CA 91604
(818) 980-9267

Prime Time Entertainment
2 Crow Canyon Court, Suite 210
San Ramon, CA 94583
(415) 820-2379

Progressive Artists
Beverly Hills, CA
(213) 553-8561

Pyramid Entertainment Group
89 Fifth Avenue, 7th Floor
New York, NY 10022
(212) 242-7274

QBQ Entertainment
48 East 50th Street, 4th floor
New York, NY 10022
(212) 752-8040

Radioactive Talent
476 Elmont Road
Elmont, NY 11003
(516) 315-1919

Rick Morgan Entertainment
132 Norwalk Avenue
Medford, NY 11763
(516) 654-0507

Roger Paul Agency
581 Ninth Avenue, Suite 3C
New York, NY 10036
(212) 268-0005

The Snikkers Agency
1905 Powers Ferry Road, Suite 240
Marietta, GA 30067
(404) 971-9292/(404) 935-3633

Spencer-De Francis
P.O. Box 5946
Denver, CO 80217
(303) 279-4310

Spotlite Enterprises, Ltd.
221 West 57th Street
New York, NY 10019
(212) 586-6750

8665 Wilshire Blvd., Suite 208
Beverly Hills, CA 90211
(213) 657-8004

Stephen Gingold Agency, The
245 El Camino Drive
Beverly Hills, CA 90212
(212) 557-1021

Terry Lichtman Co.
12456 Ventura Blvd.
Studio City, CA 91604
(818) 761-4804

T.H.E. Agency
Tracy Hubley Entertainment
125 South Clark Drive #3
Los Angeles, CA 90048
(213) 550-1125

Treehouse Comedy Productions
354 Connecticut Avenue
Norwalk, CT 06854
(203) 855-9910

Triad Artists, Inc.
10100 Santa Monica Blvd.,
   16th Floor
Los Angeles, CA 90067
(213) 556-2727

TSM Artists Management
P.O. Box 4129
Louisville, KY 40204
(502) 459-5532

Turner Talent Network
8940 North Malibu Drive
Bayside, WI 53217
(414) 351-0060

Yvette Bikoff Agency
9255 Sunset Blvd., Suite 510
Los Angeles, CA 90069
(213) 278-7490

Best iPad Apps
The Guide for Discriminating Downloaders

 Peter Meyers

O'REILLY®

Beijing · Cambridge · Farnham · Köln · Sebastopol · Tokyo

Best iPad Apps: The Guide for Discriminating Downloaders
by Peter Meyers

Copyright © 2011 Peter Meyers
Printed in Canada.

Published by O'Reilly Media, Inc., 1005 Gravenstein Highway North, Sebastopol, CA 95472.

O'Reilly books may be purchased for educational, business, or sales promotional use. Online editions are also available for most titles (*http://my.safaribooksonline.com*). For more information, contact our corporate/institutional sales department: (800) 998-9938 or *corporate@oreilly.com*.

Editor: Brian Sawyer

Production Editor: Nellie McKesson

Proofreader: Nancy Reinhardt

Indexer: Julie Hawks

Cover Design: Monica Kamsvaag

Interior Design: Josh Clark, Edie Freedman, and Nellie McKesson

Printing History:
    First Edition: December 2010

ISBN: 9781449392475

[TI]

Contents

Contents

Preface

Even before the poor thing had shipped, naysayers had their fun with it: *the iPad's nothing more than an oversized iPhone.* But now that we've all gotten are fingers on these silver-and-black beauties, this much is clear: where the iPhone's great for the little things in life—killing boredom, local lookups, and, you know, talking to people—the iPad excels at an entirely different set of tasks. Its larger screen lets you create and kick back in ways that, while possible on a smartphone, are hardly pleasurable. Its instant-on status invites you to open it more readily than a laptop and then touch what you want: put this circle over *there*; gimme a closer look at *that* nose; demon Zombie, take *that*!

In sum, it's true: the iPad's neither fish nor fowl, neither pocket PC nor portable laptop. In a very literal way it's a mobile computer that you moves as you do: from the couch to the dining room table, from the waiting room to, let's admit it, the bathroom. (The laptop travels to those spots only for the truly committed.)

With different talents come different criteria for excellence. The choices you'll encounter in the following pages look different from those crowned in this series' first installment (*Best iPhone Apps*). The guiding mission remains the same—curate a collection that will drive the average reader into an enthusiasm-igniting, download-inducing fit of "my iGadget can do that?" But a secondary set of iPad-specific factors played a big part in putting this list together. Here you'll find apps that:

Take advantage of the iPad's unique talents. This is where the radar was set on high alert for apps that made novel use of the tap, the swipe, the pinch, and the flick. (And to think some doubted this device would be a hit—if nothing else it's a chance to relive the best parts of third grade.) From virtual sculpting programs to better news browsers, you'll find apps that do things that can't easily be done on other devices (not to mention in print).

Are as beautiful as the iPad itself. Here we enter territory that's slightly subjective, but which brings to mind that famous Supreme Court opinion on pornography: you know it when you see it. The main idea here is to find programs that exhibit the same elegant design that went into the creation of the device. And it's not about ornamentation, either. It's the sweating-the-details elegance that make the best apps intuitive, responsive to your instincts, and, above all, great showcases for the content rather than buttons, menus, and other administrative levers and pulleys. Just as Mr. Fancy Accent wanted Grey Poupon for his Bentley, you want beautiful-looking apps for your iPad.

Go easy on the instructions. Great apps are those that, upon launch, are obvious to use. Got an app that will balance a checkbook or compose a sonnet but which require the user to double-tap then swipe the far-right column in a zig-zag manner? Probably not worth it to most people. To be sure, a few of the more jaw-droppingly accomplished apps (flight simulators, music studios) contain features that become clear only after spending some time in the Help section. But the juice, in those cases, better be worth the squeeze. And definite preference was given to apps that artfully integrated their guidance into their core performance by doing things like making it clear which content was tappable and layering instructions onto the screen for first-time users.

Do something better than the website. Craigslist, for example, is famous for the spartan, if not downright unfriendly, look and feel of its site. You'll find lots of apps that solve these information design problems in novel and, frequently, visual ways.

Distinguish themselves among the competition. Especially in those categories—calculators, task trackers, Sudoku players—that have attracted dozens of entrants, this book helps do some serious chaff snuffing. By tapping through hundreds and hundreds of apps, we help pick the one that's most iPad-worthy.

Are context appropriate. It's clear: the world needs apps for things like finding the best place to pee or figuring out how much to tip your waiter. But pulling out your iPad at a restaurant is—well, it's just an outrageously geeky thing to do…let's leave it at that. So while there are some things you can do on an iPad, it's not always the best tool. In the pages that follow you'll find apps that take best advantage of where and when most people are most likely to use their porta-pad.

Don't try too hard to mimic the analog version. The classic, inevitable mistake made upon the arrival of any new technology is to spend too much effort replicating its predecessor. Hence the ridiculous-looking horse heads mounted on the front of some early autos (*Cornelius, what the deuce kind of stallion has that motor wagon gone and gored?*) or the radio plays read aloud on early TV. So a sharp lookout was kept for those apps that either invented new kinds of experiences or were imaginative in how they rendered the core service being delivered.

One final note: grading was not, as it were, done on a curve: not all categories get coverage. If the current crop of contenders doesn't include a sufficiently great candidate, then why bother letting you know about who the valedictorian of summer school is? Your iPad may be for fun or for work, but it should never be a chore.

Happy downloading!

About the Author

Peter Meyers has worked at the intersection of writing and technology for more than two decades. He cofounded one of the first multimedia textbook publishers (Digital Learning Interactive, sold in 2004 to Thomson Learning) and has written about the strange and wonderful effects of computers on everyday culture for the *New York Times*, the *Wall Street Journal*, *Wired*, *Salon*, and the *Village Voice*. Peter's undergraduate degree is from Harvard, where he studied American history and literature, and he has an MFA in fiction from the Iowa Writers' Workshop. He lives with his wife and two daughters in "upstate Manhattan" (aka Washington Heights). Follow him on Twitter (@petermeyers) or check out his thoughts on the future of digital books at *www.anewkindofbook.com*.

At Work

Dare to ditch your laptop? Probably not for those of us deskbound dudes and dudettes who crank away on PCs each day, staring at mega monitors. But the road warrior world is starting to bubble up tales of those who've gone a long weekend or so packing only the 'Pad. A Bluetooth-capable external keyboard is the accessory of choice for most of these experiments, mainly for composing longish documents. You'll find apps for that kind of work in the following pages. Other, similar Microsoft Office-like activities—spreadsheets, slideshow presentations—have iPad-friendly programs that do just fine with the device's virtual, layout-changing keyboard. And it's not simply that this dog can dance. In some ways, we're beginning to see document design that gets *better* as we start putting hand to screen. To touch the thing you're creating—to be able to point and push, instructing the tools at your fingertips to move this graphic *right here*—well, that starts introducing some serious power. You'll also read about a host of other vocational activities that get darn near close to being fun when carried out on everyone's favorite 10-inch touchscreen: to-do list management, outlining, note-taking (stylus-friendly apps included), and research. Worker geeks are in for a few treats, too. Remotely access your PC? Use your iPad as an external monitor? Ditch mobile Safari for a pimped out custom web ride? Check, check, check. Finally, if you're a regular on the speaker circuit, you'll find plenty of coverage that's presenter friendly: from virtual teleprompters to online document storage, there are apps out there that'll make sure you shine.

Photo: Herval Freire

1

Best App for Basic To-Do Lists

Toodledo

$3.99
Version: 2.1 | Jake Solefsky

Do your lists have lists? Is it time to tackle to-do management in a slightly more organized way than those sticky notes sprouting on your desk? Its name may be whimsical but Toodledo is plenty capable, with three significantly crowd-pleasing virtues: low cost, ease of operation, and automatic web-based syncing—so you never have to worry about whether your iPad's list is on par with your PC's. Probably the only real downside is the service's sliding pay scale. Be prepared to pony up for a Pro ($15/year) or Pro Plus ($30/year) account if you want power goodies like file storage, goal progress trackers, and editable lists for sharing with colleagues.

ON BACKGROUND: If you've got project-wide notes, use the Notebooks, which you can associate with folders. Those folders let you bundle up associated tasks and view 'em all together. The importance rankings shown here are based on a formula that takes into account due date, priority rankings, and that final nudge, the starred to-do.

POWER PERKS: Toodledo makes it easy to import and export your data. That way, if you ever feel like switching to, say, Outlook, the web-based edition can help pluck out an Outlook-friendly CSV file. Other online treats include instructions on how to print out a foldable booklet for those times when you gotta go 'Pad-less.

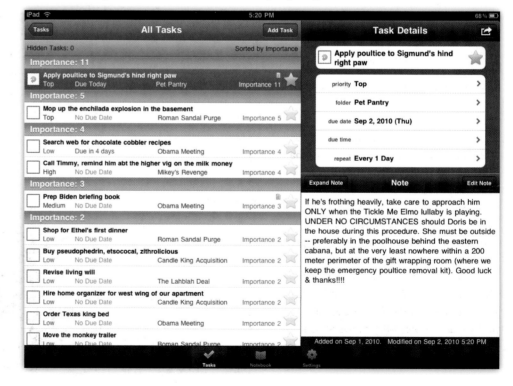

At Work

Best App for GTD-Worshipping Power Users

OmniFocus for iPad

$39.99
Version: 1.2 | The Omni Group

If the acronym up there registers as "getting things done" and you're one of the followers of this ultra-efficient productivity system, you might blink at the app's price but surely you get the pitch: a small price to pay for a "mind like water" (one of GTD guru David Allen's big promises to true adherents). This app's hard-core users are unanimous in their devotion: you simply won't find an app whose price is this high with this many 5-star ratings. So, if you're in, here's what you get: all the GTD-friendly tools you need (contexts, weekly review mode), some digital-only perks (audio notes, map views of tasks to plan errand trips), and cloud-based syncing with iPhone and Mac-only programs.

WHEN YOU GONNA CALL?: Contexts are a novel but sensible way to think about plowing through chores. It can be a place, person, or tool required to tackle your tasks. So if you're stuck in the airport, for example, being able to see a list of all the *calls* you need to make is helpful. *Errands*? Not so much. You can still group your to-dos in traditional project-specific buckets (The Kremlin Pitch, Lorna's Wedding), but this is one of several GTD concepts that, when followed, can really help.

FOREWARNED, FOREARMED, FOREVER: If each day brings new and *oh, crap*-inducing amounts of surprises, you'll love the Forecast feature. It presents a calendar-style view of incoming due dates, making it easier to spot schedule crunches before they squeeze ya. You can even—procrastinators, please avert your eyes—take advantage of light days to get ahead.

3

Best App for Making Calculations

Digits Calculator
Free lite version | $2.99
Version: 1.5.2 | Shift

The iPad's lack of a built-in calculator app has attracted countless entrants. Digits punches its way to the top of the tape by providing what most folks want for a reasonable price: easy-to-hit buttons (even for those in the Chubby Fingers club), a tally tape that's not only emailable but also—get this—editable, and a batch of memory buttons that non-calculator geeks might actually understand how to use. The default number pad color is a blaring yellow, but in the virtual land of touchscreen calculators you can subtract that problem in a jiffy: tap the lower-right corner's "i" button and dial the background color down to a less eye-jangling shade. In sum, this calculator checks out nicely.

ERASERMATE: Spot an errant entry? Summon the Tape Menu by tapping any number on the tape: Edit lets you revise, Insert pops in a new item, Total inserts a sum, and Use grabs the value for your current calculation. The Comment option's handy, too, but works only in landscape mode.

MEMORY TRICKS: Don't forget those oft-neglected "M" buttons for subtotal storage and retrieval. The Save, Read, and Delete labels do just what you'd expect. Retrieve numbers stored lower down in the memory stack (M1, say) by tapping it on the tape and then picking the M^R button. Sure, it's no spreadsheet, but sometimes you just need to crinkle rather than crunch your numbers.

At Work

Soulver for iPad

Free lite version | $5.99
Version: 1.1 | Acqualia Software

Like wristwatches, much of a calculator's job is now handled by the cellphone. But there's one problem that remains largely unsolved for the math challenged among us: percentage calculations. Sure, there are brute force methods of, say, figuring a 25% discount on $132.46, but wouldn't it be easier if your calculator could help? Soulver can. Simply enter *25% off 132.46* and voilà: 99.345. It takes a little while to master some of Soulver's slightly odd phrasing needs, but the payoff can be big. Those requests that you've previously posed to your cubicle mate, or—oh the *indignity*—your child (*what's 22 as a % of 116*)? The nonjudgmental Soulver is ready and waiting.

CANNED WISDOM: Head to the *123* tab for the app's preprogrammed smart buttons. Enter values by using the numerical keypad and then enlist whichever oracle's help you want. As you type, answers appear in the right column. Beyond the percentage magic, other layouts offer different tricks: the F(x) option features sin, cos, etc., Vars lets you create and reuse variables, and 0x1b is for hex-dec geeks.

SPEAK CLEARLY: Soulver's not perfect. Or perhaps better said: it's not an artificial intelligence genius, ready to parse any question posed in any manner. So if you want to know how much 113 increased by 22% is, you need to express that in a Soulver-friendly way: *113 + 22%* or even the slightly clunky *22% on 113*. But dang if it doesn't work. The app's help section (the book icon) has a full list of lingo tips.

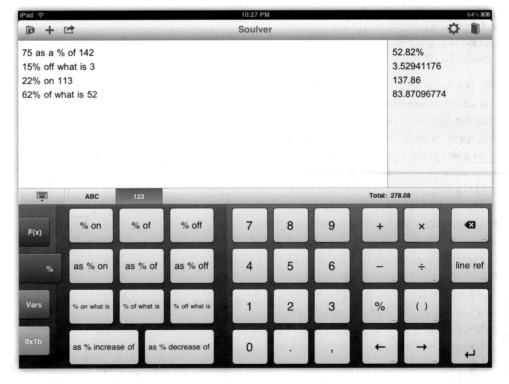

5

Best App for Database Duties

FileMaker Go for iPad

$39.99
Version: 1.1.2 | FileMaker

Database programs come in three main flavors: high-powered, programmer-help required (Oracle, IBM), sophisticated but non-geek friendly (Access, FileMaker), and a hodge-podge of simpler tools (Excel, Bento). Move along if you're in category one: the iPad's not ready for you (yet). Category two fans who are friendly to FileMaker, you're in luck. Your iPad's ready for fairly serious field work. Easy syncing features let you view, edit, and add to existing databases. And many of the high-octane tools that make the desktop version a civilian favorite—search, report, scripted fields—work on the iPad. As for those of us in category three? Steer your eyes page right: you're Bento-bound.

GETTING STARTED: You'll need the regular (Mac or Win) version of FileMaker and, of course, an existing database. The iPad app can do a mind meld with your master file in lots of ways: over a WiFi network, via the Internet (to a server-based file), or transfer the database right onto your iPad.

RECORD PLAYING: Don't plan on creating a database on the iPad. By all means, though, add records, edit existing info, and, of course, search and sort your data. Other mobile treats: you can generate and email a PDF right from your iPad (great for reports) or even email the whole database.

At Work

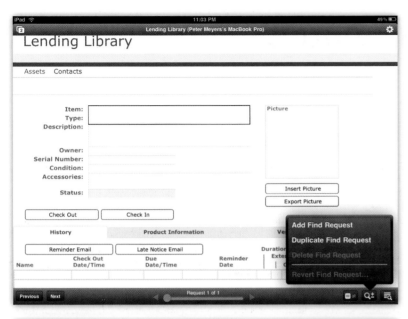

SEEK AND FIND: Drag your net quickly through the database by tapping the lower-right corner's magnifier icon and picking Quick Find; any term you enter is compared against all fields in every record. Fine-tune your search by tapping Enter Find Mode and entering your criteria in as many of the blank fields as you like. Useful key-character shortcuts include the usual less than and equal to operators; "..." for a range (5...9); and "@" for any wildcard character ("@wl" gets you "owl" and "awl").

ORDER, PLEASE: When you're ready to browse but want your records ordered just so, it's time to sort. Kick things off with the same magnifier icon and pick Sort Records. Now tap as many fields as you want to sort by; as you tap, a sort order list appears, which you can reorder. Tap each field's "greater than" arrow to pick an order method (ascending vs. descending, for example).

⊕ **HONORABLE MENTION**

Bento for iPad
$4.99
Version: 1.0.3 | FileMaker

Wanted: database users with modest needs. Esp. those who never use word "database." Looking for recipe & book collectors, home inventory obsessives, etc. Love of artful, polished apps a must. If that sounds like you, bingo: Bento's your app. Design your d'base on the iPad or import from the Mac-only desktop version. (Caveat: if you redline Bento's desktop powers, don't expect features like massive media collections and intricate layouts to make the trip to tabletville unscathed.) Two dozen or so ready-to-use in-app templates (issue tracking, equipment) make it easy to get started. Adding pictures, text, links, checkboxes, and more is a snap.

7

Best App for Brainstorming

iThoughtsHD
$9.99
Version: 1.3 | CMS

Legions of brainstorming fans swear by mindmapping: a freeform exercise for taming an unruly personal, creative, or business problem by jotting down associated words coursing through your head. As idea clusters take shape, your mass of previously jumbled thoughts starts to clarify into big-picture concepts and related tasks. Connections emerge between groups of ideas and seeing all your thoughts splayed out before you often triggers new notions. The biggest drawback of the paper exercise is the messy, hard-to-edit scrawl that results. Here's where the iPad's tap-and-drag canvas is a mindmapper's dream. Your composition remains an infinitely reshapable work in progress.

BIG PAPER: The canvas you're drawing on is nearly infinite; zoom in and out by pinching and spreading for closeup and bird's-eye views. Tap any plus (+) icon to hide a branch of "child" nodes, which is a useful way of focusing on higher-level concepts. The app auto saves a new version every five minutes or so, making it easy to wend your way back if you get lost charting unproductive territory.

NODAL NOTES: Sometimes you need more than a phrase to capture a concept. In that case, tap a node and then head to the upper-right corner's "i" button; from the drop-down menu that appears, tap the Note tab and type away. Not the most intuitive operation in the world, but once you clue into the half dozen or so input and editing tricks—check out *http://bit.ly/blz2MF* for an easy list—you'll be mindmapping like a pro.

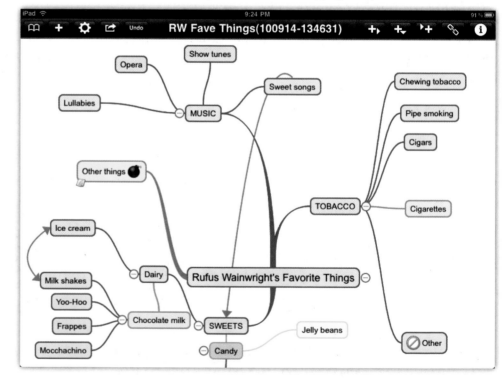

Popplet

Free lite version | $8.99
Version: 1.1.0
Notion

Even though mindmapping typically takes place on a blank, unlined page, it remains largely a text-centric affair. But why *not* include photos and drawings? Popplet's maker posed that basic question, and the resulting app liberates budding mindmappers from their usual ovals and terse phrases. Beyond being an exceedingly fun and simple app to operate, the app invites visual thinkers to merge pictures and prose in ways that are likely to spark all sorts of creative ideas.

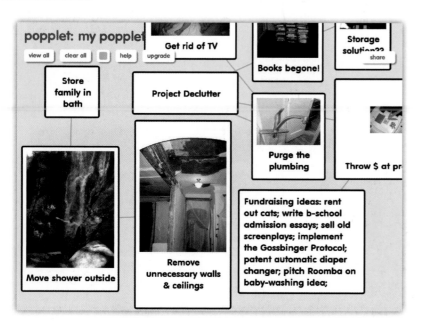

Creative Whack Pack

$1.99
Version: 5.0
Roger von Oech

Sometimes your idea planning problem lies less in organizing your messy cranial output and more in unleashing those creative juices that you know just have to be lying somewhere within you (or even more fear-inducing: within that team of subordinates, campers, schoolkids, or whoever you happen to be in charge of). If that's your pickle, here's a fun, low-cost way to try to spark the creative fire. The app's based on a best-selling business advice series of the same name, and its premise and delivery method are pretty straight-forward. Whatever kind of "issue" one or more people are working on—be it personal, professional, political, whatever—a sharp, perspective-orienting jolt can sometimes be just the thing to jostle loose some new ideas. The spur comes in the form of the app's dozens and dozens of card-based thought exercises, each of which presents a different sloganish claim, expands on that thought with a minimum of the usual business book blather, and then nudges you to use a further set of open-ended questions to reconsider your own problem.

Best App for Creating Beautiful Documents

Pages
$9.99
Version: 1.2 | Apple

CUSTOM FRAMING: The menu bar's "i" button holds lotsa fun styling options. When a photo's selected, you'll find an art store's worth of framing choices. Regular text gets its share of makeover options: you can apply styles (canned formatting rules, though they have to be created in the Mac-based Pages), set alignment and line spacing, pick font size and color—even create columns.

TAKE A SWIPE: Moving objects works just as you'd expect: tap, hold, and drag. But if you need finer-grained control, try this: while holding one finger on an object, swipe a finger on your other hand in the direction you want to move. Each swipe nudges the item one pixel; bump that up to 20 or 30 pixel increments by swiping with two or three fingers

Note the name of this award. We're not talking about simply slingin' prose here (though Pages can handle that, no problem). Instead, you're getting a forehead-smackingly easy way to mingle words and pictures. Shoot, you can actually embed movies into the documents you create. Whatever your creative ingredients, the power here is the ability to shape each page. For example, touch and hold an image with two fingers, wait a moment, and then rotate. With wonderful touchscreen controls, you're no longer stuck trying to tell a mouse and menus what you want to see. It's just you: touching and tweaking, like standing next to an art director and showing her: no, not like *that*…like *this*.

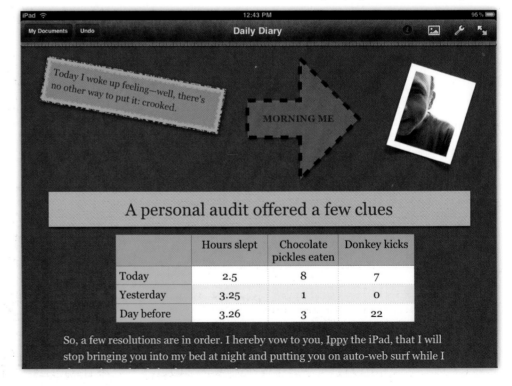

NAVIGATION'S A DRAG: The Navigator is a nifty way to browse through longish documents; touch and hold the right edge of the screen to summon it; and then drag up or down for a monocled view of earlier or later pages. The app's opening screen is where you create, import, and export files. You can save and send documents formatted as PDF, Word, or Pages files.

HIDDEN TREATS: The ready-to-use layouts in the template gallery give you a nice design boost. The choices you see here picture only the first page of each design; once you open one of these babies in Pages, scroll down in the newly created file for additional layouts (for example, the second page of the syllabus has a table layout you could use to list assignments).

Best App for Plain Prose Slinging

iA Writer

$4.99
Version: 1.0.2 | Information Architects

Stop futzing with stuff that ain't words. Let's add that Digital Age addendum to rules like *write what you know* and *show don't tell.* Hands off the style palette, step away from the font menu, and for Pete's sake, nix the Twitter feed. What you need is a barebones canvas and a dose of discipline. What you need is this app. Stripped of formatting frills, this word processor remains true to its name. You get a keyboard custom-rigged with timesavers, Dropbox integration for simple file-syncing, and typographical touches that might not jump out at you (fine-tuned leading and column width), but which contribute to the program's underlying message: the word's the thing.

KEYS PLEASE: The keyboard's top row is speedster central: on either end are buttons that'll scoot your cursor one word or character at a time. The ellipses/parentheses mashup is clever: tap once to start your aside, tap again for the closing parens. For those in search of *extreme* focus, the upper-right lock button dims all text except the three lines you're working on. Ready for your list of font choices? The iPad-optimized Nitti Light.

TIME COUNT: That time stamp in the right margin is an interesting twist: it ballparks how long an average reader would take to get there (Writer's maker thinks pagination is a not particularly useful remnant of print). When it's time to publish, the top row's share button lets you email files; the folder next to it lets you do the two-way shuttle with a Dropbox account. In either case, plain-text files are what you get.

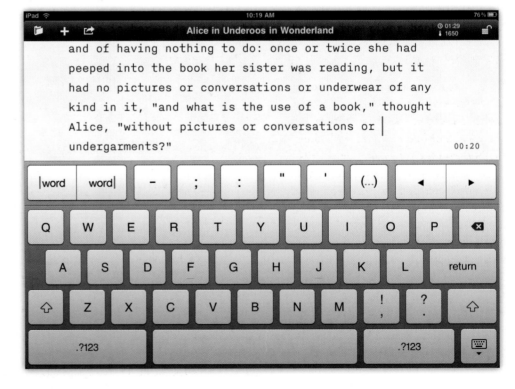

Best App for Outlining

Outliner for iPad

$4.99
Version: 2.5.0 | CarbonFin

Over there in the corner, in the room where the writers hang out, is a peculiar clique: The Outliners. These folks think in bulleted, multitiered lists, apply their method to everything from novel writing to project management, and demand much from the tools they use. This app should satisfy most of 'em. The basics are all here: you can add multiple levels; promote, demote, and move items easily; and collapse and expand what you like. Beyond that, to-do list types get some nifty add-ons (append working checkboxes to list items). Those who want to share get lots of ways to do so, including an online publishing option for collaborative editing.

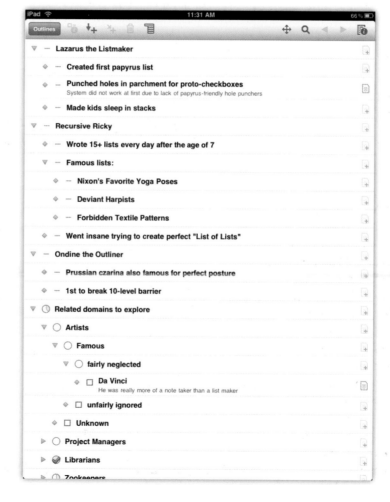

NOTES, NOTED: It is possible to write long, multiple-line entries, but in the grand tradition of terse outline writing, if you've got a lengthy disquisition to add, you're usually better off tucking it into a right-side note; that leaves you with an outline that's easier to scroll through.

LINKED LISTS: A (free) companion web-based service lets you edit and sync lists online. You can even invite others to join. Simple browser-based tools let you do everything there that you can do in the app. Speaking of sharing: the app makes it simple to copy-and-paste, or you can email or export the text in the popular OPML format favored by outlining geeks.

13

Best App for Designing Presentations

Keynote
$9.99
Version: 1.2 | Apple

Let's cut to the chase: can you create good-looking slideshows with this app? And can you use your iPad to show 'em off? Definitely and sort of. The power that Apple packs into this tool is remarkable. Artfully arrange pages filled with images and text; create lots of chart types; design pro quality animations; even add movies. As for sharing, it's close to fully useful. Your best bet—especially for Big Room regulars—is to export the show and play it from a regular computer. Apple sells an iPad-to-projector dongle, but slides only play on the big screen, not your 'Pad. Then again, iPad delivery has its own charms. From salespeople to students, it gives you a whole new way to work a room.

GET STARTED: Import existing Keynote or PowerPoint files, or fire up one of the app's predesigned templates. Reality check: don't expect PC-created presos with hugely complex build sequences to make the trip unscathed; notes are another passenger that gets left at the transfer station. If you use an app template, don't forget to tap the "add a new slide" button ("+") to see all your page design choices.

LOTSA LEARNING: Figuring out how everything works isn't trivial. Check out the "Getting Started" slideshow—a timesaving tour of 80 percent of what you need to know. That final 20? Visit Apple's decent online guide at *http://bit.ly/keynotepad*. A quick tip: object rotation's a bit tricky. Touch and hold with two fingers directly on the image or shape. A yellow line with a degree flag appears when Keynote is ready for you to rotate.

NORMALIZE: If you've edited yourself a style-clashing Frankenshow, select the text you like and, from the pop-up menu's More option, choose Copy Style. Now select the wayward text and repeat the process, picking Paste Style to finish up. Similarly, you can select multiple objects (photos, for example) and apply a single style to all.

FADE TO NEXT: Adding between-slide transitions is easy; you can pick from about two dozen styles. Start by tapping the menu bar's double-diamond icon, and then pick the slide you want to start with. In the Transitions list that appears, choose your effect. The same double-diamond tool is how you add "builds": items that arrive or leave a slide one at a time. Bulleted list items, for example, or bar graphs that you want to unveil year by year.

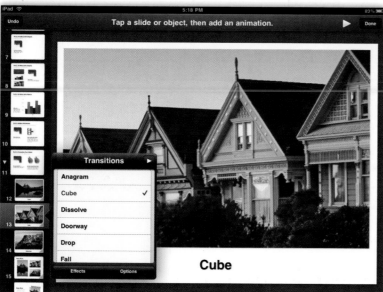

Apples to Apples: Translation Tips

You'd think Apple, being the parent of both versions of Keynote (for Mac and iPad), would make sure all your slideshow creations on the former would appear rosy on the latter. Think again. (Who says Microsoft has a monopoly on right hand/left hand communication problems?) Anyway, if you're a Mac-based Keynote veteran, you'll want to keep a few guidelines in mind for slide decks you create on the desktop. For starters, narrow your focus in the template chooser. Of the 40-plus choices you get, only the following are iPad-friendly: Black, Blackboard, Craft, Gradient, Harmony, Modern Portfolio, Moroccan, Parchment, Showroom, and White. Size-wise, set your slides' dimensions to 1024 by 768 pixels. Font choices on the iPad are decent but not exhaustive; see *http://bit.ly/iPadFonts* for the full list of what you can safely use (everything else gets auto-converted to Helvetica). You'll want to limit your master slide picks to Blank; Title; Title & Subtitle; Title & Bullets; Title, Bullets & Photo; Bullets; Photo; and Photo - Horizontal. And, last but certainly not least annoying: don't override theme backgrounds. Stick with the image fill you get.

Best App for Number-Crunching

Numbers
$9.99
Version: 1.2 | Apple

Numbers' App Store debut was met with a deafening round of…disappointment: *"You can't read or export Excel files?"* the ratings-writing masses cried. Now that *that's* been fixed, let the number-crunching fun begin. As with the Mac version, what makes this app a treat is how easy it makes mixing media: pair up a nicely designed, free-floating headline with some explanatory text, then segue into a table and graph. Top it all off with some label-bearing arrows pointing out key data. None of this is impossible in Excel, but doing it isn't easy. Here's a chance to let your data tell a story and for you to get outta grid prison.

At Work

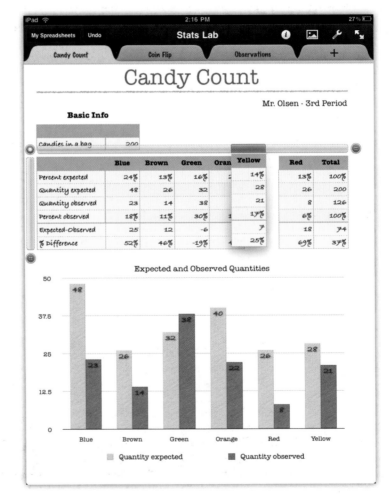

GRID GRAB: Moving columns and rows couldn't be easier. Just select any row or column (tap its tab) and then drag to its new position. Ditto for copying and moving cells. Tap a cell to highlight it and then drag its border box around any neighboring cells you want; tap the selection and then pick Cut, Copy, and so on.

IN-APP HELP: The app's Getting Started spreadsheet is a high-powered how-to guide in disguise. Each of its dozen or so tabs offers explanations on topics ranging from table basics to formulas. What's so special? The instructions incorporate live spreadsheet elements, so while the text explains how to, say, move a table, you get to practice as you read.

TRACK THIS: Numbers is happy to serve as a makeshift database, which is great news, given the frequency that folks put Excel to work tracking, say, the wedding guest list or stolen silverware. That said, the app's happy to help with most any function-powered calculation you want. Double tap any cell and the keyboard morphs to match whatever task you're doing: number, text, or data entry or formula building.

FORM FILLING: The app's also got some nifty tools to make data entry easier. Start with a regular table like the one shown at left to design what you're tracking and then tap the plus ("+") tab (which appears when the keyboard hides) and choose New Form. From here you can add an entry-friendly form where you can bang out a bunch of items.

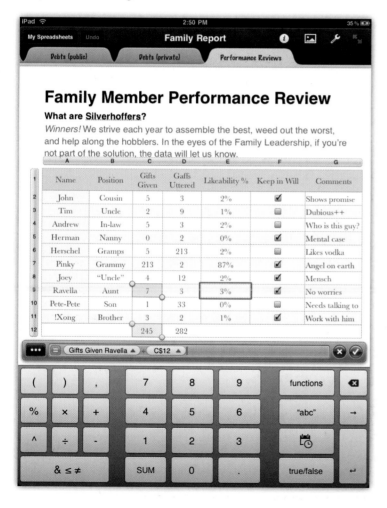

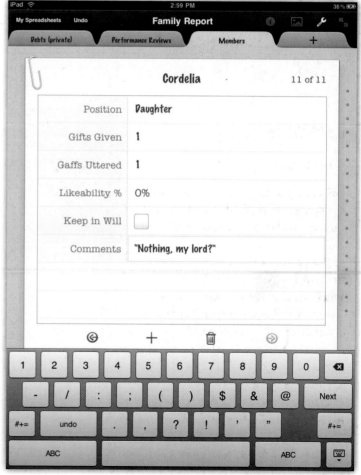

Best App for Editing Office Documents

Documents to Go

$9.99 | $16.99 Premium version
Version: 4.0.2 | DataViz

If you're looking to turn your iPad into a full-powered Office document-creating and -editing helper, the hands-down, no-brainer decision is clear: you can't. None of the current crop of contenders (including Apple's own Pages) matches what you can do on your Mac or PC. Not with fancy formatting, not with extreme number crunching, not with straightforward ease of use. So, power users: scram. You'll only be disappointed. But if most of your documents (Word, Excel, and PowerPoint files) mainly use standard formatting, by all means, download yourself a copy of Documents to Go. It services the needs of most people, most of the time. A ringing endorsement? Nope. A reality check? Roger.

FILE TYPES: You've got three ways to store 'n sync: "Local" puts the file right on your 'Pad; "Desktop" gets you a pair of clones on your regular computer and on the iPad (you need a free companion program to coordinate the process); and "Online" links you up to Google Docs, Dropbox, iDisk, and so on. The Desktop route works especially well: make a change on either copy, click the Sync button, and presto, you're copy protected. You can also create new docs from within the app.

MISSING FEATURES: Limited PowerPoint capabilities are a bummer, especially for those who shelled out extra for the Premium version's promise of compatibility. In a word: don't. You can edit and create extremely simple (think: bulleted lists, no fancy fonts) slideshows, but anything beyond that and you're headed straight to GarbledVille.

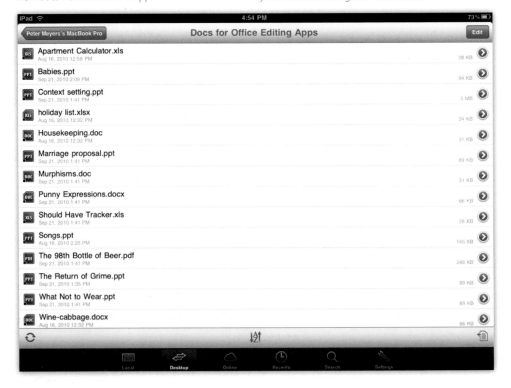

At Work

POWERPOINT IN A PINCH: To whip up a barebones presentation, pick from one of three templates: Casual, Corporate, or Simple. A slide picker in the settings menu lets you move around quickly. The other bottom-of-screen buttons give you options to save, navigate, and insert slides.

NEW FILE FUN: The rest of the Office family is represented in the app's file creation department. And especially with Word. you can create some decent-looking docs. Options include font styling, alignment, spacing, and outlining. Excel's special powers include data sorting, pane freezing and row/column hiding, and a workable Find tool.

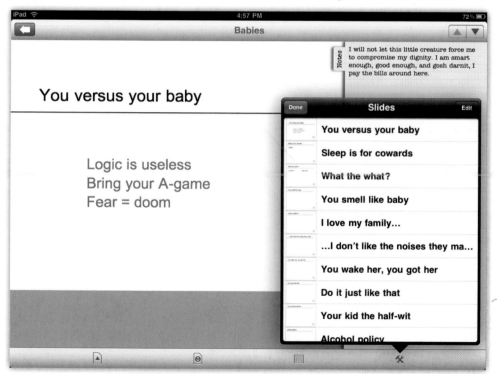

Cloud Control: Editing Google Docs

Eventually, maybe even by the time you read this, Google will make their wildly popular Google Docs service iPad-friendly. For now, while it's possible to use an iPad web browser to *view* any of the slide-shows, spreadsheets, and text files you've posted to this online alternative to Microsoft Office, there's no way to *edit* these documents. That is, not without some help. Documents to Go owners will be happy to learn their investment helps out here. Two-way editing works like a charm for the Big Three file types. Changes you make on the iPad version of a spreadsheet, for example, appear instantly to anyone looking at it from a desktop computer. (For changes heading in the *other* direction—that is, by someone using a regular computer—you may need to tap Documents to Go's Sync button to see the latest version.) By the way, among the benefits to ditching Office for Google's version: better compatibility. Remember the fancy-featured slideshow translation problems mentioned on page 18? Because Google's online slideshow tool is relatively stripped down, what you create there ends up rendering nicely in Documents to Go. And same goes for vice versa.

Best App for Gathering Research

Evernote

Free
Version: 3.4.0 | Evernote

Think Evernote's just a slightly souped-up replacement for the Notes app? Consider its many talents: you can capture any idea worth saving (web page snapshot, audio note-to-self, photo, essay outline), group these into searchable collections, and sync the whole schmeer, automatically, among pretty much every device known to gadgetkind. In truth, the power of this app lies in how it coordinates with other Team Evernote players: the desktop software, the web program and browser plug-in, the smartphone app. All free, all ready to take a multimedia memo whenever the whim hits. As you move through your digital day, grabbing and adding, the service is both scribe and personal library.

MULTIPLE VIEWS: Evernote calls each of your research collections "notebooks." What to track? How about: recipes, books to read, movies to see, proposals, you name it. The "All notes" tab gives you a calendar-style listing of when you took your notes. "Tags" are how the cool categorizers label what they save; create a tag called, say, "funny" and in an instant summon all your best laughers.

IN AND OUT: Pony up for the premium version of Evernote ($5/month or $45/year) and you get extras like the ability to attach and sync video, Word and Excel files, more storage, and no ads. Either way, though, your stuff is yours to keep. The PC and Mac programs both let you export what you've input either as HTML files or a geek-friendly XML package.

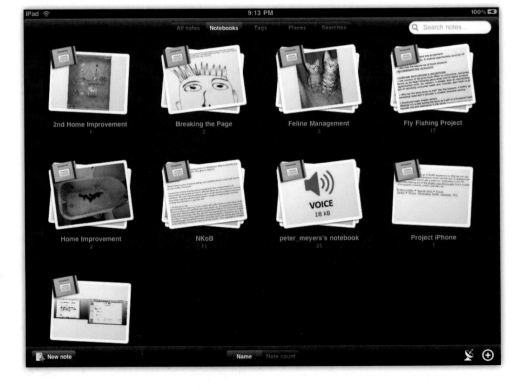

NOTE THIS: The note-taking tool works just like any other word processor: tap the main area and start typing. Pick which notebook you want to file your thoughts in and add existing tags by tapping the blue disclosure triangle; add new tags by jotting them in the Tags box, separating multiple new labels with commas. The iPad's built-in mic lets you add decent-quality voice memos.

WEB HOOKS: Saving web pages as you surf is one of the handiest research aids Evernote offers. Head to *Evernote.com* to grab their add-on for most major web browsers (alas, not yet for iPad's version of Safari). If you tap the Details link and choose the Source URL link, you can even revisit the page you saved.

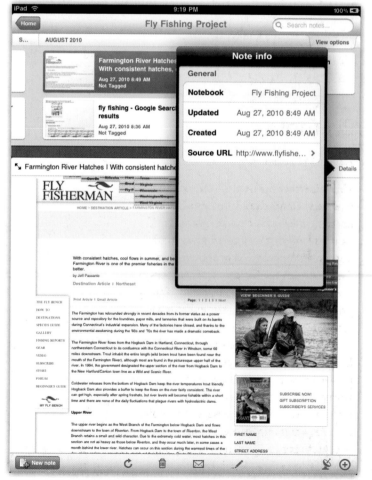

Best App for Taking Notes

Note Taker HD
$4.99
Version: 4.1 | Software Garden

iPad owners who want to handwrite on their touchscreens confront an ugly truth about their beloved devices: sketching apps are lousy for scribes who want to scribble. Enter Note Taker HD, an ingenious solution that really works for most people. Its main innovation: a secondary, zoomed-in-view writing pane that lets you compose on a magnified section of the canvas. It's kind of like having a magnifying glass to write on. You write in this enlarged area and what you add shows up simultaneously, normal sized, on the main canvas. It sounds complicated, but in practice it's not. You also can highlight text and draw diagrams, but writing legible text: that's the show stopper.

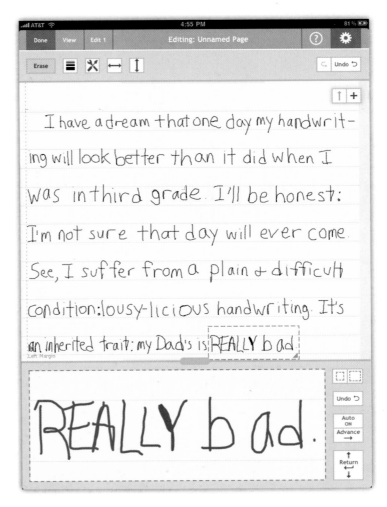

PENMANSHIP TIP: The app's page or so of instructions is worth reading—nothing complicated, but the special mini-editing frame takes some getting used to. A how-to video (http://bit.ly/bxpy2s) shows the basic steps. Highlights: Tap the Edit 2 button to summon the magnifier pane. When your writing reaches the edge, tap Advance to jump the magnifier ahead on the main canvas.

FINGER OR STYLUS: Fat-fingered folks may want to experiment with some of the iPad-friendly styluses sold by firms like Pogo. Many find them helpful, but approach with realistic expectations. It's more like writing with an extra thumb than a pencil: its fat nub has to occupy that width for the touchscreen to recognize it.

At Work

22

Penultimate

$2.99
Version: 2.1.1
Ben Zotto

Sketchbook doodlers, this one's for you. Don't expect to get a significant amount of handwriting done; if, say, you're a student taking lecture notes, you're much better off using a writing app's onscreen keyboard (or an external, Bluetooth one). But when words are only a small part of your idea-catching toolkit—if you like to doodle, sketch, and illustrate in a way that comes closest to what visual types have done for ages—this elegantly designed, simple-to-use app is picture perfect. Press and hold the pen icon to choose different ink colors and line widths; the eraser's next to it. Not much else to know other than that: just draw.

Noterize

$2.99
Version: 3.4 | Robert Stretch

Noterize is noteworthy for its wide range of talents. Lecturegoers will love its built-in audio recorder, which works as you type or write (yep, you can do both). PDF regulars will love how the app makes hay of importing, adding a signature, and then exporting a page with your John Hancock. Research types will wanna write home about the web page clipping tool: grab anything you see online by using the built-in browser, slap a note on it, and add it to any project you're working on. Everyone will appreciate the app's integration with online doc sharing services Box.net and Dropbox. So where does the app fall short? Only in the slightly steep learning curve; you'll want to spend some time with the fairly readable user's guide while making that journey.

Best App for Index Card Writers

Index Card

$2.99
Version: 1.4.2 | DenVog

This app is pitched at the screenplay set; its App Store page even has a blurb from a genuine A-list TV writer! But in truth, anyone whose writing or note-taking would benefit from a corkboard and index card setup will find a lot to like here. Its signature talent is the same one you get with the real-world version: as your board fills up with cards, you can move 'em around with ease. That's especially useful for new-idea mavens and plot reordering junkies. Each time inspiration strikes all you need to do is fire up a fresh card or reorder the existing sequence. When your agent calls (or you want to polish your prose on a desktop computer) the app also lets you export your gem.

At Work

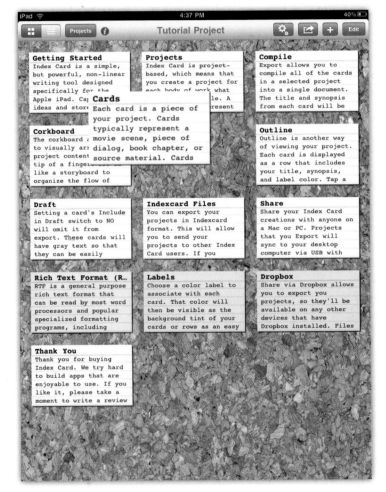

CARD CATALOG: Create projects for each collection of related cards (one for that screenplay, another for your *Ulysses* travel guide); each gets its own corkboard. A handful of card colors are available, so within a project you can identify related themes (red for love scenes, green for accounting). Moving is simple: tap and hold till the card enlarges and then drag to reposition.

EXIT ALL: The upper-right share icon is your cards' ticket out of the app. Export options include the fairly common RTF format; the app assembles your cards into an outline-style compilation (you can tag any you don't want making the trip). Dropbox support is also included for those who use it to sync multiple devices.

DATA ENTRY: Here's where you actually unload your best ideas. (Bonus typing tip: hit the keyboard's ".?123" button to reveal an "undo" option on the numerical keyboard.) Tap the slanted white arrow for the back of the card, where you can stick additional notes. Flip off the "Include in Draft" switch if you don't want to export a card.

OUTLINE VIEW: Tap the icon with three stacked lines in the upper-left corner to reach this barebones list layout; it's where you should head for searches. Enter your query in the search bar. This view also shows, at bottom, a word and character summary for an entire project's collection of cards.

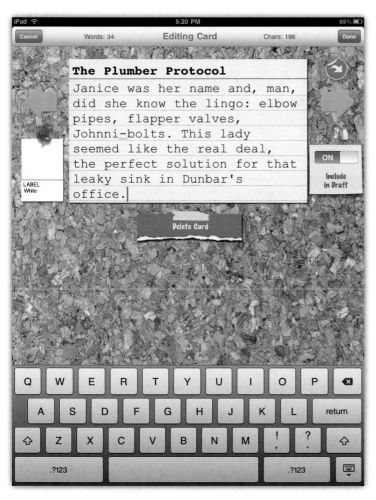

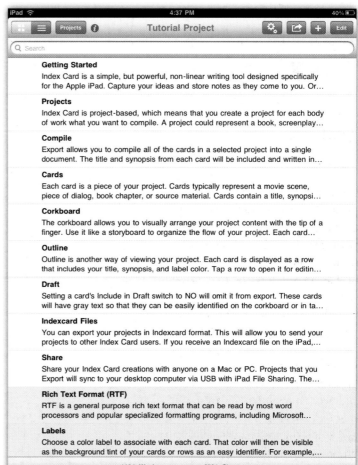

Best App for Documents on the Go

ReaddleDocs for iPad
$4.99
Version: 1.6.1 | Readdle

Apple's goal of shielding iPad owners from file and folder management hassles has been a great success. Who needs to futz with all *that* when you can live a safe and uncluttered life within each app you use? Except for, uh, when the real world intrudes and you have four Word files with notes about your vacation plans, a Power-Point deck for that speech you're giving, a PDF of that ebook you just bought, and the spreadsheet with the guest list for next month's wedding. *Now* wouldn't it be nice to have something resembling your PC's ability to store and view different files? ReaddleDocs is a polished, simple-to-use solution that turns your iPad into a big combo flash drive/file viewer.

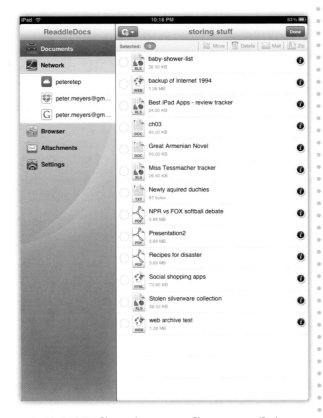

FILE DIVERSITY: Plenty o' ways to get files onto your 'Pad: open email attachments, transfer from your PC via WiFi, or pipe 'em over next time you've plugged your iPad into iTunes using a USB cable. Or sync with online storage services like Google Docs and Dropbox. The list of files you can view (but not edit) is lengthy: pretty much all Office files (including .docx and .xlsx), PDF, and all the most popular image and video files. PDF reading comes with a special treat: you can highlight and add notes.

+ HONORABLE MENTION

GoodReader for iPad
$1.99
Version: 3.1.0 | Good.iWare

GoodReader grabbed early and well deserved kudos for its widely popular iPhone file manager. Following in its footsteps, the iPad app edition makes for a helpful download, especially for power users who appreciate the chance to customize in ways that might strike many mortals as overkill. For example, want to change the red/blue/green mix on the background canvas of text files you create using the app? GoodReader's happy to help. More useful tweaks include the ability to set custom next- and previous-page tap spots.

Best App for Teleprompting

Teleprompt+ for iPad

$9.99
Version: 2.1 | Bombing Brain Interactive

Toastmasters, speechmakers, junior class president candidates: stop fumbling with note cards or finger-licking your way to the next page of *your* Gettysburg Address. Till you're teleprompter-worthy, pop your iPad on the iPodium and pontificate like a pro with this helpful app. Chief among its virtues: the two minutes or less you'll need to get up to speed—especially important for Nervous Nellies or technophobes who want to focus on their talk and not on gadget wrangling. What you'll find are a handful of orator-friendly tools: speed-of-scroll control, a "reading guide" highlighter box for better focus, and an in-app recorder for at-home rehearsal.

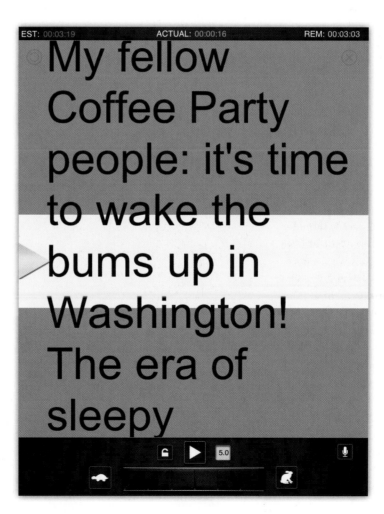

EST: 00:03:19   ACTUAL: 00:00:16   REM: 00:03:03

My fellow Coffee Party people: it's time to wake the bums up in Washington! The era of sleepy

5.0

TEXT TO SPEECH:
Two main entry methods for inputting your speech: via Google Docs (tap Import) or through iTunes. You can also compose a talk right in the app, but a more realistic use of the in-app keyboard is last-minute wordsmithing when your speechwriters are gone and you're on rewrite duty.

PRIMP THE PROMPT:
Font size choices range from big (24 point) to "we're gonna need a bigger iPad" (204 point). Speed controls also come in plenty o' sizes: from 1.0 to a Spinal Tap-happy 11.0. Once you've started your speech, a simple two-fingered tap lets you pause the scroll for questions, catcalls, or applause.

27

Best App for Trendspotting

Cool Hunting

Free
Version: 2.0.2 | Captain Lucas

If your cool quest hasn't stopped since high school, you probably know—or should know—about Cool Hunting. The website presents an eclectic mix of trendy tips grouped into categories like tech, travel, and culture. The small team behind this venture curates its picks with a shared sensibility for good design, which extends to what you get in this app. Namely, most of what's on the website, but in a package that's better for browsing: easier, more photo-rich layouts for flipping through the latest posts, a great screen for the service's well-done mini documentaries, and an in-app browser that lets you follow links of interest without leaving behind the cool vibe that lured you here in the first place.

POST HUNTING: Pick between two main browsing modes: scroll through photo/blurb pairs for a bird's-eye view of everything on offer, or head into article mode where you read and then swipe between stories. If you go the latter route, you'll probably prefer portrait mode, which gives the text more canvas. However your iPad is oriented, swipe across article images for a gallery of other post-related photos.

TRAVEL TIPS: For a small group of trend-friendly cities, the Local tab offers hotspot tips that won't show up on most tourist lists. For what you pay, this hunting guide overall is a nice add to any trendwatcher's toolkit. But beware: the service is not flawless. The app's got bugs (the search feature comes up empty), but the developer has a record of improvement with each release so additional polish is likely on its way.

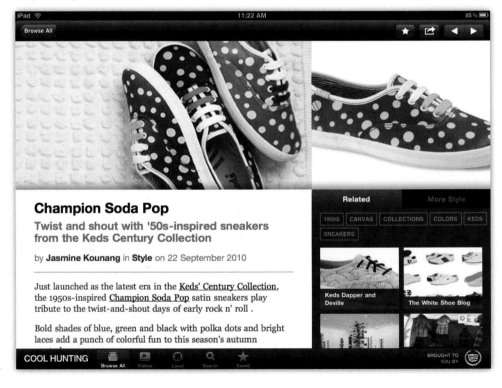

Best App for Simulating a Great View

Magic Window
$1.99
Version: 1.3 | Jetson Creative

That windowless cube at work getting you down? Sure, you could flick on your dormant iPad's photo slideshow. But do you really want Ingrid from accounting to see all *that?* Give her—and, more importantly, *you*—a Calgon moment by illuminating your black slate with some seriously soothing nature footage. More than just a series of great outdoorsy shots (the App Store's littered with those), Magic Window does something different: it stitches together thousands of time lapse photos for each of its 20 scenes and then lets you control the speed at which they "play." Add in an (optional) ambient audio track (seagulls, wind, whatever matches the view) and office life suddenly ain't so bad.

FLIPBOOK PHOTOS: The lower-right control strip is where you control the speed of this visual time travel. Anywhere around Slow and you'll barely notice the scenery changing; push the circle either right or left and you'll see the pace pick up. To manually step through the frame fest, drag your finger anywhere on the main image—right to move ahead, left to view history.

SCENE SAVER: The left-side Scene button holds the catalog of viewable destinations. At launch, it presents four Quick View options, preloaded and ready to start playing at your tap. Head to Browse More Scenes for the remaining crew. You can preview any of these, but for the full play, you'll need to download 'em (for free); the developer says their filesize (a few dozen MBs) makes including them all prohibitively large.

Best App for Remote Desktop Access

LogMeIn Ignition
$29.99
Version: 1.2.184 | LogMeIn

You will in all likelihood find this app a frustrating waste of $30 should you install it on your iPad (and a PC-based version on the machine you wish to control), launch it, and then dive right in. But take the time to learn a few simple swipe and tap gestures and—shazaam!—you're sitting behind the controls of one wickedly cool and convenient way to remotely control any Mac or Windows PC in your computer arsenal. And unlike many of its competitors, setup couldn't be simpler. The PC software is a free download, and the wizards behind this production have green-curtained the network setting wonkery. Log yourself in, flip on the ignition, and steer remotely.

REMOTE CONTROL 101: Pinch or spread to zoom in and out. To pan across a zoomed-in screen drag *away* from where you want to go: head left, for example, and the screen moves right. And to control the onscreen pointer, it sounds weird, but don't try to tap directly on the pointer. Instead, pick a spot a few inches below and to the side of it, and then tap and drag or flick to push the pointer around quickly.

TAP DANCE TRICKS: What takes a little getting used to, because of the marionette-like distance you maintain from the onscreen pointer, is that your finger on the iPad is usually tapping a location that's several inches away from, say, that menu that you actually want to click. Yes, it sounds complicated. But have faith: it's really straightforward once you get the hang of it.

Best App for iPad as External Display

Air Display
$9.99
Version: 1.2 | Avatron

Trying to get lots done on a cramped, smallish display stuffed with lots of open windows is a drag. All that mousing, clicking, and constant window shuffling: it's a real time suck. Join the multi-monitor owning masses…without having to buy a second screen. Air Display transforms your iPad into a dedicated viewport that extends your main computer's desktop real estate. Then stock this second screen with whatever you like: an IM or Twitter feed to occasionally glance at, the outline to that book you're writing, a slow-moving chess game. It's a mini-monitor for multitaskers.

SIMPLE SETUP: Start by installing the freely downloadable helper program on your computer. Then launch the app on the iPad and flip the system on using a control switch on your Mac or PC. You can also activate mirror mode, so that both displays show the same image—useful, for example, for teachers who want to pass around a photo for the class to inspect.

MAC TIP: If you're working on a Mac, put the permanent Apple menu bar (the one that always appears on top of the display) on the computer's monitor, rather than on top of the iPad. Do that in Display Preferences by using the Arrangement tab; drag the white menu bar to wherever you want it to appear.

Best App for Safari Haters

Perfect Web Browser
$2.99
Version: 1.2 | Ingenious Creations

This app might not quite live up to its name (an option to import existing Safari bookmarks feels like a big miss), but for power surfers frustrated by the iPad's built-in browser, this guy's worth a try. For starters, if you're peeved by sites that dish up their mobile selves, tap the gear icon and switch to "Safari Mac" (via the Desktop Web Rendering option). Now you'll see, for example, Gmail as it was meant to appear on a big display. Tabbed browsing is likely to be the main draw for most comers. Now you can tap and hold links and then launch them in new tabs, easily accessible at the top of the screen. If the Web's where you do most of your iPad-ding, that trick alone might be a clincher.

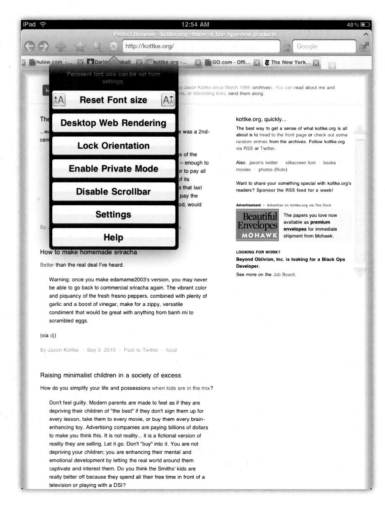

BROWSE BETTER: Tap the upper-right blue arrow box to enter fullscreen mode and reclaim the top 1/2 inch or so that Safari devotes to the address bar. In-page search lets you look for a word or phrase on a page. And scroll noticeably faster (compared to flicking) by using the right-side scrollbar.

TAP TIPS: Swipe left or right with two fingers to switch between open tabs. Three-finger swipes keep you on the same tab but act like the back (left swipe) or forward (right swipe) buttons. Bonus tip: tap the chunky green plus button to save an offline copy of any page. Nice.

At Leisure

 That big black chair Steve Jobs settled into during the iPad's unveiling wasn't there because he doesn't like standing. The unmistakeable message he sought to convey with legs crossed and device in lap: the iPad's a living room-friendly gadget. Whether you're in the mood to read, watch, or listen, when you leave the laptop behind and enter instant-on, browse-by-swiping mode, the distance between you and your media shrinks. Exhibit A is the kind of social-powered entertainment snacking that's currently sending shivers down the spines of Big Media Moguls everywhere: Twitter, Facebook, Flickr, and co. These photo- and link-rich status update factories have drawn great gobs of viewer interest in today's info-overloaded environment. Apps that offer a swipe- and touch-friendly view of these collections have a way of making that couch cushion even more comfortable. Mainstream media, of course, isn't going anywhere. Old-guard providers see a chance not only to deliver their traditional product, but sprinkle it with New Media pixie dust (adding things like how-to animations and live updates). Meanwhile, upstarts in radio and music aim to give the people what they want, which translates to a lot of personalized playlist making and eye-candy beat visualizers. And the big screen makes its own appearance on the littler screen; the tablet's rich display and long battery makes for great movie watching. Finally, our poor old friend, the book: perpetually declared having breathed its last breath, gets, yet again, a chance to resuscitate itself. From plain ol' prose to new kinds of storytelling, the iPad's proving to be quite a screen turner.

Photo: Maerten Prins

Best App for Reading Books

Kindle

Free
Version: 2.3.1 | Amazon.com

The Kindle's early success seemed to earn Amazon victory in the Great Ebook War, but then—pow!—came the iPad, its multi-talents a worrisome blow to the rainforest retailer. Not so fast. Amazon's stealth counterpunch comes in the form of its ebook-reading app. Paired with a huge, competition-beating selection (quality, not just quantity counts) and syncing options to pretty much any mainstream device (PC, Mac, Blackberry, Android, iPhone). The clincher: the reader-friendly choice to dispense with all that distracting, faux print-book chrome that other apps go for. Instead you get plain ol' prose, center stage, all by itself.

At Leisure

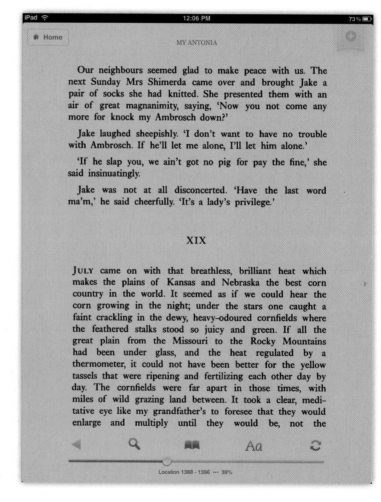

FOCAL POINTS: Everything you see on this screen, save for the book's title and its text, takes a hike—either when you tap anywhere or advance the page. That lets you lose yourself in the book without real-life worries like what time it is or a useless reminder of the name of your device (iPad? Thanks, I thought I was holding a cheeseburger.)

COLLECTED WORKS: Click that upper-left Home button and you'll see all the Kindle books you've purchased that currently reside on your iPad. If you've got other Kindle book reading gadgets (a Blackberry, say) your full list of Amazon purchased ebooks can be reached and downloaded by tapping Archived Items.

LOOK DOWN, LOOKUP: The built-in dictionary means you're only a tap away from the handy definition box that appears at the bottom of the screen. Links in the lower-left corner of that box let you continue the search on either Google, Wikipedia, or, if you want a deep-dive explanation, tap Full Definition for the full scoop from the *New Oxford American Dictionary*.

BONUS BOOK: Speaking of the *New Oxford* and its full explanatory powers: don't forget you've got access to it as full-fledged, searchable and browsable dictionary—separate from any ebook you're reading. Just go to the Kindle app's home screen and you'll see it listed. Tap to open, and use the magnifying glass Search icon to look up a word, bookmark favorites, and add notes.

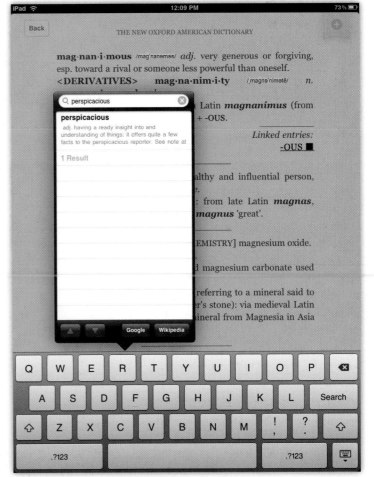

Best App for Reading Textbooks

Inkling

Free
Version: 1.1 | Inkling

The demise of the $100-plus, backpack-straining textbook can't come soon enough for those forced to buy those beasts. Inkling's trying to fix matters in two ways: by selling individual chapters and by redesigning the layout and reading experience in an iPad-friendly way. Each chapter gets chunked up into "cards"— vertically scrollable sections that do away with the page-based layout of a print book and can be read in either landscape or portrait orientation. (Print page numbers, however, are still pegged into the margins for times when that's important.) Some nifty note-sharing and in-text diagnostic tools provide a further glimpse of how these books can do more than print.

HIDDEN TREATS: Embedded, pop-up glossary definitions give students a quick way to look up unfamiliar terms. Other items, waiting to be summoned on an as-needed basis, include sidebars (like Tip #5, which explains note-taking in detail) and full-sized images. By presenting smaller versions of both elements, the page showcases the main flow of info; readers can further investigate tangential stuff when they're ready.

ATTENTION READERS: The book's not just for text and static images. *The Elements of Style* sampler (completely rewritten, it should be noted for the sake of its grave-rolling original author, William Strunk) has a video sidebar that shows how the app's note-taking and highlighting tool works. It demonstrates a relatively simple process, but the embeddable video gives a glimpse of one helpful way to integrate video into how-to texts.

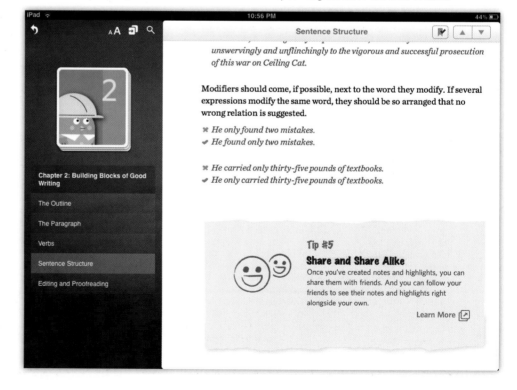

NOTED: A social, shareable notes feature puts to the test the idea that it'd be useful to see the marginal jottings of other (presumably smarter) pals. A permissions-request system plays gatekeeper to who gets to follow you. Color coding helps differentiate notes you made (yellow), from those of your classmates (blue) and your teacher (purple).

NAVIGATION AIDS: Each vertical line segment in the left-side column (Inkling calls it the "spine") represents a section within a chapter; the length of the line reflects the length of the section and the white dot pinpoints your current location. Tap the line for a pop-up menu that lets you jump to any section within the chapter.

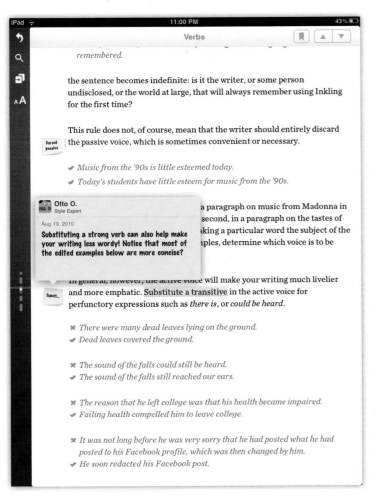

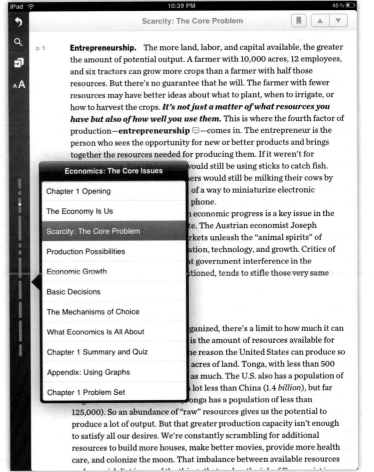

Best App for Reading Wikipedia

Simplepedia for iPad

Free
Version: 2.0.1 | Lazyapps.com

For a volunteer effort, Wikipedia's sure got a lot of folks trying to make some coin off it. Close to a dozen apps, for example, offer to repackage—with various amounts of design polish and download-now, read-later features—this treasure trove of report writing. Keep your wallet in your pocket and grab a copy of Simplepedia, an elegant implementation that stays true to its name (man, this app couldn't be easier to use) *and* the free-for-all mission of the site's article-creating army. What you get is what you need: auto-saved storage of articles you've read, scrollable tables of contents for each entry, and the ability to search within each entry (as well as, of course, the entire encyclopedia).

READING HISTORY: The Offline Articles tool automatically hangs onto several dozen of your most recently viewed entries. Tap the button to see a menu of what you've been browsing. If the factory-set English Wikipedia isn't enough for your polyglot tastes, hit the search oval's English label to pick from a few dozen other Wikipedian languages.

BROWSE BETTER: Each article's pop-up table of contents works like a charm. Though it might seem like a small detail, the developer has taken care to line-wrap section headers; that means you don't have to puzzle your way through truncated TOC entries when trying to figure out where to jump in an article. Nice.

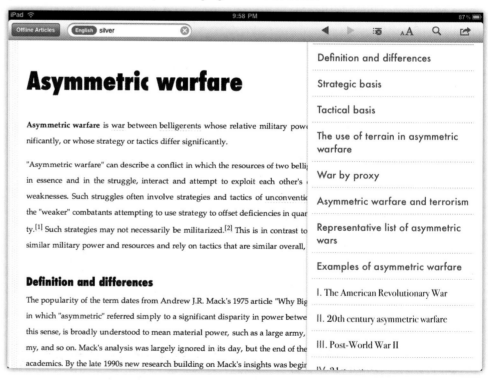

At Leisure

Best App for Reading Shakespeare

Shakespeare

Free lite version | $9.99
Version: 1.3.0 | Readdle

The Hamlet-style question you'll face with this app is much simpler than our indecisive hero's famous angst: to get the Pro version or not? Let us count the ways it serves serious Shakepeareans: loads of factual geekery (top 20 characters by total number of lines, for example), a greatest quotes browser, and, most usefully, a reading experience–changing embedded glossary that beats print by a mile (tap to view annotations). Either way, you get a searchable concordance, 40-something plays, a handful of poems, and a wooer's worth of sonnets. The finishing touch is a lovely layout (including meter-preserving indentation) that puts this collection a cut above any freebie you can find online.

TAP & LEARN: A best-ever implementation of a seriously useful 40,000-word glossary: you're only a tap away from easy-to-consult, easy-to-dismiss pop-up boxes linked to the dotted words and phrases peppering the text. (And the annotations are no crowd-sourced, scrape-the-Web job: they're pulled from the well-regarded *Shakespeare's Words*.)

SEARCH FRIENDLY: The app's concordance highlights found terms in yellow and gives you a nice chunk of surrounding material in the results list, so you can scan search results before diving into a particular play. Another reader treat (Pro only): an option to flip on "Long names" in the Settings button so that our pal Ham becomes Hamlet.

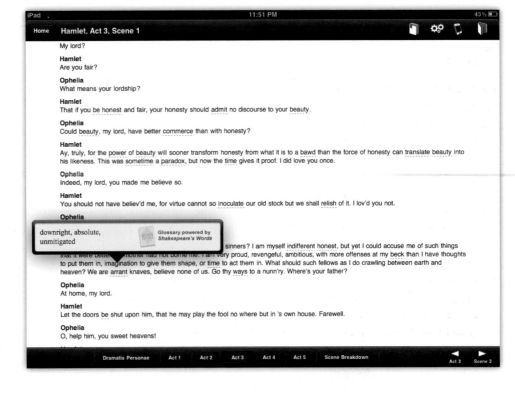

Best Dictionary and Thesaurus App

Wordbook XL

$2.99
Version: 4.3 | TranCreative Software

Are you a word gawker? Do trips to the dictionary lead past your original target? Skip today's Starbucks and spend it on an app that's perfect for English language explorers. On the surface, it looks and acts like a dictionary—one that's powered by Princeton's WordNet project, which specializes in identifying meaningful relations between words. It's the extra treats that'll woo word hounds: bookmarkable favorites, a pad for adding notes to words, links to more- and less-specific neighbors (plus plain ol' synonyms), emailable definitions, and an in-app web browser with built-in links for each term to other online dictionaries. It's a wonderful way to explore your mother (or other) tongue.

WORD WANDER: Cool: most terms come with not only synonyms, but also less- and more-specific lists. Water down *azure*, for example, and you get *blue* and *blueness*. A *cozenage* is a specific type of *swindle*, whereas *fraud* is the more general category of intentional deception. Climbing the definitional tree in this manner from root to leaf is a thoroughly fun way for word geeks to boost their word count. Tip: don't like the "Words of the Day" lineup? Tap the refresh icon in the lower-left corner for a new batch.

PROSE CONS: Bummer: some definitions get reused for related words: *nobble* and *hornswoggle* both offer as their primary definition: "deprive by deceit." The overlap, which stems from the underlying WordNet archive, means WordBook is probably less reliable as a high-powered premium dictionary and more handy for more mainstream explorations. But don't forget the handy outbound links. Click Google, for example, and you're one link away from the generally reliable Merriam-Webster website.

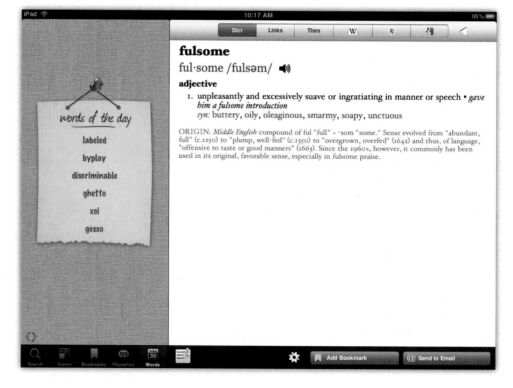

At Leisure

Oxford American Dictionary & Thesaurus

$9.99
Version: 2.0.3 | Handmark

While your favorite word wonk waits for the *Oxford English Dictionary* to go app (surely that's gonna happen now that they've nixed future printings of the 20-volume beast), check out its nicely equipped junior partner. It's stocked with a full complement of modern and classic finding, browsing, and savoring tools: an integrated dictionary and thesaurus, usage notes and example sentences, "fuzzy" word search (where you enter wildcard characters for letters you're not sure about), sharing (via email, Facebook, and Twitter), and the ability to tag words and see the tags others have applied. All in all, an ambitious offering that, in the non-app world, reading fans wouldn't blink paying 10 bucks for.

Dictionary.com

Free
Version: 1.1 | Dictionary.com

Maybe you're not a language lover. You think about your dictionary like any other office supply: there when you need it, nothin' fancy, and as close to free as possible. If that's the case, you'll want to flip open the Dictionary.com app, a just-the-words-ma'am offering, but powered by the respectable wordsmiths at Random House (it's based on their unabridged dictionary, which is paired with a thesaurus). An Internet connection is required for most of the fun frills like audio pronunciations and Word of the Day listings, but the main listings are on tap regardless of where you are. Lookups couldn't be simpler: enter the first few letters of what you're looking for in the search bar and the app shows a list of the dozen or so words that begin that way. If you enter a word it doesn't recognize, the app presents you with similarly spelled words.

Best App for Bible Studies

Logos Bible Software

Free
Version: 1.4.4 | Logos Bible Software

While the Bible's likely to continue its run as the bestselling print book of all time, the depth, breadth, and hyperlinked goodies available in this app may well turn a few page flippers into screen tappers. The outfit behind this offering sells a variety of PC-based Biblical tools and you can link the app to that software. But what you get for free is bountiful. About 60 titles appear in the built-in library and include familiar editions (King James), many translations (Arabic, Spanish), and a wide variety of reader aids (*Summarized Bible: Complete Summary of the New Testament*). Most require an Internet connection, but a handful, including the King James, are available free for offline reading.

THE FIRST DAY: Finding *In the beginning* is a little confusing amidst the wealth of info on offer here. Start at the Library icon, scroll to the edition you want and then tap the book's title. Once the text appears onscreen, navigation works like most other ebooks: tap or swipe to move from page to page. A single tap in the middle of the screen summons navigation and search tools. The Verse button lets you flip to a particular book, chapter, or verse.

HYPERLINK HELP: Different editions have different annotation symbols, but in general you'll find that large bold numbers indicate the chapter, superscript numbers pinpoint verses, hyperlinked letters connect to other passages that echo the linked phrase (tap once to see the passage location, tap again to see a preview), and hyperlinked numbers offer quick notes on translation issues or modern variations.

BEHIND THE SCENES: The sharing and textual analysis you get for a free app are pretty impressive. For example, you can email a link to an online version of any passage (swipe upward and pick Share from the pop-up menu). Other aids available via that pop-up menu include a passage guide (a CliffsNotes-style summary) and a text comparison (with other editions, complete with key phrasing variations highlighted).

LIBRARY BROWSING: Among the many supplementary titles, *Easton's Bible Dictionary* offers an alphabetized guide to pretty much any term you need background on; tappable links within each definition make traversing the collection easy and useful. Other good reads to help with the Good Book: *The Pilgrim's Progress*, *Young's Literal Translation*, and *Commentary Critical and Explanatory on the Whole Bible*.

additional month (ve-Adar) was inserted, so as to make the months coincide with the seasons.

"The Hebrews and Phoenicians had no word for month save 'moon,' and only saved their calendar from becoming vague like that of the Moslems by the interpolation of an additional month. There is no evidence at all that they ever used a true solar year such as the Egyptians possessed. The latter had twelve months of thirty days and five epagomenac or odd days.", Palestine Quarterly, January 1889.

MOON — heb. yareah, from its paleness (Ezra 6:15), and lebanah, the "white" (Cant. 6:10; Isa. 24:23), was appointed by the Creator to be with the sun "for signs, and for seasons, and for days, and years" (Gen. 1:14–16). A lunation was among the Jews the period of a month, and several of their festivals were held on the day of the new moon. It is frequently referred to along with the sun (Josh. 10:12; Ps. 72:5, 7, 17; 89:36, 37; Eccl. 12:2; Isa. 24:23, etc.), and also by itself (Ps. 8:3; 121:6).

The great brilliance of the moon in Eastern countries led to its being early an object of idolatrous worship (Deut. 4:19; 17:3; Job 31:26), a form of idolatry against which the Jews were warned (Deut. 4:19; 17:3). They, however, fell into thi[s] Jer. 8:2), and also cakes of 25).

> **Deuteronomy 4:19**
> 19 And beware lest you raise your eyes to heaven, and when you see the sun and the moon and the stars, all the host of heaven, you be drawn away and bow down to them and serve them, things that the LORD your God has allotted to all the peoples under the whole heaven.
>
> Jump to reference »

MORDECAI — the son of [...] alleged that he was carried [...] he must have been at least [...] twelfth year of Ahasuerus ([...]) necessarily lead to this conclusion. It was probably Kish of whom it is said (ver. 6) that he "had been carried away with the captivity."

He resided at Susa, the metropolis of Persia. He adopted his cousin Hadassah (Esther), an orphan child, whom he tenderly brought up as his

Best App for Reading Comics

Comixology

Free
Version: 1.6.2 | Iconology

Comic book fans welcomed the iPad's arrival: finally, a portable gadget large enough to show off their favorite titles. Their parents and spouses celebrated, too: finally, an end to those shelf-hogging collections. Comixology's maker, Iconology, is the programming outfit behind most of the App Store's leading comics apps. This app offers the same service: a storefront from which to buy and a reader to get down to business. A decent assortment of free titles makes sampling easy. Plus, its neutral catalog reaches, if not quite as deep as some of its competitors, then about as wide as you'll find.

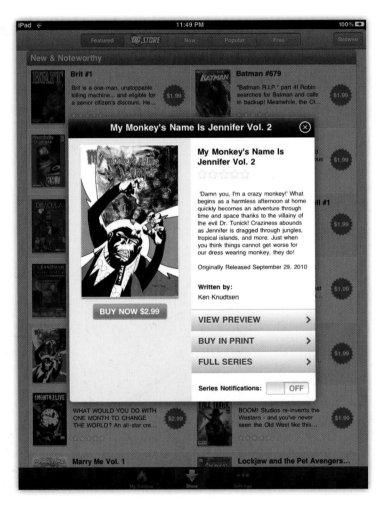

EASY READING: Guided View lets you quickly pan and zoom in sequence through each page's panels. While the technique is mainly designed for iPhone owners who want to read full-sized comics, it offers a nice focused reading experience on the iPad (which, at about 10 inches, is still smaller than the 12 inches occupied by most print comics).

WANDERING EYES: Like Comixology, but wish its selection of, say, DC or Marvel comics were a bit larger? Check out the apps from both those publishers; they're powered by the same code under this app's hood, so everything's pretty similar—you just get a different catalog of buying choices.

At Leisure

Best App for Comics…Set in Motion

Motion Comic Superare

$1.99
Version: 1.0.1 | Amo Tarzi

As artists begin to compose expressly for tablets, expect to see more productions like this one: a comic book that takes an old form and recreates it for the digital display. We've seen animated funnies on the Web for years now, but this is something different—a clearly talented comic artist working to modernize his métier. He's taken the sequential framing of the comic, kept the structure that guides the reader's progress, and then added what the iPad makes possible: ambient sound, motion (a character walking down the street), and even movement across a series of panels, creating a kind of visual relay (a suit, flung, tumbles across the screen).

TIMING: The story's pacing is itself an accomplishment. The panels unveil themselves like advent calendar windows on auto-open, each providing enough time for you to digest what it features before the next frame appears. A pause button lets you stop, review, re-read—a key tool for giving the viewer a sense of control.

TROUBLED TALE: Alas, things are a bit buggy (page turning stutters) and the promised content updates aren't coming quite as quickly as the artist is aiming for. But for a glimpse at so-called "born digital" content and, worth mentioning, a touching story about a bereft widower, this app is definitely worth checking out.

45

Best App for How Magazines Should Look

Popular Mechanics Interactive Edition

$3.99 per issue
Version: 1.0 | Hearst Communications

Magazines are scrambling to find their place in AppLand. Apple's 30% cut and data-sharing policies have slowed the pace of experimentation among the biggies (Conde Nast, Time), but a clear front runner in the race to recreate has emerged: Hearst's *Popular Mechanics*. Not a gear head or DIYer? The only thing you need to fall for this app is an interest in, uh, the future of reading. What they're doing here will be standard issue in the issues of the future: user-controllable animations to clarify how-to instructions, a navigation system that requires no help guide, and a sharing feature that —news flash!—actually lets you spread the stuff you enjoyed.

THIS WAY, PLEASE: Table of contents and page-by-page browsing options each do their own thing well: the first offers a drop-down menu that scrolls vertically with one blurb per article, and the second presents a row of horizontally swipable page miniatures of the entire mag. And see those horizontal lines stacked in the upper-right? Drag 'em up or down to change the page icon size.

RETIRE THE HELP WRITERS: No one has ever wanted to spend their time on a page called "how to use this magazine/book/ etc." *Popular Mechanics* recognizes this and inserts minimally intrusive, maximally useful usage tips and integrated design elements (arrows, for example, pointing which way to swipe).

ASSEMBLY LANGUAGE: Some incredibly useful animation work here helps how-toers turn into get-it-doners. A DIY feature on building a hanging hallway shelf and coat rack comes with three visuals: a materials inventory; a 3D model of the finished cabinet that you can twirl around; and, most helpfully, an animation of the assembly sequence with key parts highlighted. Use the scrubber bar to review key steps after the video plays.

QUAKER MAKER: An earthquake visualizer (from the demo issue) amounts to an app-within-the-app. It does two things: presents a continuously updated, sequentially unfolding display of noteworthy quakes over the past seven days, and, in a separate mode, shows the top 10 biggies of the past 150 years. Brilliant touch: two-finger drag and tilt mode lets you shift your viewing angle from bird's-eye (of the whole U.S., as shown here) to "your nose is on the earth's surface" (lets you see how deep each bang reverbs underground).

① 3D MODEL   ② ASSEMBLY SEQUENCE   ③ MATERIALS

⏸ 0:17 ————————————○———————— -0:10 ⤢

hallway. Its three cubbyholes provide more than enough space to store everything from car keys and harmonicas to a porkpie hat (if you're so inclined). For most of us, though, it means a place to stash gloves, sunglasses, dog leashes and mail. Coats hang below.

I mounted my minicabinet near the front door, but it would also be useful in a mudroom, breezeway, front hallway, enclosed porch or garage—any area in the home that begs to be transformed from a scene of confusion into a

gateway for calm and quick exits to the outside world.

Building the Case

→ The heart of this project is nothing more than an open box. Moldings and shaped edges help conceal that fact, as do subtle proportions. I began by crosscutting the ends using a miter saw, but you could just as easily use a circular saw and guide. Next, I marked the arch on each end and cut it using a jigsaw.

TECH WATCH

Interactive Earthquake Finder

After devastating earthquakes in Haiti, Chile, China and Mexico in the past few months, it may seem as if 2010 has been an unusually active year for the earth's crust. Not so, says Dr. Michael Blanpied, associate coordinator for earthquake hazards at the U.S. Geological Survey. "The death and destruction in 2010 is unusual

and unfortunate," he says. "But in a typical year, the earth gets between 12 and 16 magnitude 7 or greater earthquakes. So far, we've had six."

In fact, earthquakes are surprisingly common events. The earth experiences almost constant seismic activity—the U.S. alone sees a magnitude 5 or greater quake about once every five days, often far from the obvious location of California's San Andreas Fault. *Popular Mechanics* commissioned data-visualization wizards Jonathan Cousins and

Nick Sears to create a highly interactive map that taps into USGS data to reveal this subterranean drama. Users can browse through the past week's seismic activity, zooming in on particular regions of the country, or bear witness to the biggest quakes of the past 150 years. We also display population data—and the regions below our biggest cities show a distressing level of seismic activity. Tap the launch button in the center of the page to begin your exploration.
— *GLENN DERENE*

TAP TO PLAY, THEN ROTATE YOUR IPAD

WEDNESDAY, MAY 5, 2010 04:07:49 AM AT EPICENTER
BAJA CALIFORNIA, MEXICO
MAGNITUDE 3.7
DEPTH 7.6 MILES

Inside the Quake Finder

Our earthquake map has two modes. *The first is* Latest U.S. Seismic Activity. *The utility downloads all USGS quake data from the previous seven days for events measuring at least magnitude 3.25. The map then displays each quake sequentially. The second mode is* Top Ten Quakes, *which shows the biggest seismic events in the lower 48 states from the past 150 years. Both modes display the time, date, location, magnitude and depth (if available) of the quake.*

Best App for Public Radio Fans

NPR for iPad

Free
Version: 1.3 | NPR

National Public Radio has long done a great job streaming its signal online. This iPad app continues its digital winning streak. Pulling from a deep well of coverage, the app tidily organizes stories into three fun-to-scroll rows of article "cards." You're rarely more than one swipe away from finding a new item worth your time; the app's a great way to catch up on missed morning treats. Combined with some nice customization options (you can build your own playlist, for example), a handy offline reading switch, and built-in Facebook and Twitter sharing, the free app is sure to make noncontributors feel even more guilty come next season's fundraising drive.

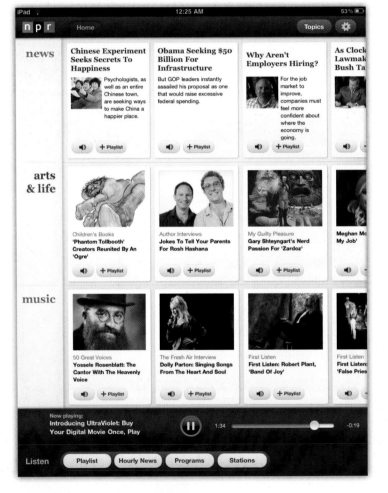

NEWS GRID: The app presents its main offerings front and center via the three main (scrollable, left-to-right) categories: News, Arts & Life, and Music. To drill down into subcategories, tap the upper-right corner's Topics button and make your picks from there.

TRAVELLER TREATS: When you're on the road and need an NPR fix, sure you can dial up your hometown station, but sometimes it's nice to go local: tap the Stations button, then Locate, then Nearest, and say goodbye to fiddling with that radio in your hotel.

RADIO PLAYLIST: Listen to each story (and continue browsing the app while listening) or build your own playlist. You also get easy access to a couple dozen popular programs (*Car Talk; Wait Wait, Don't Tell Me*)—all of which you can either add to your playlist or head off to iTunes and download the podcast. (Bonus: once you've plucked the stories you want, tap the Playlist button and then Edit, and just drag the items into the order you like.)

LISTEN NOW OR READ LATER: A handy "read offline" feature is perfect for flights and other Internet-less excursions. Tap the upper-right Topics button and choose which categories you want the app to slurp down (sorry, audio doesn't make the trip). When you're ready to read, head back to this same menu.

Best App for Congress Watching

MyCongress

Free
Version: 1.1 | ObjectiveApps

Lawyers, journalists, and CEOs rejoice! Americans tell pollsters they now respect you *more* than their elected officials. But before we all throw the bums out of office, ask yourself: how well do you actually know what it is your Congress peeps are doing? If you don't feel like committing policy wonk-like amounts of time to rep-tracking, download a copy of My-Congress. This handy tool helps lever pullers of all political persuasions keep tabs on Washington's finest. Everything in here is available online, but the insta-collection of rep-specific articles, videos, and tweets make campaign promises and job performance easier than ever to track.

CONGRESSIONAL PAGES: The Members panel lets you browse by name, state, party, or chamber. Or punch in a ZIP code to see which representatives cover that area. An auto-locate tool uses the iPad's location-finding ability if you're traveling. Bookmark reps you want to follow for quick access from the home screen.

SOURCES SAY: Here's what you get: scrollable lists with links to recent news articles, YouTube videos, and tweets. The range of websites the app pulls from is truly fair and balanced: from Fox News to the *New York Times*, and, even more usefully, small local papers. Best of all are links to the rep's listing in OpenCongress: an independent watchdog site that itself has a treasure trove of info.

Best App for Reading It Later

Instapaper

$4.99
Version: 2.3 | Marco Arment

Know what the flip side of "information overload" is? Those guilt-inducing chunks of free time when you *wish* you had something good to read. That's what this personalized clipping service is perfect for. Instapaper sucks down items you pick while web browsing and bundles 'em into a handy collection, ready for reading, whether you're offline or simply sick of surfing. The developer's built an easy-to-install arsenal of "Read Later" buttons, which clip onto all your browsers (Mac, PC, iPhone, iPad). Plus, a small but growing number of other apps (Tweetie, for example) now have built-in buttons to funnel their haul to Instapaper. Save more, read better.

HIDDEN GEMS: Don't miss some of the app's not-so-obvious goodies. Forward too-long-to-read-now emails to your Instapaper account (head to *instapaper.com* for your dedicated email address). And add another Instapaper account's starred items to keep up with super-smart pals who have a talent for curating. To set that up, tap the "+" icon next to the Folders button and enter your buddy's Instapaper username.

GOOD READS: Each article gets stripped of gunky formatting and most ads; what you're left with is good, meaty prose. Once you've opened an article, tap its upper-right corner's folded paper icon to toggle between two views: scrolling (one long page) and split-into-pages mode. Serious news collectors will also probably want to set up multiple storage folders—a great way to build an archive of favorite reads.

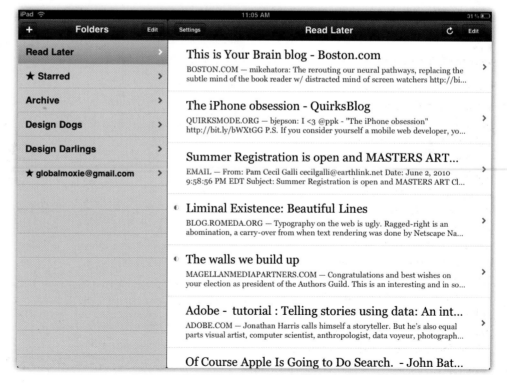

Best App for RSS Feed Wrangling

Reeder for iPad

$4.99
Version: 1.2 | Silvio Rizzi

Lotta action happening in AppLand for people who want to browse news visually. But RSS pros don't have time for a prettified visual layout of the hundreds of feeds firehosing their way. For them, a specialized, heavy-on-the-text, feed reader is what's needed—one that gobbles down great big web gulps and presents 'em all in an easy-to-speed-through format. Reeder's barebones interface offers an info hierarchy that lets you move quickly from high-level categories (Typography, Usability) on into the actual articles, letting a newshound do what she must with that great torrent of mind data: read it, pass it by, save it for later, or share it. This app gets it just right.

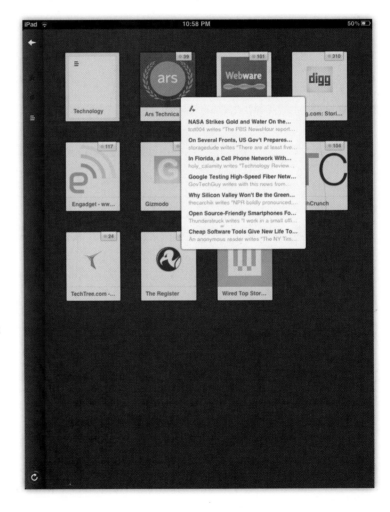

DRILLING DOWN: Check out this handy tool for quickly browsing a feed and seeing whether its articles are worth dipping into: two-finger spread the feed name and up emerges a headline-only list of what's on tap. The number in the upper right of each box shows how many unread articles await.

FEED THE FEED: Reeder auto syncs with Google Reader. In fact, Google's RSS tool (a richly powered web-based tool in its own right) is the *only* way you can get feeds into Reeder. For tips on how to get other feed reader subscriptions into Google Reader so you can then use Reeder, check out *http://bit. ly/9Vr1SY*.

SPEED READ: Lotsa ways to move through a feed's article list: tap the left column's up or down arrows, flick-scroll through the mini-blurb list (landscape view only), or tap-hold-'n-pull up or down the main article. Tap and hold any link to summon a pop-up window of sharing options (Delicious, Instapaper, and so on—you can change what appears here in the iPad's Settings app).

READING RECORD: A few helpful icons to know about: a small, dark circle indicates an unread item (an empty white circle equals "I've read it"). Stars let you put a virtual sticker on particular faves. If you're big on shucking off each article's unread marker, then don't miss this handy trick: you can toggle the marker off (or back on) by dragging an article blurb from left to right.

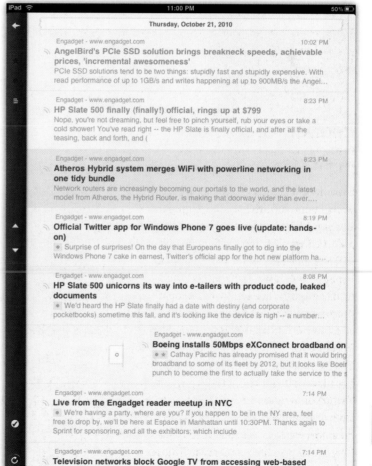

Best App for Flipping Through Web Feeds

Flipboard

Free
Version: 1.0.2 | Flipboard

Time was, a "social magazine" was one you shared with friends. But Flipboard's creators bill its version as one culled from all that mental matter swirling about your various social networks. How it works: the app takes your Twitter and Facebook feeds and fashions, on the fly, an appified magazine from that geyser of tips, tweets, and blurbs. Rather than a terse update pointing to, say, a *New York Times* article, Flipboard grabs the linked-to headline, the first couple paragraphs and accompanying photo, and lays it all out next to a few other similarly assembled nuggets. As its name suggests, Flipboard's final touch is a virtual page-turning feature, which lets you flip through the whole collection.

FANCY FLIPPING: In one respect, the app's no different from the oodles of custom aggregators out there (Friendfeed, RSS readers, and so on)—not to mention, um, that thing our grandparents used: a web browser to poke around the Internet and read what's interesting. But if you're looking for a new, iPad-friendly method of browsing (swipeable articles, build-your-own readlist) and enjoy a presentation that looks more like a shopping catalog than a shopping list, this app's fun.

HOME PAGE: The Contents page is the entry point into all the sources you're following. Double tap any box to read the feed. Don't like the current layout? Tap, hold, and drag a box to reposition.

Best App for Scrolling Through Web Feeds

Pulse News Reader

Free
Version: 2.0 | Alphonso Labs

Regular people never much cottoned to RSS, that abbreviation-ugly way to have websites send you automatic updates whenever they publish a new article. It wasn't, frankly, much fun for normal civilians to scroll through what amounted to a long list of web articles—with those awful, nagging reminders of how many you haven't yet read! Here's an RSS reading tool that in one fell swoop manages to never mention that geeky term and, more importantly, presents each source in a simple to browse, visual grid layout (they call it a "moveable mosaic"—nice) that might well beat the standard web page presentation for most people.

SOURCE CONTROL: The app gives you plenty of ways to load your library: pull in Google Reader feeds (one by one only, alas) or search for new ones using keywords, Twitter names, or RSS addresses. To bring in your Facebook and Twitter feeds, head to the Categories tab, scroll down to the Social listing, and sign onto both services.

PLAIN OR FANCY: Toggle between a text-only or full-on web view of any article you've tapped by picking from the buttons in the upper-right corner. The latter is great for websites that offer only a limited snippet of each article in the underlying RSS feed that Pulse grabs. As a timesaving bonus, the app grabs the web version automatically, so switching to look at it doesn't mean having to wait.

Best App for Financial News

Bloomberg for iPad

Free
Version: 1.0.1 | Bloomberg

This app's main appeal, beyond its reliable source material, is its easy-to-navigate, dashboard-style layout. That'll please the wide range of info grazers likely to launch it: personal portfolio watchers trying to make sure their next investment decision's a good one; business people with a vested interest in industry happenings; and financial service pros, who might turn to the app as a kind of lightweight snack while sitting at Starbucks or on the couch at night. Who it's not for: Bloomberg subscribers looking for an iPad-based version of their insanely powerful terminals and day traders looking to sniff out tips or quant trends they can capitalize on.

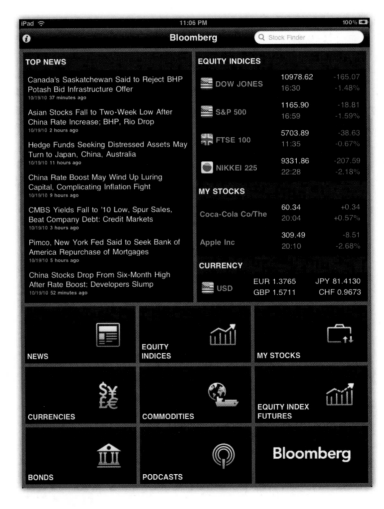

MARKET MAKERS:
News updates arrive more or less nonstop, but rather than dumping them in a long list, the app divvies the posts into three dozen categories, ranging from Asia, bonds, and China to tech, stocks, and worldwide matters. Tap the News section's Edit button to customize the order in which the categories get laid out.

MARKET REPORT:
Those keen on tracking various markets' ups and downs can pick from the same list Mayor Bloomberg *used to* check in the morning paper before he hatched his info empire: stocks, bonds, and so on. You can also manually enter a watch list of stocks. Each market gives you five viewing options (daily, monthly, 6 months, last year, last 5 years).

Financial Times iPad Edition

Free
Version: 1.4.1 | The Financial Times

Global-oriented money watchers might prefer the *FT*'s take on markets and other business matters. If you read more than 10 articles every 30 days, you'll have to pony up for a subscription plan (starts at $22/month), but the door's always open to quantitative goodies like a portfolio tracker (set it up at *FT.com*); a global market "macromap;" and a page filled with key global benchmarks (treasuries, gold), market movers, and currency info. Tap any company name for an even more customizable chart (change the tracking period, for example). Those paying full freight can download for offline viewing any of the paper's five worldwide regional editions.

Wall Street Journal

Free
Version: 2.0.1 | Dow Jones & Company

Whether you think new owner Rupert Murdoch has sprinkled pixie dust or ashes on the Diary of the American Dream, it remains the newspaper of record for financiers and others committed to capitalism. Like the *FT*, it frowns on freeloaders: you'll need a subscription to *WSJ.com* or be willing to pay a monthly fee (around $17). The app edition presents a familiar face to print edition regulars; more so than most digital efforts, it uses its print sections (Marketplace, Money & Investing) to divvy up its contents. A "My Watchlist" tool lets you compile a custom collection of stocks, markets, and futures to track. And for those who've fallen behind, the app's stocked with an offline-friendly archive of the previous seven day's papers.

57

Best App for Finding New Websites

StumbleUpon

Free
Version: 1.31 | StumbleUpon

Seems crazy that with all the info snacks out there online, finding good stuff is still hard. A guiding hand helps. Stumble-Upon's old news for web veterans: a site that's been serving up suggestions for almost a decade. But on the iPad, it's found a serving tray perfectly suited for its recommendation-slinging talents. The lever you press for more web pellets is the prominent Stumble! button. Those who suffer from the web-browsing equivalent of the Insatiable Channel Surfing Syndrome might either want to flee immediately…or hope there's fodder here to satisfy your clicklust. Repeated stress-testing suggests this site's devilishly accurate.

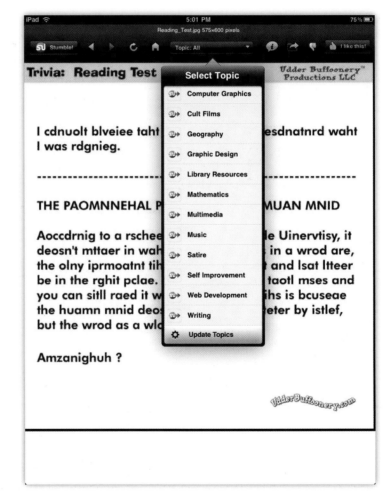

BESPOKE BREW: No account's necessary to use the service, but those who create one get to pick from a long topic list (Action Movies to Yoga, Bizarre/Oddities to Zoology) to personalize their results. You also get a couple other ways to customize the site stream, including an option that excludes sites that use iPad-unfriendly Flash. Cool.

REFINE, REPEAT: Growing bored with the latest suggestion crop? Time to tweak your preferences list. Do so by heading to the bottom of the Topic menu, where you'll find a choice called Update Topics. On the page that appears, pick the categories that catch your eye; when you're done, hit the Start Stumbling button.

GRID-BASED GREATS: The "Recommended for you" grid offers a way to have a hand in where you head next. Tap the Home icon at the top of the page to spin the screen and see it. The left-side column has all the categories you've expressed interest in; on the right is a tapworthy temptation of links to pick from.

POWER TO THE PEOPLE: StumbleUpon is very much a people-powered affair; the recommendations you get are influenced by the "I like this!" votes cast by fellow users. To peek behind this opinion-casting curtain, tap the "i" button and a magic wall spins to open another very tempting collection of sites to sink your fingertips into.

Best App for Amazing Speeches

TED

Free
Version: 1.0.2 | TED Conferences

So much of what you find online is eye- and mind-candy—not to mention outright junk food. This app's a good way to gobble up some tasty veggies. For those not yet familiar, each of the variously themed TED conferences host a sparkling roster of presenters who talk about some aspect of technology, education, or design. (In truth, the criteria's really: are you enormously, if not yet famously, successful at what you do.) The speaker videos themselves are the main event here. But what distinguishes this collection from what you can easily get on the event's website is how the app helps you discover new videos and find your way through the show's "ideas worth spreading."

SPEAKER SURFING: The Featured page is a good place to start exploring. Each swipable video grid is stocked with headline-style blurbs that promo each talk. Another entry point into the collection: fifty or so themed collections (Media With Meaning, Design Like You Give a Damn) that bundle up a couple dozen videos all mining similar territory.

RATING REPORT: With speakers that range from Bill Gates to Billy Graham and from James Cameron to Jane Goodall, it's hard to find a dud anywhere in this app. That said, drill down in the Themes section; there you'll find each talk labeled with three honest assessments, voted on by viewers. So while many earn adjectives like "Fascinating" and "Jaw-dropping," a few get the "Longwinded" tag from the crowd.

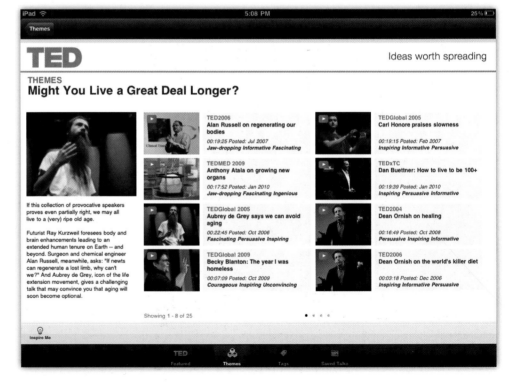

At Leisure

WHAT'S ON: An Inspire Me button sits on the lower-left corner of most pages, ready to assist with even more concierge-style suggestions. Tap it and you're presented with a list of adjectives (Courageous, Funny) from which to pick; then use the clock face to tell the app how much time you've got. It responds by stitching together a suitably themed and timed playlist.

TALK TO TED: To join the conversation, click the "visit TED.com" link in any video's "About this talk" section. An in-app browser whisks you off to a well-trafficked, noticeably thoughtful dialogue on almost all of the talks. One nifty treat on these web-based pages: "Interactive Transcripts" that are instantly translatable into a handful of languages and, even cooler, feature clickable text that, when tapped, take you to that spot in the video.

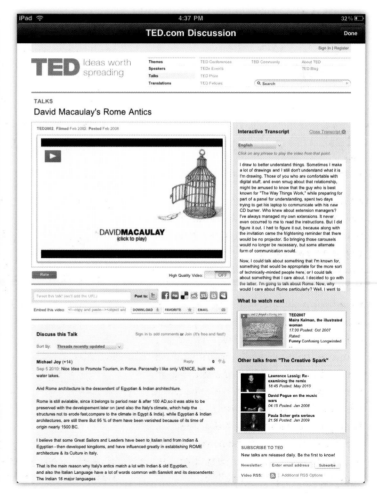

Best App for Naming That Tune

Shazam for iPad

Free
Version: 2.0.0 | Shazam Entertainment

Tip-of-your-tongue sufferers, rejoice. This App Store veteran first found fame as an iPhone app. Now it's here to help iPad-owning music lovers figure out what's playing. Fire it up, situate your device reasonably near a radio, inside your favorite soundtrack-powered store, or anywhere else that's got a song playing. Then click the upper-right Shazam icon. The app proceeds to match a brief sound snippet to its enormous collection (requiring an Internet connection to do so) and, ping: the song title, usually, appears. Shazam's finding skills work remarkably well, though with limitations: it's not so good at classical music, ambient beats, and, predictably, polka.

FIND MORE: The app also works as a decent browse and discover tool. Top of screen, center, is a Tag Stream button, which, when tapped, shows what other app users are currently liking and listening to. Tap any songs you like to add 'em to your own tagged list and, in many cases, you can also play 30-second snippets or buy the song in iTunes.

OTHER TREATS: A Similar Tracks feature digs into the Shazam catalog and offers up suggestions; results are pretty good with a few notable clunkers. (Coldplay is related to Marlene Dietrich exactly how?) A lyrics lookup tool is great fun. It works most of the time, though it is hobbled by one serious shortcoming: there's no way to add what the app finds to your iTunes collection.

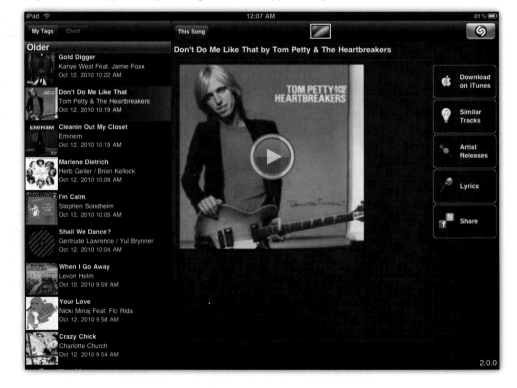

SoundHound
Free lite version | $4.99
Version: 3.4.1 | Melodis

Where Shazam's main mission is ID'ing songs, SoundHound takes this business of discovering new music seriously and plasters your screen with all sorts of What's Hot Right Now suggestions. It also helps scoop up fun finds related to the music you already own, by showing YouTube videos, linking to ringtones, and listing tour date info. All this might turn off those who just wanna figure out what song's playing, but frequent forgetters might still want to add this app to their memory-nudging kit. It performs a couple tricks Shazam doesn't: you can hum or sing a song and it'll try to find a match, and you can type in lyric phrases—it does a pretty good job with that, too.

PARTY TRICKS: Tap that big orange-y box and start humming. You don't even need to know all or even any of the words. Tested using one of humanity's most tuneless voices, it actually worked. Some reviewers moan about the freebie limit of five searches (after that you have to pay $1 for five additional searches or $5 for unlimited finds), but you can always test it out for free.

NOW PLAYING-PLUS: For all its links to other music services (iTunes, Pandora), this is an app that wants you to spend time inside its four walls. A lyric lookup tool uses an in-app browser to send your query to a number of specialty sites; music videos are also presented inside the app. You can even tap into and control your iTunes collection.

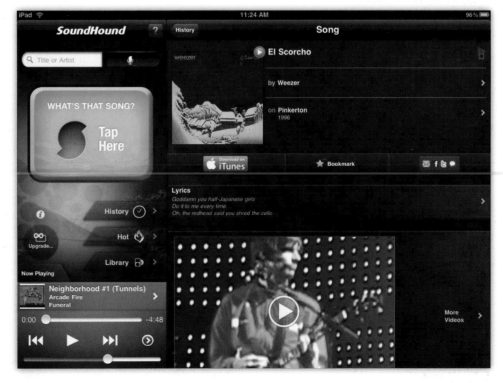

Best App for Personalized Radio

Pandora

Free
Version: 3.1.4 | Pandora Music

You've heard about Pandora, right? It's the music service that lets you customize an endless dial's worth of radio stations, each organized around a song or artist that you pick. From ABBA to ZZ Top, each "station" plays a list of tunes that match certain characteristics of your selection (piano style, say). It's free, addictive, and better than the shuffle button for expanding your musical know-how. The iPad app offers a stripped-down version of the more customizable web-based offering, but it lets you do the things that will put a sweet song in any music lover's ears: add new stations and rate each song (to help refine what songs come your way).

PLAYTIME: The fast-forward button flips the action ahead to the next song in your queue. Publisher restrictions prevent you from doing this skip step more than five times an hour in any one station; go figure how the lawyers cooked up that formula, but if you're desperate for, say, more Patsy Cline-ish songs, you can always hop over to the web version (not from your iPad, alas).

WEB EXTRAS: Speaking of the Web: hop online to *Pandora.com* for some extra personalizing: edit station names, refine your mixes (by adding additional artists or songs), see lyrics for most songs. And wherever you are, hitting the QuickMix button pulls together songs from all your different stations.

At Leisure

Best App for Traditional Radio

Spark Radio
$1.99
Version: 1.91 | HandCast Media

You might not realize how lame your kitchen radio is till you fire up an app like Spark. Among its talents: 24,000-plus stations worldwide (including local AM and FM), browse by genre (kids, blues, conservative talk), tune in police department scanners, and, of course, play Internet-only programs like Cockroach Radio, Naughty Comedy, and Greek's own Radio Kokkinoskufitsa. What makes this app a winner is its lovely coat of design polish; you never feel like you're wading through a wasteland of confusingly categorized stations; instead, browsing and discovery are a pleasure.

SOUND SOURCES: The News & Talk category is where you'll find a gabfest's worth of chatter: from conservative to progressive, from entertainment to religion. Buried in the News section are emergency service scanner listings, traffic reports, and continuous weather updates. Or take an audio tour of the world by browsing through the Music category's World section. Several dozen smaller groupings await: Arabic, Brazilian, Reggae, Turkish—the list is huge. And if you want something fun to watch while listening, tap the Visuals button: a virtual starburst takes over your screen.

Wunder Radio
$6.99
Version: 1.94 | Weather Underground

Radio diehards might want to pony up a few bucks more for this app, stuffed as it is with power-user extras. You can go beyond, say, just searching for French music and instead explore specific regions (from Bordeaux to Toulouse). Talk radio fans will like the way widely syndicated figures (Dave Ramsey, Dennis Miller) are presented according to how much time is left in each show. Songsters will like the iTunes links that appear beside most currently playing tunes. Like what you're hearing? Head over to the tunes shop and grab it.

Best App for Discovering New Music

Aweditorium

Free
Version: 1.0 | Thesixtyone

"What kind of backwards society do we live in where we limit the genius of a Thom Yorke or Trent Reznor to a single vertical column?" asks this app's evangelical creator, making a fair point about iTunes' grid prison and other lame digital music album art. Enter Aweditorium, a daring attempt to remedy this problem. At heart it offers a way to discover and listen to new music. But what's new and delightful here are the multimedia extras woven into each song. You get: a fun-to-browse mosaic of album art; nicely rendered lyrics-as-subtitles; video interviews; pop-up blurbs about the band's history and influence; and sharing, bookmarking, and buying options. Prepare to be entranced.

STYLE GUIDE: At launch the app's stocked exclusively with tunes aimed mainly at the admittedly amorphous hipster set. That still gets you a wide swath of sounds, from angsty mellow to angry metal. (If you really feel at home, add *www.thesixtyone.com* to your web browser; it's an online sibling of this app.) Artists get included by application only, which is how the app gets its goodies (the info blurbs, lyrics, and so on).

NAVIGATION STATION: Lots of different ways to explore: tap any photo; finger pan around the large mosaic; or, once you're listening to a song, swipe in any direction. That box in the upper-left corner is a miniature of the collection—tap any spot to move there. The green dot represents the center of your screen, gray bars are songs you've heard. Other colors show the exploratory locations of fellow listeners (great for seeing clusters of interest).

Glaciers
Anni Rossi *from* Chicago, IL

Started by Chris Chu in a moment of magical bliss, just listening to the music of these four men combined will cure any disease known to man.

waiting for a war
the morning benders *from* Berkeley, CA

THE STAIN, IT WON'T COME OUT

FUN FACTS: Your treats play out while the song plays. You can finger drag the pop-up info boxes, which appear at random intervals. The lower-right icon goodies let you: pause/play; share and collect your faves; find other songs by the same artist and shop on iTunes; watch video interviews while listening to the song; watch full-screen videos; and head back to the main grid.

LYRIC LIST: When you're in full screen photo mode, tap the screen once any time to see the lyrics at the bottom of the screen. If you do nothing at the song's end, the app scrolls a new one onscreen for you. But the whole point is to poke around. If you don't like what you're hearing, pinch or swipe for something new; there's a nice fade-out/fade-in effect as you move between songs.

⊕ **HONORABLE MENTION**

BandMate: Concert Tipster HD

$2.99
Version: 3.4 | WellAlright

So Aweditorium's got you in a musical sort of mood. Ready for the real thing? Here's a wonderful way to discover who's playing live. The app starts with a deep tissue study of your iPad's music. The Events tab then lists where and when each band is playing, along with other acts Bandmate thinks you'll like. (Use the Artists tab to turn off musicians you *don't* want the app to factor in. Or, manually add in ones not in your iTunes collection.) You can instruct the app to search for events near your current location or in another city. Oddly precise strength-of-match percentages appear next to each recommendation (Pink Floyd is 71% similar to ex-lead singer Roger Waters, which, on second thought, sounds just about right).

Best App for Watching Music Videos

MySpace Music Romeo

Free
Version: 1.3 | MySpace

MySpace is in a pickle. The former social networking star is now fading in the Age of Facebook and Twitter. What to do? Return to its music-loving roots, which is great news for iPad owners who love music videos. This app delivers a playful twist on recommendations: tell it your musical tastes and your current mood and it serves up music vids tailored for you. The service isn't perfect (clearly lacking high-quality video servers) or for everyone (the site's efforts to target the under-35 set shows in the song choices). But there's enough here to remind us all what life was like back when you could flip on MTV and watch videos any time you wanted.

PICK A SONG: Tap the settings icon and pick from a dozen genres (alternative to world) and as many moods (studying, partying, exercising). Some silly combos crop up—"Play me some Christian Music" and "I'm feeling naughty"—but the app's game to try. For the record: all-girl band Point of Grade sings the country spiritual "I Wish," which does, to be fair, have the line: "my jeans fit a little bit looser."

GIVE AND TAKE: Other downsides: you can't fast forward or rewind, and you have to sit through an ad every 10 songs or so. (Memo to bean counters: get more advertisers!) But you can tag songs as favorites (tap the heart icon) and links take you to iTunes if you want to buy what you like. To fine-tune the videos, head to the Loves tab in Settings and tap "Play More Like This".

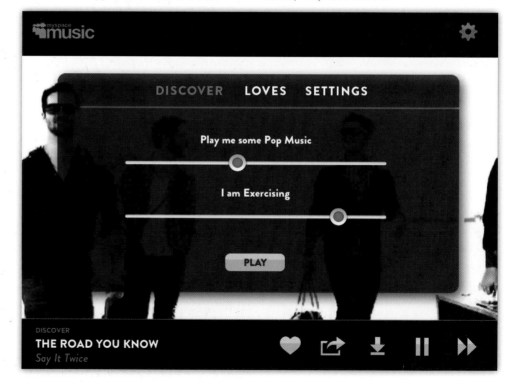

Best App for *TV Guide* Replacement

Yahoo! Entertainment

Free
Version: 1.1.1 | Yahoo!

First things first: why do you need a TV directory on your iPad when you've already got one on the boob tube? Two words: flick scrolling. Everyone's favorite new navigational gesture is about a zillion times better than the remote-controlled grid crawl we've gotten used to. (Now, of course, you can't actually watch live TV on your iPad—yet. We're just talking about finding out what's on.) Speaking of that ridiculously overlong grid: probably the most useful feature in the app is how it lets you custom build a list of the channels that, you know, you actually watch. All those other must-skip channels? Don't give 'em a second look.

CUSTOM LINEUP: Beyond simply weeding out duds, HD fans can nix the nuisance of never-watched standard-def stations. Head to the gear-shaped Settings icon, where you'll find the Channel Lineup that lets you pick and choose. (Hint: start with "Deselect All" and then flick on the 20, 30, or however many channels you want.)

FILTER ON: Plenty of tools await when you're ready to browse better. The upper-right search oval does just what you'd expect (plus gives you an easy on ramp to web search a few sites that specialize in TV info). The bottom bar lets you narrow your target watch time window and specify the kinds of shows you're looking for.

Best App for Movie Lovers

IMDb

Free
Version: 2.0 | IMDB.com

The granddaddy of movie info sites, IMDb's app also deserves top billing in Why Apps Often Beat Websites. In a phrase: less is more. In the web version, you're assaulted with blinking ads and a confusing mass of options (it is the Internet Movie Database, after all). In the more streamlined app, movie fans can flick more easily through what's fun, including, of course, movie trailers, showtimes, and detailed cast and crew info. But it's the minor morsels—all just an easy tap away—that keep you dipping into this app like a big bucket of popcorn: trivia (who knew Dolph Lundgren was a chemical engineering whiz?), actor quotes, and all-time best and worst movie lists.

At Leisure

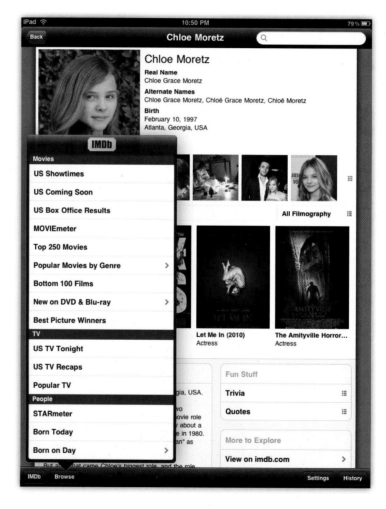

BROWSING BASICS:
The lower-left Browse button is your ticket to everything that's playing in this app. Each category in the left-side pop-up menu offers browse-inducing ways to flesh out your what-to-see-next list. The MOVIE- and STARmeters, for example, put you face to face with a gallery of what and who's most popular on the IMDb website.

DID YOU KNOW?:
Each movie gets its own dedicated page, where you'll find the good stuff: goofs (continuity gaffs, geography errors, visible crew), plot summary *and* a synopsis (including—you've been warned!—spoilers), Oscar winners, "born today" calendar for your favorite stars, and a parental guide with specific examples for different categories.

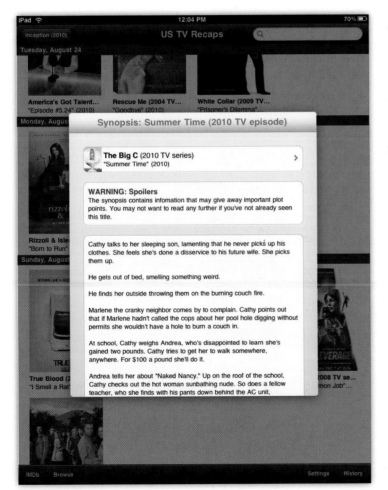

TV TIME: Serious cinephiles know that TV is not a diversion from what they love but a healthy palate cleanser between all those Fassbender retrospectives. That means the tube gets the full IMDb treatment.

WHAT'S ON: If you need to catch up on missed episodes dial up the spoiler-flagging synopses. Other TV treats: a profile of what's on to-night (US TV Tonight, in the Browse button) and Series Fun Stuff (trivia, transcripts of amusing exchanges from the script).

Movies

Free
Version: 4.22 | Flixster

Rotten Tomatoes and Flixter are two websites especially popular with the no-time-for-papers and share-everything sets. The first compiles a collection of popular mainstream critics' reviews and from that issues a thumbs up (fresh tomato icon) or down (same fruit, spoiled). The second is a heavily trafficked movie discussion site. Both team up in this app, and while its info well doesn't run as deep as IMDb's, Rotten Tomato lovers might favor this app for its well-integrated mix of that rating service (owned by the same parent company as Flixter). Other nifty touches: each critic's key quote gets good-for-scanning marquee treatment; a built-in Yelp tool shows restaurants near your theater of choice; links to iTunes purchasing options; and—in the "coming soon" department— the ability to manage your Netflix queue.

Best App for Watching Hollywood Movies

iTunes

Free
Apple

Picture the perfect movie-watching app: it's kinda like the iTunes Music Store, no? Any movie, any time after its release, reasonably priced ($10 for cinema-synced releases? Betcha about 10 million new parents would pony up for that), without viewer-hostile watching restrictions. Once you return from la-la land, the closest you can get to that is an app you don't have to download, and which many iPad owners forget about: the iTunes app, and specifically, its Movies tab. You'll find a decent selection of buck-a-pop rentals, plus a surprisingly good collection of movies that seems to keep growing.

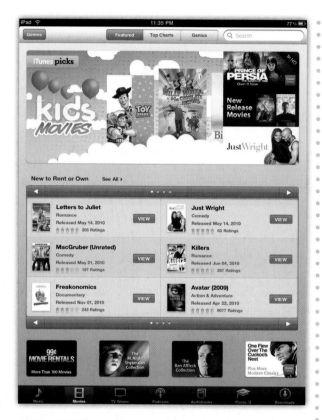

GENRE GENIUS: Don't forget the Genres button (top left), where you'll find well-stocked classics (*Gone With the Wind*, *La Dolce Vita*), most available for rent ($3 standard def, $4 HD; newer releases a buck extra). Need inspiration? The Genius tab tracks your previous purchases and rentals and suggests more. Not all movies are available for rental, but most are. To watch the movies, open the Videos app, where you'll see your download waiting after about 15 minutes. Bummer: you can't start watching till the download's done.

⊕ HONORABLE MENTION

Netflix

Free
Version: 1.1.2 | Netflix

Want a somewhat larger (though not necessarily better) movie selection than iTunes? Want instant-on satisfaction and the modern surfer's ability to start, stop, and switch to something different? Then Netflix is for you, and it comes with only two asterisk-worthy qualifications. First, you have to be a regular paying member; plans start at $10/month, which also gets you one DVD at a time by mail. Next caveat concerns the selection. Netflix is constantly paying for more and better movies, but the pickings are slim-ish.

Best App for Big League Baseball

At Bat for iPad

$14.99
Version: 1.3.1 | MLB Advanced Media

While this app currently doesn't deliver hot dogs and beer, there's not much else it leaves out—an impressive feat, considering it's the only game in town (no other app has the right to deliver MLB's signature product). What you get is a stats-at-your-fingertips, play-by-play animation of every game—perfect for info junkies who crave answers while watching the live game on the boob tube, on-the-road types who can't bear missing the home team (and are willing to pony up extra for a live broadcast signal), and radio lovers who'll appreciate the choice of hearing home and away team announcers. Next game you're watching, don't be surprised to see a manager or two with this in the dugout.

RUNS, HITS... You get in-game video of key highlights (even if you're not paying for the full broadcast service); field diagrams indicating runners, batters, and fielders; and player cards that give you everything but the gum: measurements, birthdate, handedness, today's performance, and longer term measures like batting average with men on, with runners in scoring position, and vs. left-handed pitchers.

...AND ERRORS: Hardcore fans (and iPhone app owners—that's a separate app) will be miffed to find missing from the iPad version things like archived and searchable video library (available on the iPhone version), full team schedules, and a lag in the audio broadcasts (probably not the app's fault, but it makes using it as an alternate announcer source impractical).

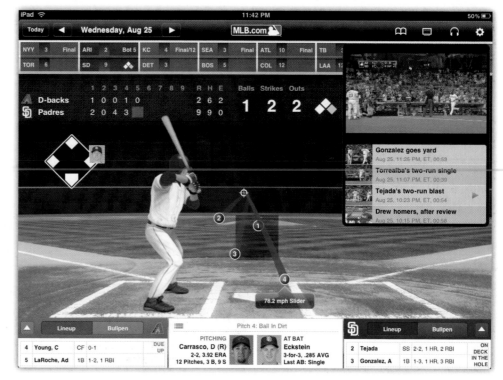

Best App for Twitter

Twitter

Free
Version: 3.1.1 | Twitter

Beyond its day job of getting humanity to stop being so wordy, Twitter's also an app developer. Their flagship effort offers a slick way to blow through your tweets *and* the web pages most of 'em link to. Its signature feature is the seamlessness with which it lets you move between your timeline (stream of tweets) and the web pages that most of those mini-missives mention. Turns out that by serving up both tweet and linked page, your Twitter account delivers a deeper, more satisfying read. Rather than flittering through blip after 140-character blip, this app's convenient side-saddle presentation of tweeted links gives you a chance to consume more of your followees' mental nourishment.

PICK A CARD: The app's interface takes some getting used to, but the basic design is nothing more complex than columns: the left one for your account's key tools (search, direct messages), middle one for your timeline, and the right side for viewing the outward-pointing links. The latter two are actually more like stacked, movable cards; swipe 'em left or right to make one or the other center screen.

IN THE STACKS: If you want to return to your main timeline—the one with just your latest list of tweets showing, tap the chat bubble icon on the left side of the screen. For extended web reading, expand the page to full screen by tapping the lower-right corner's diagonal, two-headed arrow. In this minibrowser, links are live and ready for tappin' (though you can't type in a new web address).

OVERHEARD: A disorienting aspect to life on Planet Twitter are those random chat snippets you sometimes run across (*@oprah we liked the texmex!*). These tend to be part of a longer exchange, but you're only viewing one snappy portion. Find the missing pieces by tapping the fragment in question, or even do a two-finger drag down, like a window shade (shown here in the three bottom messages). Twitter will lay out the full dialogue for your reading pleasure.

BACKGROUND: If you run across a tweet from someone you don't know (perhaps someone you follow has retweeted them), get the 411 on them, quickly: just do a two-finger spread across the unfamiliar tweet and out pops, 3D-style, a profile card listing their key details. From there, you can find all sorts of interesting details, including a browsable history of their tweets, who follows them, and who they follow.

More Apps for Twitter

➕ **HONORABLE MENTION**

Tweet Library
$9.99
Version: 1.1.1 | Riverfold Software

You tweet for the benefit of others, but as a collection, these micro-messages also serve as a kind of diary: where you went, what you did, and especially for power tweeters, what you found interesting. Problem is, Twitter doesn't make it easy to preserve this increasingly vital knowledge trail. (Sure, you can search online, but c'mon, who has the time?) Among Tweet Library's handful of nifty features is a system for sucking down the 3,000 most recent posts you've let fly. Now you've got a searchable, on-your-iPad record of your brain's best bursts. And if that's not enough, an export button lets you email a file of your collected works—great for serious archivists.

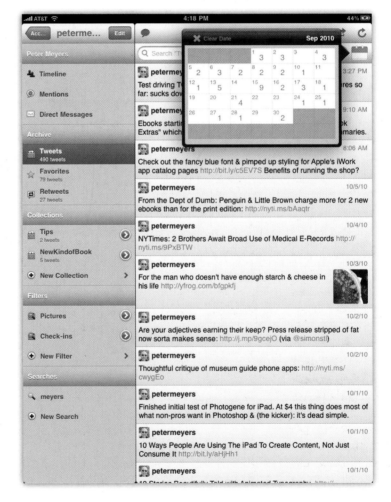

CALENDAR TIME: Interested in seeing how much writing you did on a particular day? Tap the calendar icon and up pops a visual with a number logged whenever you posted. Click any day to see just those posts and swipe left or right to move through the months.

FREQUENT FILERS: Those who like to organize might like another twist that this app introduces: "Collections." Stockpile thematically related tweets in these custom folders. And if you think the world deserves a glimpse of your curatorial talents, the share icon's also got a Publish option, which lets you post your (and others') gems online.

Best App for Avatar Making

Facemakr Avatar Creator HD

$3.99
Version: 1.2.1 | Dadako

That image you stick on your Twitter or Facebook account can rack up more views than your mug gets in real life. Put your best face forward—or some whimsical twist thereof—with this Mr. Potato Head-style drawing kit. Good news for those whose self-portrait skills stopped in stick figure class: with so many facial parts to pick from, simply cycling through the stock catalog is likely to get you close. Talented sculptors will have a field day with the customization options: colors, of course, but also the ability to pinch, spread, and rotate. A closet full of accessories (hats, glasses, and, of course, surgical masks) takes this virtual dress-up game anywhere you like.

MUG MAKER: You start off with an empty canvas; work your way down the right-side object list to select each part. At each stop along the way, you have the option to go male or female; choices in the left side parts palette adjust according to your pick. Shrink or enlarge anything using the usual pinch and spread. Certain items (eyes, ears) respond to other gestures, like dragging left or right to change the distance between pairs.

NIPS AND TUCKS: To remove an item you've added—facial hair, say—tap the blank square in the top-left cell. Use the "Save to Presets" button for portraits you'd like to polish further. When you're ready to go public, tap the upper-right Settings icon and prepare for the wave of comments from the avatar fanatics in your crowd (they're there, you'll see!).

Best App for Friend Photo Browsing

Flickpad

Free lite version | $4.99
Version: 2.1.3 | Shacked

This one's for those of us who travel in photo-happy circles. We've gotten a taste of what the iPad can do with loads of pictures (Exhibit A: the Photos app and its nifty stack-of-pix and scrolling grid layouts). Now we want the same treatment for those other two big sources of picture plenty: Facebook and Flickr. Flickpad is a special-purpose viewing, sharing, and commenting tool. Its name reveals its main method: you "flick" photos on and off a screenwide lightbox. Especially when you're flooded with new pix, the app's review-and-release system (you flick viewed photos offscreen and a replacement from the same album instantly appears) is not just efficient, but also great fun.

78

PICK & PRESERVE: The app's calendar-based approach (you can view this week's haul, last week's, or move day by day) is great for catching up on photo-viewing chores you've had to put aside for things like, you know, work. Save the gems you like best to a Flickpad favorites album and email any pic you like to anyone, even if they're not a member of one of these networks (yep, still a few of 'em out there).

TONS O' TOOLS: Other treats: double-tap any picture to see the full album it belongs to; hide friends whose photos you don't want to see; and, in the Flickr icon, tap Explore to see a greatest hits selection—sorta like a tour through your friends' best pix…if your friends were all pro photographers.

Qubical

$0.99
Version: 1.0 | Aleryon

Half the fun of Facebook comes from the photos your pals share. But unless you're on full-time news feed patrol, it's easy to miss the latest pix. And even the ones you do see show up in that boring "click Previous, click Next" layout. This app stakes its future on a pretty distinct bet: photo browsing's more fun when pictures get laid out like tiles on a twirlable 3D cube. And you know what? They're onto something. As you exit the Land of Lists and feast your eyes and fingers on the app's photo-filled cube, the temptation to tap, to pinch, to—whoa, there, fella…these are your friends—well, let's leave it at this: Qubical's a fun way to browse.

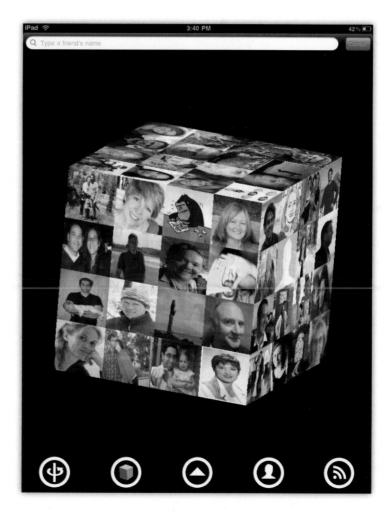

CUBE CONTROL: Grab the cube by tapping and holding anywhere onscreen (not just on the cube itself) and pivot it by moving your finger. Shrink or enlarge the box by pinching or spreading. For your autorotating pleasure, tap the arrow-around-the-pole icon. The app's also got Facebook's commenting hooks built in, so you can add comments.

PICTURE POWER: Double-tap any friend whose photos you want to see and then head to the Albums icon. Here's where you can roll through whatever photo collections your buds have broadcast. See something you like and wanna view it, uh, normally? Just tap the picture for a regular shot frozen in plain ol' 2D space across your screen.

79

Best App for Instant Messaging

IM+

Free lite version | $9.99
Version: 4.5 | Shape

Tweeting and texting might be how the cool kids stay in touch, but sometimes those tools just won't do. If you don't want the whole world listening in on your conversation, have more than 140 characters' worth of wisdom to impart, and socialize or work with a chat dependent crew, you're gonna need an instant message app. (IM being another name for *chat*, that scrolling list of dialogue-style back and forths that many devotees regard as superior to email.) This app connects with all the major services (AIM, Google, MSN, plus a half dozen others), offers simple setup, and makes it easy for even the chattiest Cathies to converse between multiple conversations.

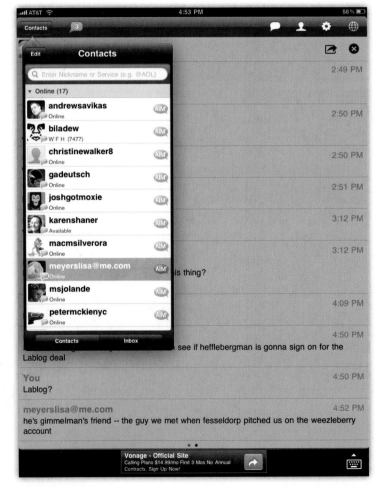

FRIEND FEED: Head to the head-and-shoulders icon to plug into any IM network you want to tap keyboards with. (You can only sign into an existing account; if you need to create a handle on, say, Yahoo, first head to their website to do so.) The app also lets you pipe in your Twitter feed for folks who like mixing their message modes.

MULTIMEDIA: Pepper your prose with IM+'s other communicatory talents. A full palette of emoticons are of course available, plus you can record and send audio, transfer files (a photo from your iPad's library, for example), and even fire off your location by using the Share icon's "Send Location" tool, which gives your recipient a map link for where you are.

Creative Corner

They said the iPad was gonna be a watch-only device. They said Generation iPad was gonna grow up sapped of creative know-how, their will to make stuff pretty much zombied out of them by the brain-leeching effects of staring at The Man's Media all day long. Man, were they wrong. The apps you'll meet in this chapter may well be one of creative kind's most inspiring, empowering, and flat-out fun collections of digital tools that we've seen since the arrival of the computer. In the music department, what's available ranges from multi-instrument-powered mobile recording studios to vocal-boosting makeovers, and from neophyte-friendly tune makers to strange new music machines. Visual artists and photographers are in for all kinds of treats. Painters and sketchers are getting awfully close to the day when those white pulp pads are simply not necessary; your black 'Pad can do the same thing, plus a whole lot more. Shutterbugs get a moveable darkroom that puts Photoshop-style power literally in your hands. (Advance preview: selecting areas by tracing them was never easier than on a touchscreen.) Sculptors, time to pinch and spread in a whole new way. From potterymaking to 3D models to virtual firework shows, you're working here with a medium that's both familiar and utterly new. And for our youngest artists, the intuitive operation of the tappable canvas means they can start creating pronto (stickers and stick figures are only the beginning). The best part for the adult iPad owner? Nothing to clean up when playtime is over.

Best App for One-Man Band

Music Studio

Free lite version | $14.99
Version: 1.5.1 | Alexander Gross

You don't need a PhD to understand this basic bit of economics: what you get in the freebie version of this app is a steal: nine fully functioning instruments (grand piano, flute, guitar), a layout-morphable keyboard to play each of 'em on, crazy fun and legitimately powerful effects to sculpt your music-making (reverb, pitch control), a multiple-track editor, and a recording tool to capture what you create. Fork over 15 clams and turn this ensemble into something close to a multi-thousand dollar studio. The full version lets you export editable files to a Mac or PC, quadruples your instrument count, and gets you equalizer and amplifier effects, to name just a few of the premium extras.

PLAYTIME: Wanna start by goofing around with different sounds? Easy, just pick an instrument from the tab of that name (test your options there by tapping Preview), then switch over to the Keyboard tab and use that to tickle whatever flavored ivories you've chosen. To hear a canned composition, pick a demo from the Projects tab and then head back to the keyboard, where a tap of the green play button turns your iPad into an auto-player.

KEYBOARD CONTROL: You've got a couple ways to control which keys appear onscreen: pinching and spreading (to squeeze in more or present just a fat few) or by stacking two keyboards. If you go the latter route, use the Instruments tab's "Keyboard row assignment" controller to pick which sound each row unleashes. Musicians in training can turn on the key labels so they know where the right notes lie.

THE EDIT ROOM: The Tracks tab lets you exert some serious instrument control, as well as learn a heckuva lot simply by watching. Each track gets its own horizontal row, representing a particular instrument. Isolate any one by tapping its icon on the left side and then pressing the S (for "solo") button. Silencing works similarly; just hit M (for "mute"). The vertical bar dancing across the screen identifies the song's current spot.

STACCATO TO LEGATO: If your flow sounds fractured, lengthen the track's "release time" (basically: the time a note continues after hitting the key). Do this in the Instruments panel, using the Release control. Other fun effects: the "pitch bend" lets you shape the current note's pitch by tilting and turning the iPad. Turn that on in the Effects tab, where you'll find plenty of other ways to colorize and warp your music.

⊕ **HONORABLE MENTION**

ThumbJam
$6.99
Version: 1.3 | Jesse Chappell

If the Music Studio's standard keyboard and instrument lineup is too common for ya, give this hugely popular alternative a try. Not only do you get substantially more eclectic sound options (*darabukka* or a *round sine,* anyone?), each comes with its own uniquely designed "play area." Some sorta/kinda look like a piano (picture the keys arranged in a vertical stack of rows). Others offer a big chunky grid. Hundreds of included scales, from common ones like major and minor to Javanese Pentachord, puts music-making within reach of amateurs and pros alike. Shape the sound further by moving your iPad: shake for vibrato, for example. Recording and sharing options aplenty make this some truly social—not to mention creativity-enhancing—software.

Best App for Making Meditative Music

Bloom HD
$3.99
Version: 1.0 | Opal Limited

Brian Eno fans will want this ethereal, lava lamp-ish music-creation app for a glimpse at how the famous ambient sound guru combines visuals with the aural gems he's built his career on. Everyone else should consider it for their app collection simply because of its otherworldly soothing properties. On the one hand, it's nothing more than a stream of cool tones—some triggered by you, others "played" by the app itself—accompanied by visual bubbles. But that's like mistaking yoga for mere stretching. There's something as soothing as a scuba dive going on here.

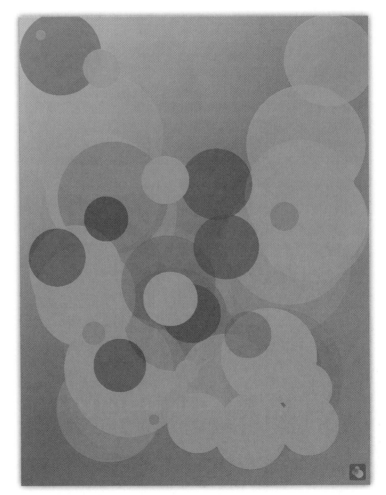

BREATHE DEEP: Start, simply, by listening and looking. You might think you've wandered into a hearing test, but soon the trance of ping-pongy tones takes on a Zen flavor. Meantime, the multicolored bubbles expand and evaporate like raindrops on a pond.

MAGIC FINGERS: Next, swirl your finger in this multimedia koi pond by tapping the screen, and watch as your finger placement generates its own sounds and circles—each an echo, a kind of tap-and-response pattern to your input. It all gets software-magically woven into a spell that's partly your creation and part trip to EnoVille. It's like a xylophone that's impossible to play incorrectly.

CUSTOM MIX: To shift into a slightly more advanced composition mode, tap the lower-right corner's Create icon. The screen that appears contains its own bubble display, center stage, plus a collection of custom—if somewhat opaquely named—controls.

MOOD SWINGING: The various Mood options, for example, read like a psycho-pharmacological dispensary from the 25th Century: Labdanum, Vetiver, Tolu. Ambient aficionados might discern a difference in each of these options (the app makers say the choices reflect different color schemes and musical keys), but if the subtleties evade you, no matter. Everything here is set on maximum soothe.

Bubble Harp
$0.99
Version: 2.1 | Scott Snibbe

This odd, charming duck of an app will fascinate as many people as it frustrates. Nominally, it's a—heck, let's turn the mic over to the developer, because this thing's just too weird for words: "It's a combination of drawing, animation, music, art, geometry, and gaming. You can record long movements of a single point, or stream many points out of your fingertips like ink." Yeah, you know: for those of us spiderpeople whose wrists spray multi-colored music-making webs. Back in iPadLand, what you'll mainly do is swipe the screen and watch the pulsing line (representing the current note being played) spider across the web you've helped make. Tap the note-shaped icon to adjust the chords that play. It's wacky, it's wonderful, it's worth a buck.

Best App for Making Music in a Grid

SoundSketch

$0.99
Version: 1.1 | Glowdot Productions

Do you visualize patterns—geometrical, graphical, psychedelic—when you hear music? If the answer's yes and the only instrument you know how to play is your iPod, then this simple-to-use electronic music composer is for you. You lay down patterns by tapping them out in the grid; hit Play to hear your concoction. Experiment with symmetrical arrangements or drop scattershot clumps and hear the notes bunch together as sequences jump around. Heck, see what your name "written" on the grid sounds like. For a certain type of music fan—especially members of the Information Visualization Band—this snack of an app is a fun treat.

TAP AND PLAY: Start by punching out a pattern on three grids: one for an electronically funky "lead" track and one each for bass and drums. The cells you tap-to-select represent notes. As you listen to your creations play, the correlation between note location and generated sound becomes clear. Spots lower on the grid get you low beats, midway up the y-axis are the mid tones, and so on as you climb the scales toward the top row.

SONGSMITHING: You can even edit as the thing plays, plucking out discordant notes, smoothing over clunky spots—let your eyes guide what your ears want to hear. The app's designer advises minimalism, especially in the bass and drum tracks, and that's advice generally well heeded. You can save (but, alas, not share—c'mon fellas, add that!) eight separate sequences and it's a trifle to trim back when you've overtapped.

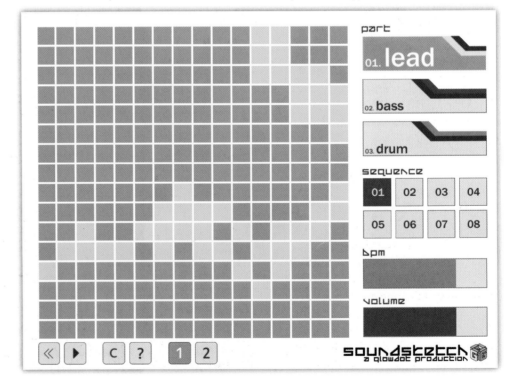

Best App for DJ Mixmasters

GrooveMaker

Free lite version | $9.99
Version: 1.0.2 | IK Multimedia

Back in the day, DJs stitched their mixes out of vinyl, weaving their works from supermarket-swiped, record-holding milk containers. Modern mixmasters, of course, work digitally, and you can too with this portable beat-spinning station. But what's most impressive is what's within reach of newbie MCs. After familiarizing yourself with the cockpit-complex console (flatten the learning curve by checking out the tutorials at *http://bit.ly/ GMdemo*), the soundscapes you can create are stunning. Fill up to eight tracks with an almost infinitely customizable assortment of loops (prerecorded snippets) and listen 'n learn as you discover the artistry that goes into digital music making.

WKRU: Pick your loops from a few dozen that come free with the app, or buy genre-specific collections: hip hop, reggae, and so on. When you've got your track collection just so, save it for the final step: sequencing, where you stitch together and then export to a WiFi-connected computer a high-quality version of the mix you've made.

LIVE OR MEMOREX: Unleash your groove via a pair of powered speakers and then tweak as it plays. Or shack up in the studio (with a pair of headphones works fine, too) and spit out a recording to share with friends or laydown as soundtrack to that movie you're working on—royalty-free raw material means whatever you make here is yours to use, gratis.

Best App for Musical Geometry

Soundrop

Free lite version | $1.99
Version: 1.2.1 | Develoe

I used to be a productive member of society, confesses iTunes reviewer Dr. Fong. If you're into eyeballing refraction angles, enjoy instrumental compositions, and find a certain charm in the 70's video game Pong, the good doctor's warning is worth heeding. This simple-to-operate, impossible-to-exhaust take on tune building will lure you into work- and love-life-jeopardizing amounts of time spent with your iPad. You "compose" by positioning one or many line segments beneath a drip-drop cascade of music-creating pellets. As each dot hits the various lines, the app plays a note. Add more lines, tweak their positions, and watch this you-made-it-yourself production unfold.

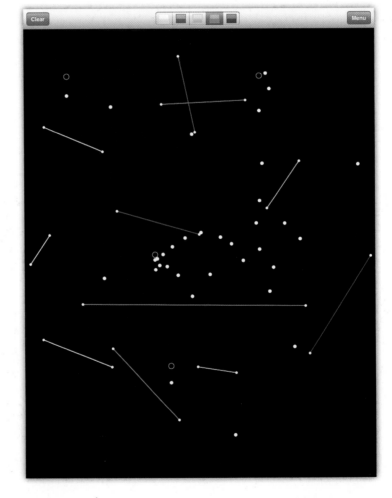

PAY TO PLAY: The free version offers a stripped down palette: line-segments produce one sound only (part wind chime, part marimba). Upgrade to the Pro edition via an in-app purchase for the real goodies: multiple instruments (piano, saxophone, and synthesizer), tempo and beats-per-minute controls, and the ability to save your creations.

COMPOSITION CONTROLS: Each note's pitch changes according to its velocity: increase the distance between the pellet dropping node and the chime-inducing line segments gets you a higher, more tinkly sound. Don't forget to play with the gravity, friction, and bounce settings to alter your notes in similar ways.

Best App for Improving Your Voice

ImproVox
$7.99
Version: 1.5 | MuseAmi

Today's music stars famously benefit from the vocal equivalent of plastic surgery: a little AutoTune-aided voice sprucing. So there's no shame in us musically-challenged crooners seeking a similar boost. The remarkable thing about this app is that its assistance is delivered *as you sing*. Some serious wizardry went into this feat, as most music magic is added post production. Here, you simply plug in any earphones with a mic, start singing, and add harmonies and effects. Save and export when you're done. And don't forget to bring your iPad next time you go caroling.

IMPROVE YOUR IMPROV: Pick the key you want to sing in or have the app I.D. your native note by tapping the "key" section's Use Voice button and singing for two seconds. The app's now ready to back up your best Bono. All you need to do, aside from singing, is drag the harmony and effects' dots to whichever position sounds best. Achieve further tweaks by picking styles (jazz, barbershop) and mood (happy, sad). Reveal more effects by double-tapping the screen's right side. Now you've got your auto-wah, flanger, and—every kid's favorite—the "you won't hear this sound in nature but it sure sounds freaky-deaky" bit crusher.

⊕ HONORABLE MENTION

Glee Karaoke
$0.99
Version: 2.2 | SonicMule

Karaoke has never been less humiliating with this voice-pimping singalong software. Among its other talents, the app software-magically keeps you on pitch, adds optional harmonies, and turns your 'Pad into a 'prompter: highlighted lyrics appear as the instrument track plays. Three songs come with the app; buy others that have appeared in the namesake show for a buck a pop. Bonus treats include the chance to listen to recordings made worldwide by other app-using fans, share your own efforts, or add your voice to songs other fans have posted.

Best App for Sheet Music Reading

forScore
$4.99
Version: 2.1 | MGS Development

You know one thing musicians won't miss years from now when the digital revolution concludes and they're sitting at home in their player pods, pecking out remotely broadcast chamber music on the iPad XV? Sheet music. Really, what could be more annoying than, mid-*mezzo forte*, having to reach up from the piano to flip to the next page? This app gets you paperless and tosses in a few nifty tricks to boot: a free collection of 100-plus well-known scores, an easy system for importing new files (via email or iTunes) or grabbing 'em off the Web, a handy way to add notes, and, for an applause-generating finale: it all just works as you'd expect. Bravo.

TURN TURN TURN: Of course, job number one for an app like this is making page turning easy. One quick tap anywhere on the right side of the screen gets you to the next page. Kill the page transitions effect (in the Settings menu) to shave some microseconds off the turn time. A page-browser slider at the bottom of the screen is an easy way to move through long scores. A built-in metronome also has an auto-turn option (enter BPM and the app does the flipping for you).

TAP TAP: The app's filled with lotsa nice, someone-was-sweatin'-the-details touches: if you have the iPad in landscape mode, and you're at the top of the page, your first tap on the right side scoots the page up so you see the hidden, bottom half; next tap advances the page where the cycle continues. (In other words, no having to scroll manually. You can make your way through a score using just taps.)

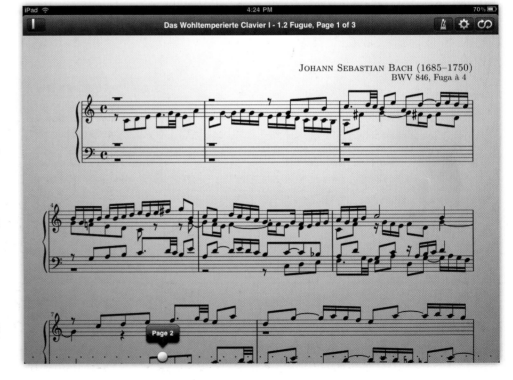

Creative Corner

LISTEN & LEARN: Tap the title in the menu bar and down drops a window where you can add all sorts of "metadata": genre and rating stars, for example. These are helpful as you build your sheet library and are looking for ways to sort and search. You can even link any piece to a song in your iTunes library and play the tune while you follow along (tap the cover art to shrink the size of the iTunes player window).

NOTATION STATION: Unlock a full complement of annotation tools by tapping and holding one finger. From the overlay that appears, you highlight phrases, add your own musical symbols (accidentals, dynamics), or just add comments for the benefit of you or other musicians in training. When finished, your notes remain part of the score.

Best App for Creating Comic Strips

Strip Designer
$2.99
Version: 1.8.4 | Vivid Apps

Ka-pow! Here's the knockout winner for anyone looking to crank out their own photo-based comic strips. The app lets you compose everything from single frames tagged with silly speech bubbles to multi-paned layouts ready for complex stories. Start with the pix in your photo library and then adorn and edit using an inventive and highly customizable catalog of tools. The best include special effects filters (Comic, Sketch), editable stickers (Wham! Bif!); and dozens of ready-to-use template designs (three squares in a row with a filmstrip border, six plain rectangles). Fun for the whole family, guaranteed.

COMIC CANVAS: First pick a layout and import one or more pix. Add and adjust speech bubbles and then write your dialogue. Wanna shrink the font size? Just resize the thought bubble, wait a sec, and then the program automatically picks a smaller font. Lots of sharing options: copy to the iPad's clipboard, email a JPEG or PDF, save to your Photos library, or post to Facebook or Flickr.

FILTER FUN: The Halftone filter lays a Roy Lichtenstein-style pointillist mesh over your pic; Invert adds a photo-negative meets X-ray glow. Add more than one filter at a time and adjust the intensity of each by using the slider below the filter bar. Go crazy experimenting: you can remove any effect by tapping the button of the same name.

Best App for Swapping Faces in Photos

iSwap Faces

Free lite version/$1.99
Version: 3.0.3 | Black Frog Industries

Much like plastic surgery, this app can boost or butcher anyone's looks. Most folks will amuse themselves by exploring the latter route. It's just too tempting when a handful of simple finger taps is all that stands between you and photo-surgically implanting your college roommate's face on your toddler's body (*"Who's your daddy now?"*). Those less puckish can opt for ego-helping photo fixes: improving that family photo by editing in a better-looking version of poor, photogenically challenged Uncle Stan. Of course, Photoshop and its ilk can make all this happen on your PC. But aside from cost, those tools require time to learn. This app's been crafted in an easy-to-use, easy-to-make-look-great way.

FACIAL FUN: It's a three-step dance, then you're done: open one or two photos (use the Load and Load 2 buttons); adjust the goalie-style masks on swapped areas one and two; tweak the results using the color and contrast edit sliders. Zoom in (by spreading your fingers) to help fine-tune mask placement.

SELECTIVE SURGERY: Once you've mastered the basic swapping maneuver, play with a few odd, guffaw-inducing variations: swap the pairs' mouth and nose or, um, different body parts. Summon your inner seventh grader and don't forget to share your best creations. Save the results to your photo library or upload directly to Facebook.

Best App for Adding Spot Color

Color Splash for iPad
$1.99
Version: 1.2 | Pocket Pixels

Photo pros play all sorts of "Yo, viewer, look here, at this spot" image-editing tricks—especially in the digital darkroom. One favorite: spot color, whereby a dollop of color adds punch to some segment of a grayscale image. In addition to requiring special software, the toughest challenge in targeted colorizing is picking what you want to illuminate. Enter ColorSplash, which, teamed up with the iPad's my-screen-is-your-controller solves this problem just about perfectly. What's that? You haven't shot black and white since the last century? No problem. ColorSplash starts with color pix, drains the rainbow right outta them, and gives you the tools you need to fingerpaint-I.D. what to color.

COLOR BY FINGERS: Start by loading up a suitable picture—ideal candidates include those with reflections (a pond, mirror sunglasses) or key areas featuring bright colors. Tap the Color button and then trace wherever you want your Kodachrome moments to shine. "Gray" lets you repaint b&w on spots you've mistakenly colored. Zoom in (you can go as far as the pixel level) for hard-to-select areas.

BETTER BRUSHING: You can adjust the brush size, but it's better to leave it at roughly the size of your fingertip and then zoom in and out to sweep across different-sized areas. In the same spot, you can also adjust things like opacity and edge settings (hard vs. soft). Don't miss the wonderful in-app video tutorial for a full spectrum of tips and tricks.

Creative Corner

Best App for Filter Afficionados

Photo fx Ultra

$4.99
Version: 2.0.1 | The Tiffen Company

Filter fanatics—photo gurus who require dozens of special effect choices and the ability to customize each option—will want to tap into this nearly bottomless toolkit. Where the pro power really becomes clear is in the volume and tweakability of the edit controls: Eight top-level categories (Film Lab, Diffusion), around a dozen effects within each group, and, to make sure you have no one to blame but yourself for the final result, yet another level of style variations for each filter. (Example: in the Light category, if you pick Windows, you get two dozen-plus simulated shiners—Crooked Blinds to Stained Glass.) Go forth and filter.

SPECIAL EFFECTS:
Pick the filter you want by traversing the category collection at bottom. The lower-right sliders let you control settings like brightness and blur. For quick before-and-after comparisons, tap the menu bar's lightning bolt icon. Cropping and straightening tools also await via the menu bar's middle icons.

FOCAL POINT:
You can even limit the filter's effect to specific areas. The dot-surrounded-by-dashes icon gets you a size- and location-adjustable area selector; adjust however you like to focus the effect. Similarly, the paint brush icon lets you mask out areas you want to protect from the filter (or vice versa).

Best App for Oil Painting Your Photos

PhotoArtistaHD—Oil

$4.99
Version: 1.1 | JixiPix Software

Truth be told, this app should be called "Photoshop Filters: Oil Painting's Greatest Hits." (Filters, in case you're not a member of the image-editing cool club, are ready-made effects that transform pictures.) But you know what? For those of us who aren't graphics gurus and get a kick out of giving our favorite pictures the Monet treatment, this single-purpose specialist is worth a few bucks. True, some of the effects belong in the Chemical Accident category, but overall, the ratio of work required to stunning result achieved is pretty impressive. And it couldn't be easier: start with a photo of your own, pick a style you like like, tweak if you like, and presto: you are now an Artista.

STUDIO SETUP: Your order of operations is helpfully laid out in the buttons from left to right. Start Project Pisarro in the Get Photo button where you pick the image to transform. Garbage-in, garbage-out holds true, but don't be afraid to pick a fuzzy miss; image composition is more important than sharpness when you're heading for the Land of Impressionism.

FILTER FUN: The Paint Style pop-up menu is where you'll find a catalog of a couple dozen effects, grouped into categories (impressionism, realism, abstract). The icons above the labels give you a rough idea of what you'll end up with. Don't go crazy trying to discern the difference between, say, Impressionism 06 and Impressionism 07; most noticeable are the color tones. If the effect icon looks greenish, then that's what you'll end up with.

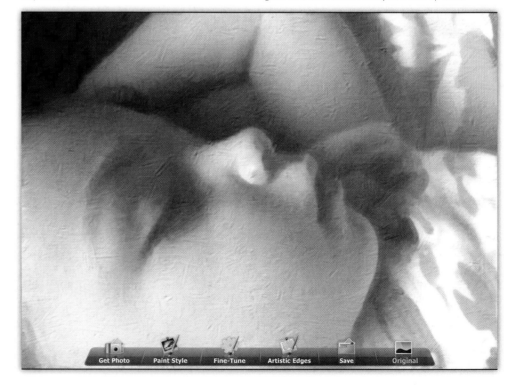

TOUCH UPS: The buttons marked Fine-Tune and Artistic Edges do what their names imply. In the first one, your tuning opportunities are greatest with the Tone color box and slider; pick a new shade and you'll see noticeable differences in the filter-painted result. Get edgy in the second pop-up menu by applying an assortment of borders.

BEFORE & AFTER: For maximum wow, hold your finger on the button marked Original; when pressed, it reveals your starting point. Anyone who plans on becoming an Artista regular, should be sure to use the Save Preset option in the Save menu; it captures whatever settings you've applied and lets you reuse it via a newly created entry in the Paint Style gallery.

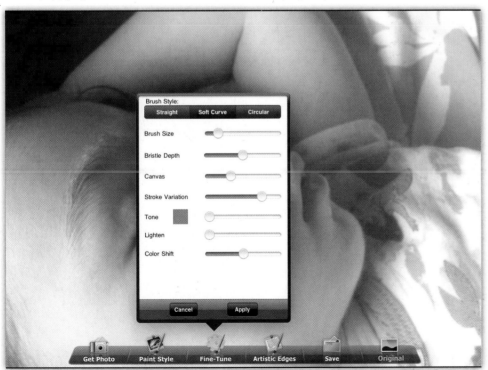

FX Photo Studio HD

$3.99
Version: 1.2.0 | MacPhun

Filter fans with absolutely no interest in tweaking sliders: here's a one-tap way to join the party. This app's kinda like hiring a Photoshop pro to show you 150 or so variations of any photo you feel like messing around with. The names of most effects are fairly descriptive (*cool blue*, *startdust frame*), though a few (*Amsterdam*, *Crosspro 3*) make the accompanying thumbnail demo an essential visual aid. All you have to do is pick a pic from your photo library and then tap the filter name that you want to apply. A live preview makes auditioning a snap. The dice icon in the upper-right corner lets random walk fans go for a stroll. Overall, the quality's good, though the cheese-o-meter redlines every so often (*Teddy Bear*, *Scary Face 2*).

Best App for General Image Editing

Photogene for iPad

$3.99
Version: 1.3 | Mobile-Pond

That screaming you hear in the distance? It's Adobe's Photoshop team, fear shrieking at the thought of how their $600 program will fare against this pocket change photo-editing competitor. To be sure, no high-end Photoshop jockey will ditch his workhorse for this. But everyone else? Photogene's toolkit is really deep. You can crop, rotate, apply filters, adjust color and exposure, treat red-eye, add text and shapes—even photo geek maneuvers like levels and curves are here. And you want to know the real kicker, the thing that should send shivers down the spine of any purveyor of image-editing software? This app is darn near dead-simple to use.

PICK A BUTTON: The tool bar at top offers quick access to undo/redo, plus the basic choices you'd find in a File menu: open, save, share. Bottom of the screen is where you summon each of the app's different edit tools: crop, rotate, and so on. Pick different effects in the right-side panel.

FILTER YOUR FRIENDS: The Filter tool puts you one tap away from applying any of the changes previewed in miniature on the right side. No, you don't get the 87 different customization settings that many photo editing programs come with, but that also means 87 fewer choices you need to make. The Adjust slider at bottom does let you dial back the filter's intensity.

Creative Corner

LABEL MAKER: The shapes menu (the star button at bottom) has a grab bag's worth of arrows, thought bubbles, hearts, and so on. It's also where to go if you just want to add a simple title or headline. Primp any text you add using the text color and font options stacked in the Custom area.

RINSE, REPEAT: If you're pleased with your work on a particular photo (frame just so, color adjustments spot on), then head over to the Macros button in the tab bar. At the bottom of the list of canned settings (Lomo, 40s Vintage) you can save, for instant reuse, the settings from a previous editing session.

Best App for Making Movies

ReelDirector

$3.99
Version: 3.2 | Nexvio

Hey, who cares if your last name's not Spielberg or Scorsese? You've got plenty of cute home videos on your iPad and nothing but crappy snacks and time to kill between now and when your flight lands. *Action!* ReelDirector keeps things simple: import movies and pix from your Photo library; lay 'em out on a timeline; add titles, transitions, and tunes; lightly edit as necessary…and you're done. Even if you don't have a lick of video, there's plenty of fun to be had whipping up photo slideshows, which can be spruced up with Ken Burns–style pan-and-zooming. Seatmates of the world, be warned: a new type of in-flight video is coming.

RAW FOOTAGE: Import videos and photos by tapping the plus button in the upper-right corner; each appears in the timeline at the top of the screen. Tap any timeline item to summon its editing options—for example, splitting video clips in half or trimming 'em (adjusting start and end points).

OUTPUT OPTIONS: When you're happy with the results, order a large beverage: rendering requires some serious patience (count on waiting about three times as long as your actual video to generate a final copy). Once you've got that you can email it, save it to your Photo library, or post to YouTube.

Best App for Making Animations

Animation Creator HD

Free lite version | $1.99
Version: 1.3 | Red Software

From junior John Lasseters looking to block out their own virtual toy stories to doodlers in search of a more dynamic canvas, this app's perfect for turning an iPad into a portable animation studio. Pixar's probably not going out of business anytime soon due to the stick figure confections made possible here, but then again, check out some of the creations (*http://bit.ly/d5zFNY*) that a few of these 21st century Walt Disneys have cooked up. Drawing and editing options are pretty limited, but that's not necessarily a bad thing. Think of this app as a sketchbook for animators: an always handy idea catcher out of which, who knows what may bloom?

PRE PRODUCTION: Start and finish with a blank frame or two (tap the toolkit menu's Add button) for that professional look you get from a screen white fade-in. Pick your drawing tools and colors from the buttons of the same names. Once you've composed the initial action—a sun dipping its way into view from the top of the screen, say—press Add to move onto the next frame. Shadow replicas of the previous frame's shapes linger around to help maintain continuity as you work on each subsequent step.

CONTINUITY: For images you want onscreen a blip or two longer than your heart-of-the-movie action (an opening title, for instance), tap the copy button once or twice to duplicate what's in those frames. Or do the same for an object that you want to dispatch across the screen. Just replicate it, use the Positioner tool from the Tools palette to nudge it to a new location, and then maybe add a dash or two of something new (wavy lines are great for suggesting motion or to represent steam boiling out of your mom's ears).

Best App for Major Photo Distortion

Fluid FX
$0.99
Version: 1.2 | Autodesk

Sergey's having a tough day. His right eye is dripping halfway down his cheek, he's got a mouth that looks like a crushed tomato, and his nose is within sniffing distance of his ear. That'll happen when you crank the knobs in Fluid FX's control center just so. If it all looks a little Hollywood special effect-ish, that's because the software smarts behind this app power many of the movies you've probably seen. True to its name, these aren't fingerpaint-style fix-and-set-in-paint distortions. The changes remain in motion like so many different paint colors swirling together in a bucket. Operate on the images that come with the app or import your own; when you're done, dial up Dr. Ripley.

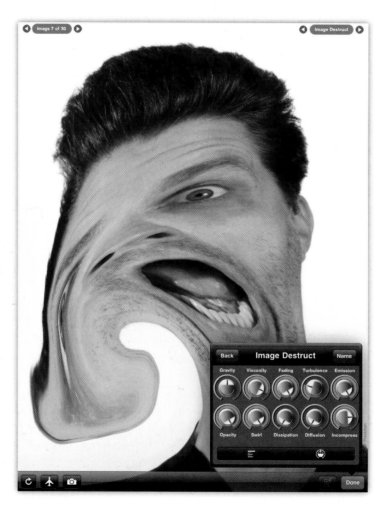

FREAKSHOWTIME: Sample the settings' circus by tapping the lower-left airplane icon: that gets you an AutoPilot menu, which plays a wild collection of effects. You can also manually pick from three dozen stock images (use the upper-left's arrows) and a similar number of canned effects (upper-right arrows).

ROLL YOUR OWN: Once you get bored—not easy!—with these basic options, move on to custom futzing: import your own photos, tweak the dials (tap- and-hold and then move your finger up or down), and swipe your fingers across the photo to coax these warbled images in new directions.

Best App for Depth of Field Trickery

TiltShift Generator for iPad

$2.99
Version: 1.07 | Takayuki Fukatsu & Takuma Mori

Welcome to the land of wee. Tilt-shift photography takes normal-sized objects and makes 'em look like they came from *Honey, I Shrunk the Kids*. In reality, the scenes are of everyday life, faux miniaturized through the use of some lens-shifting and -tilting wizardry. Or the use of iPad apps like this one. Yep, you can get much of the same effects *after the fact* simply by goosing digital photo settings like saturation, focus, and contrast. You're basically picking a portion of the image whose focus you want to spotlight and whose overall richness you want to enhance. It generates small things, but this app offers a giant dose of micro magic.

SIZE MATTERS: Suitable subject matter is key: parking lots and crowded stadiums, for example, both work well. Next, decide which focal point-picking tool to apply: Radial for oval-shaped objects (like stadiums) or Linear (car rows). Then finger drag and resize whatever shaped band you've picked to roughly match what you want on center focal stage. Play with blur size and value sliders to control the area covered and focal intensity.

HIDDEN DETAILS: When you're done becoming the master of the mini, pop in other kinds of pix: portrait closeups, family photos, whatever. Fiddle with the sliders and soon you'll be simulating all kinds of digital SLR effects. Other settings like saturation, contrast, and vignetting can work subtle high- and spotlights into your creation. You'll soon discover the extraordinary amount of detail that's packed into your photos' digital bits.

Best App for 3D-ifying Photos

OutColor for iPad

$1.99
Version: 1.7 | Vizros Software

Some photos are so action-packed the subjects look like they're practically leaping out of the frame. Others need a little software-powered nudge to hop from 2- to 3D. That's where this app kicks in. Using civilian-friendly controls that are perfectly suited for touchscreen tweaking, you can take nearly any photo and amplify its appearance. Innards spill outwards, jaws drop southwards. There's even a Flickr collection devoted to these so-called "out of bounds" images (*http://bit.ly/OOBipad*; don't miss the discussion area for OOB tips). Use the app's built-in sharing tools to post your best results. If James Cameron has an iPad, this app should be on his home screen.

TAP THIS WAY: The app's bottom row buttons offer an implicit guide: once you pick your image (via the Review tab's Load button), the easiest path forward is to follow the buttons from left to right. Choose a background, position the frame wherever you want the action to emerge *from*, identify your foreground starring attractions, give the shadows a fluff, and then review.

REVIEWER'S GUIDE: The Review tab is worth a special note. Head here for a don't-miss tutorial that'll save you buckets of time. Later, come back: Share lets you broadcast your baby, and Save contains the mighty useful Session option, so you can take a break and restart where you left off.

FRAMING THE ACTION: A one-finger tap-and-drag lets you reposition the overall frame; hold-and-drag any corner to resize. It's a bit of a duet between you and the app's 3D–frame rendering engine; play with each corner till you find a good spot. Flip back and forth between Frame and Review to see how you like the results.

FINGER SELECTING: The Foreground button is where you do with your finger what your PC-based ancestors struggled with for hours using the mouse. Tap the Color Brush button and then "paint" what you want in the final image; spread your fingers to zoom in and hit Eraser to fix mistakes. The Brush drop-down menu lets you change things like size and opacity.

Best App for Organizing What Inspires You

Moodboard
Free lite version | $6.99
Version: 1.3.1 | A Tiny Tribe

Explaining *what* you can do with this app is a little easier than tackling *why* or *how* you'd use it. You can: import your photos and lightly edit, rotate, resize, and frame 'em; cruise the Web in a special-powered browser that lets you clip and paste any image, portion of a page, whatever; compose notes and headline-y quips; and arrange all those items wherever you like onscreen by dragging and using Photoshop-style "layers" to stack objects one atop the other. Meant for designer types in search of inspiration, the app could easily prove useful to scrapbookers, photo collage fans, event planners—the list is pretty endless.

WEB CLIPPINGS: Spot something online that's lineup-worthy for the board you're creating? Hop in the custom web browser, tap the "Crop and Save" button, and finger-adjust the marquee around the item you want to corral.

TOP TO BOTTOM: The layers palette is where you designate the stacking order of overlapping items. Tap and drag the right-side bar grips to bump an object up or down the stack; tap to close the left-hand lock if you want to fix an item on the canvas and prevent it from accidental moves.

Best App for Virtual Potterymaking

Let's Create Pottery HD
Free lite version | $4.99
Version: 1.13 | Infinite Dreams

When you first launch this app, you might be forgiven for thinking you've downloaded a $5 wet lump of clay. Sure, you can use your fingers to shape a spinning muddy glob and then "fire" it to a finish. But where are the color choices for prettily painting your patiently spun shapes? And the patterns that, for millenia, have made potting the artform of choice for this handsculpting performance art? Spin and ye shall find. The developers have woven in a decently engaging build-and-sell-it virtual shopping game, the rewards for which are more patterns and colors. They've even managed to build in a series of mini tutorials that arrive in the guise of email request from your "Aunt Chloe."

TIP JAR: Follow their tips successfully and your toolkit grows. Send them mud splotches (or even designs that don't match their requests) and they'll politely send you back to the studio. It's really not as hokey as it sounds. And while some digital clay-shaping perks (an Undo button; unlimited reset chances) might cause real-world potters to fire off a frown, there is definitely room for some kind of true finger-shaping and color-selecting artistry here. The best measure of this? How easy it is to botch your mud block into toddler art.

SUPPLY SIDE: The app comes stocked with a supply cabinet full of colors and patterns, none of which you can touch—until you get shopping points from kindly Chloe *or* start "selling" your stuff in the app's built-in shop. Unlike most other apps' virtual exchanges, this one doesn't actually appear to be a lure for you to fork over real dinero. While it seems likely the developers will add a real-life commerce element, for now, it's a make-and-take exchange. The more stuff you build and submit, the more tools you get. Fun.

Best App for Drawing and Painting

ArtStudio for iPad
$2.99
Version: 2.11 | Lucky Clan

Pro and amateur artists alike are starting to view the iPad as a tool every bit as useful as their computer, not to mention the ol' reliable brush. Some high-profile oldtimers like David Hockney even tout the advantages of touchscreen painting, since he can capture early morning vistas without any light other than the screen's glow (he uses a really fine app called Brushes). Art Studio has earned rave reviews not simply because of its discount price, but because it offers nuanced tools that also happen to be easy to tweak and control. If you've ever been turned off by the complexity of digital drawing, give this app a tap and a whirl.

ART SUPPLIES: The app's toolkit is neatly (but not overly) stocked with a finger painting–friendly lineup: pencils, brushes, spray paint cans, tube squirters, scatter patterns, and burn, dodge, and smudge implements. Hold any tool to fine-tune settings like brush size, opacity, and jitter (which does just what its name implies).

POWER PACKED: Photoshop veterans rejoice: go deep into the canvas with clone stamps, layers, layer masks, and blend modes (ten of 'em). About the only big item missing as of this writing is a selection tool, and that's on the developer's to-do list. He's more or less a one-man shop but releases new features frequently.

FILTER FUN: Half the treat of digital artistry lies in *filters*, canned effects that let you apply painterly themes across the entire canvas. A dozen or so await, and some—Gaussian blur, Pixelize, and Posterize—give you adjustable settings, letting you do things like control the dimensions of the pixels used to "paint" the effects. For some quirky looks, try applying a filter multiple times by tapping its button repeatedly.

LOOK & LEARN: This app's even got built-in tutorials that teach basics like animals, faces, and one- and two-point perspective. There's nothing incredibly sophisticated going on here: the app draws a stroke and asks you to repeat. And while art instructors may question the pedagogical value of this kind of watch-and-trace approach, it works for those willing to repeat the steps frequently enough to capture them in muscle memory.

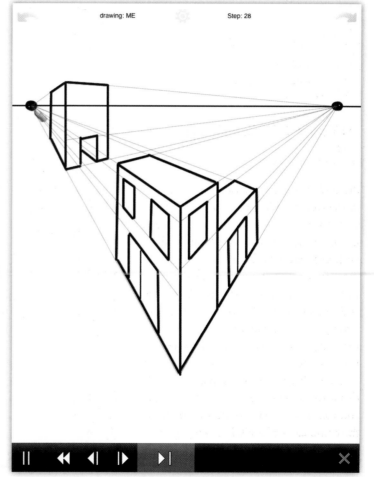

Best App for Drawing Time for Kids

Drawing Pad
$1.99
Version: 1.7 | Darren Murtha Design

White drawing pad? Check. Tray stocked with markers, crayons, and multicolored sparkly glue dispensers? Check. Toddler ready to make some art, but who suddenly spots that irresistible couch, just *begging* to be drawn on even though the concept of "no-no" is firmly lodged in said toddler's pea-brain head? Ruh-roh. Friend, you need yourself a virtual canvas on which your precious Picasso can splatter the messy fury of her art. You need Drawing Pad. This delightfully usable, kid-friendly app is a creativity-encouraging vortex from which your child will not soon emerge.

TOOLS FOR TOTS: The app's designers made the brilliant decision to forgo options you'd find in painting programs for grownups: separating color choices in a different toolbox, layers (a concept many *adults* don't understand), and brush size controls. Instead, the app shows the tool as is: paint it or leave it. The main choices: paint brushes, colored pencils, crayons, markers, pattern stamps, stickers, and paper.

STICKERS!: Resize and rotate any of these guys by pinching, spreading, and twisting your fingers. The most complex moment in the entire app is when the sticker-specific tools appear after you tap an object. From left to right they: lock the item's position, place it either in front of or behind other stickers, flip it horizontally, stamp it onto the canvas (so it can no longer be resized or moved), and trash it.

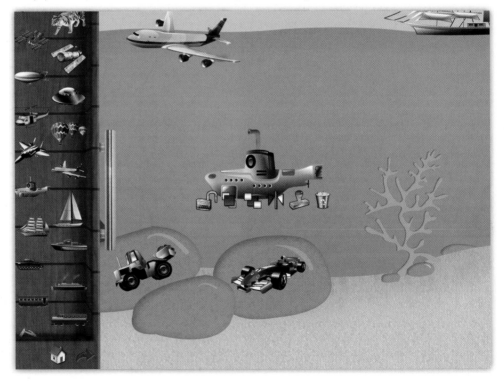

Best App for Drawings that Move

Art of Glow
Free lite version | $1.99
Version: 1.1.0 | Natenai Ariyatrakool

The best apps let us do what's not possible on paper. If a white sketchpad is your goal, by all means, head for a drawing app like the one shown on page 108. But if you want to compose "kinetic art"—wavy and warbling lines that jiggle as and after you draw 'em—this app's for you. The toolkit you draw from is considerably more limited than most painterly programs, but the brush choices signal that something's new here: *lifetime* (how long each stroke remains onscreen), *speed* (roughly: the velocity of sparks unleashed), and *rebirth* (a way to replay the stroke after it fades). The pro version lets you replay a video of what you've concocted—a snazzy way to preserve this moving art.

STUDIO PREP: Start by tapping the lower-right tools icon and then head to the settings tab to choose from a half dozen-ish shapes and colors. Either pick specific ones to compose with, or let the app cycle through or randomize the styles that splurt out of your finger. You can start recording from a virgin canvas, or once you've got a composition cooking, head back to the tools icon and grab the action from the video tab. When you replay the vid, you get to see the evolution of what you made from start to, well, it never really finishes.

Space Crayons
$1.99
Version: 1.0 | Zidware

For tots not yet ready for Art of Glow's full suite of options, here's a tyke-friendly collection of two dozen or so premade drawings on top and around which they can compose the goofiest-looking moving pix they've probably ever seen. The three screen-top crayons adjust the effects. Kids can also pick from a lineup of different colored crayons. Silly robot sounds add a nice touch. Unfortunately there's no way to save and share these amazing creations, but forward-looking art lovers (and their kids) will find this a glimpse of doodling's future.

Best App for Drawings that Disappear

Magic Ink

Magic Ink
Free
Version: 1.0 | Karl Stiefvater

How surprising to encounter an app that does so little and yet is such elegant, captivating fun. Nominally, Magic Ink is a finger-painting tool. But it's as much a piece of interactive performance art; a philosophical gesture from its creator to each of us harried, sensory-overloaded iPad owners. If that all sounds too touchy-feely, at a lifelong guaranteed price of free, there's really not much to lose in trying this out. Your reward lies in an app that gently helps you lay down an almost calligraphic stroke. The kicker? What you write begins to disappear as soon as your finger leaves the screen. The message is clear: like life, some art, too, is fleeting. A lovely thought from a lovely app.

MAGIC MOMENT: The slower you go, the thinner your line becomes. A fast swipe, by contrast, lays down a fat teardrop of a stroke, inside of which, as the fade begins, you'll see concentric circles with increasingly reduced opacity. It's like coming across, in the midst of a hectic, info-overloaded day, a haiku that soothes, clarifies, slows you down.

LEANWARE: Multiple brush options and color pickers…where can they be hiding? The answer: nowhere. You will find no controls in the iPad's Settings app and no secret multi-touch gestures. Even the app's approach to launching is minimalist. Tap its icon on your iPad's home screen and, with no delay, you face a bare white canvas. Go.

Creative Corner

Best App for Software-Assisted Sketching

ASKetch

$0.99
Version: 1.4.2 | Andrew Kern

Toddlers use training wheels, pseudo-singers turn to AutoTune, and now the graphically challenged have some line-steadying and curve-smoothing assistance. This black-and-white-only sketching app is like drawing with a cleanup crew trailing your strokes, gently coaxing your curves onto a more harmonious path and sometimes filling in gaps where the app guesses you need help. Amazingly, it's often right. The artist behind the drawing on the right, for example, has a history of creating art that belongs to the school of Second Gradism. And while that self-portrait won't win any awards, the lines have a fluidity and coherence that would never have happened without a nudge.

TOOL TIPS: A two-finger tap summons the app's barebones toolkit: sketch, erase, undo, save, and trash. Modify your line and eraser size by pinching or spreading the canvas: the size of the purple circle boosts or shrinks your brush size. Draw with one finger for a line, two for a shaved-iron look.

LINE DESIGN: Lines drawn roughly in parallel to each other sprout slightly paler cross-hatched connecting segments that look like spider webs. Do a two-finger rotate (you'll see a dot appear) to control how much inter-line latticework appears; turn clockwise for more, counterclockwise for less.

Best App for Virtual Sculpting

iDough
$4.99
Version: 1.0.2 | CrateSoft

What you make of the virtual green clay lump this app starts you off with depends on a) how well you did with Play-Doh, and b) picking up some basics on how this 3D modeling app works. The first is a matter between you and your fingers. But even those whose instincts tend toward pinch and mutilate will likely enjoy prodding the green glob. The point of all this poking can range from idle fun (*look Ma! my first alien*) to some serious sculpting: you can export files that mesh well with serious modeling programs. So the drafts you build on the iPad are ready for, say, Photoshop's finer-grained coloring, shading, and further beautification.

Creative Corner

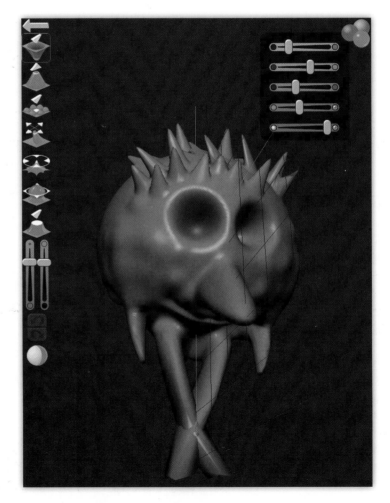

PIXEL PUSHERS: The left-side vertical slider controls "finger size": how large a divot you get when pressing the screen. The right-side counterpart lets you adjust pressure: how hard your virtual finger presses. In both cases, the lower you position the tab, the more intense its effect. Colorize things by tapping the upper-right 3-circled icon.

MIRROR MIRROR: The thin, red grid bisects whatever you're making; activate or disable the bottom Symmetry button to control whether the adjustments you make on one side get mirrored on the other. When finished, you have an email-ready *.obj* file: a popular 3D modeling file format that programs like SketchUp, Maya, and Inkscape are happy to play with.

Best App for Drawing with Letters

TypeDrawing for iPad
$4.99
Version: 1.3.1 | Hansol Huh

Publishing wonks and designers know that *typography*—text styling and its placement on a page—is an art form in its own right. But how about deploying words as brushstrokes? Ladies and gentleman, meet TypeDrawing. You could call it a word lover's app, but this one's really got hybrid appeal. Drawing types will enjoy how letters spackle the screen in ways that no traditional brush can match. The alphabet set, on the other hand, will love the chance to draw puns that are, literally, visual. (For a tasty sampling of TypeDrawing fan-made creations, check out the Flickr group of the same name at *http://bit.ly/iPadType*).

ALPHABET PREP: Enter the text, phrase, or letter mishmash you want to compose with by tapping the T button. Next, pick a font (button: F) and finish the drill by choosing a color from the color-picker square. Fun frill: the color menu's Random tab shows a grid of hues the app will cycle through as you draw.

COLOR BY LETTER: To draw, drag slowly for a thin line; speed up if you want to go chunky. Or pick a fixed size by heading to the Font drop-down menu and turning *off* "Vary size by speed"; now set the size and tracking (spacing between letters). Tucked in among the several saving options (high-res PNG, PDF), you can also replay an animation of your strokes.

Best App for Designing Your Own Font

iFontMaker

$7.99
Version: 1.6.1 | The 2TTF

Want to add a personal touch to typewriting? Doesn't get much more custom than designing your own font. This app lets you finger paint an A to Z font family. And then—get this—download a fully functional, computer-ready version for composition in programs like Word and Pages. How this all works involves a dance between the app, a web-based rendering engine, and a popular font standard—the details of which you need to know precisely nothing about. Your job is simply to trace out the letters, numbers, and special characters that you want your creation to have. Handwriting may be dead, but here's a chance to escape HelveticaVille and add some flair to your fonts.

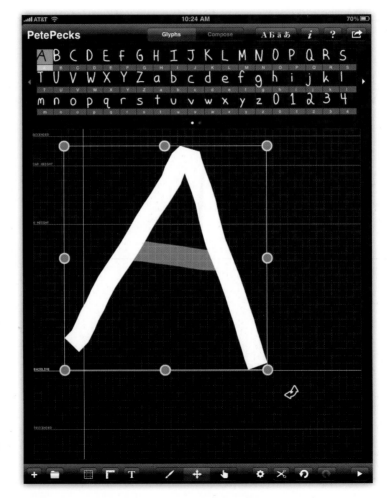

PHASE ONE: In broad strokes, the creation process goes like this: on a blank canvas (Glyphs tab, the "+" button), pick the brush you want to compose with. In the drawing window's center, tap or trace your version of whichever letter is highlighted in the top row; select the next target letter and repeat.

PHASE TWO: You can edit your work at any point by tapping the tab bar's four-headed arrow (one-finger tap for the resize or rotate box) or the hand icon (to tweak individual strokes). Hit the menu bar's Compose tab to test draw some letters. When you're ready to publish, head back to Glyphs and in the Share menu, choose "Build Font…" and follow the instructions from there.

Creative Corner

116

FONT CHECK: Here's a prepublication chance to see what your creation looks like. Use the spacing slider to tighten or loosen kerning (space between letters). Keep an eye out for odd alignments (the "i" here needs a leftward nudge) or descenders ("g", "y") whose tails get clipped. Head back to the Glyphs tab to make those adjustments.

TYPEFACE PLACE: The public gallery of finished fonts (*http://2ttf.com/gallery*) serves a few purposes: a sharing ground to see and download other font fanatics' creations, a venue for trumpeting your own work (via the social networks in the Share section), and a handy code generator for CSS geeks (click any font's Web Font button for some ready to use *font-face* code).

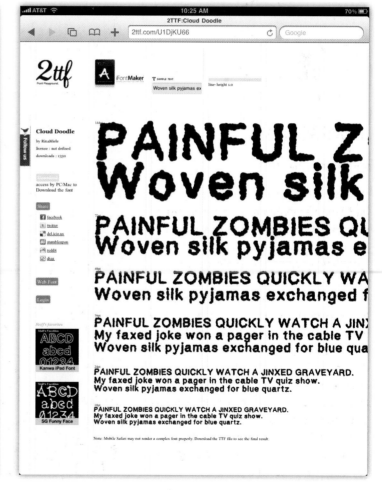

Best App for Sculpting Virtual Fireworks

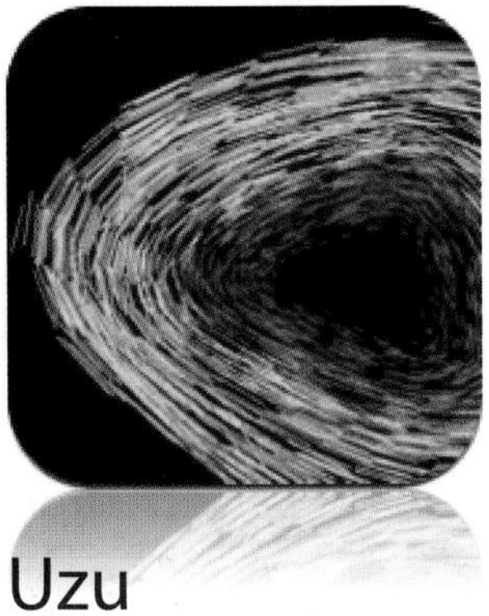

Uzu

$0.99
Version: 1.2.1 | Jason K. Smith

A "kinetic multitouch particle visualizer" is the tagline on this app's start screen, but once you enter, it looks more like thousands of tiny mites have invaded your iPad—ewww! But wait. Flick your finger across the surface and watch as these multicolored bugs scatter like so many iron shavings disturbed by a magnet. Next: do a two-finger pinch or spread and a mini fireworks-style starburst erupts. For double fun, do the same gesture with two pairs of fingers in two different spots. The lightstorm that erupts is, well, the technical term is: neato.

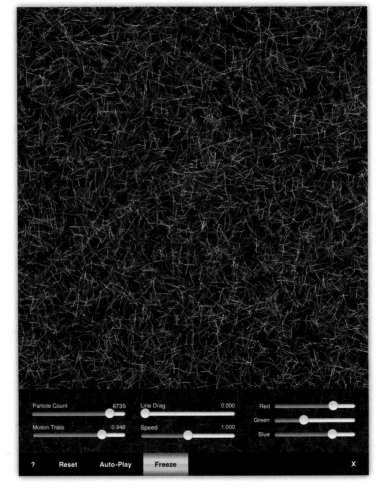

TAP THAT: Start by tapping random spots on the screen in quick succession and you've got yourself a 4th of July–style constellation of starbursts. Don't miss the five-finger flick: it slings a comet ball of whatever's onscreen at hyperspeed. Syncopate your hand gestures for crazy effects: tickle the screen with a downward, lefthand swipe and then cross paint the ensuing rainbow eruption with two fingers from your right hand. Double tap any corner to summon the settings.

GO WILD: This app invites a spasm of gestures that would get you in trouble in nearly any other context: grope, pinch, tickle, flick. If your iPad could giggle, it might just erupt in hysterics.

THE MUSIC OF MOTION: The jaw droppers start once you unleash your hands conductor-style on the display. The more touches, the more movement, the more your fingers jab, swipe, and poke, the better. Knead the screen—heck, if you're independently wealthy, you might even want to punch the dang thing. No doubt this app has some amazing visual treat awaiting the most creative gestures.

SWIPE SLOW: When you're tired of jabbing, slow down and even—hard as it may be—stop. That's right, press and hold any collection of fingers in an on-screen pose and the app rewards you with a wide variety of warbling shapes that match your fingers' positions. Now add in another finger or move one that's onscreen and that muffin-sized oval turns into a spinning taffy vortex through which a new dimension might well await.

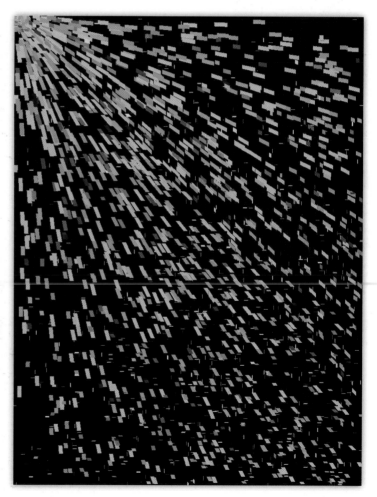

Best App for iPad Wallpaper

Granimator

Free
Version: 1.6.0 | Ustwo

Maybe your locker-decorating, skateboard-stickering days are over, but who says your iPad has to sport the same background image as everyone else's? Certainly not the lads at Granimator, the U.K. graphics shop behind this custom wallpaper maker. Get started on their dime with a grab bag of freebie designs: Mentalism, Best Box, and Sweet Tooth are some of the pattern packages the app ships with and which you use to stamp out your vision. To expand your palette visit the in-app Pack Store, where for a buck or two you can add other artists' themes. The creation process is finger-painting simple and you can share favorite creations online for others to download.

120

YOUR TOOLKIT: Before jumping finger first onto the canvas, begin here in the Tools menu. Pick the Shapes you want to lay down; active shapes are outlined in white. To turn a selection off, tap it again. Styles work the same way; you're basically picking fill patterns that end up inside each shape. Finally, pick your one and only background.

FURTHER TOOLING: Don't worry too much about finalizing your choices in the Tools or Shape Size sections; once you send the Tools menu packin', you'll still have easy access to a smaller menu stocked with those frequently used implements.

YOUR CANVAS: Two main ways to draw: just tap the screen and out pops a single style-filled shape; alternatively, trace your finger across the screen to string out a stream of objects. Tap the hand tool when you're ready to shape shift: tap and then drag, rotate, or change an object's size. The Share button at the bottom of the screen lets you broadcast your creation to Flickr, Facebook, and, most importantly, save it to your photo album.

TWEAKER'S TIP: Save what you make, and see how it looks as your background (head to the iPad's Settings app and choose Brightness & Wallpaper). If you want to make any adjustments, come back to the app to work on whatever image you left on the canvas. Remember, too, that not every home screen needs to have a full grid of app icons. Remove a few, if you like, to give what you created maximum shining room.

Best App for Creating Digital Banners

Marquee

$1.99
Version: 2.2 | Yodel Code

You probably will need Marquee about three times during the course of your iPad ownership: when stuck roadside and in need of a flashing *HELP* sign, to shame that creepy window-staring neighbor (*I SEE YOU*), and to taunt soon-to-be ex-colleagues after giving your two weeks' notice (*SEE YA, SUCKERS!*). But for these and any other supersized scrolling banner needs, this app puts your message up in the big lights. A full suite of custom controls—speed of scrolling, font type and size, and some basic animation effects—ensures you'll get noticed when you're in need of attention.

BIG MEDIUM: Tap the dark gray rectangle at the top of the screen to enter your mega message. In addition to regular text, you can also include things like the time, date, photos from your library, and an impressively large collection of emoticons, including the much-needed purple-headed pointy-eared frowny face. Once you start stockpiling messages, divide 'em up into groups; use the left-side pane to add, edit, and delete collections.

MESSAGE CONTROL: If you want each word to get its own billing, switch from a horizontal scroll to a fade or zoom; plenty of similar formatting choices await on the Edit Message screen. Rainbow colored text is available, but serious marquee writers frown on such gaudy effects. Instead, pick a single text and background color and, when in doubt, follow the first rule of design (do no harm) and go with white text on a black background.

At Play

Mention video games to most gainfully employed people and the dominant image that pops to mind is the 20-something dude, a Red Bull at his side, fingers furiously working that inscrutable controller thingie. Sure, Nintendo broadened the audience a bit with the Wii and its civilian-friendly just-wave-it wand, but video games are still primarily a hobby for couch creatures with time enough to master these admittedly marvelous creations. The iPad continues what the Wii began. Thanks to its stunning display and customized high-powered video engine, the iPad's ready to host some jaw-dropping video effects. (Check out the freebie Epic Citadel if you haven't gotten a proper glimpse yet.) It might not quite match what X-Boxers enjoy, but on a long car ride, that's a multi-hour teen-sitter you've got there. Coverage of those kinds of games is kept to a minimum, mainly because the typical (insert your Blockbuster Gaming Franchise here) fan needs no review. Madden NFL just came out on the iPad? Madden NFL is getting downloaded. What you will find in the pages that follow is help on two big fronts. First, categories overcrowded with choices. Brain benders like Sudoku seem to have attracted entrants from every computer science student looking to showcase her first app experiment. A guide to which ones are worth it awaits. Perhaps more interesting is a tour through those innovative games that mainly don't exist on the big consoles and which take advantage of the iPad's touchscreen talents. Here we enter the wild precincts of the weird and wacky, as orbs and swords match up against pigs and ninjas. Game on.

Photo: Emery Way

123

Best Tower Defense Game

Plants vs. Zombies HD
$9.99
Version: 1.0.2 | PopCap

Who versus *what?* Never mind if the setup seems straight outta B-movie Land. The gameplay is wave after wave of unstoppable fun. Your job: as zombies slump toward your house, you need to strategically place specially powered plants. The former groan every few steps ("brains," "we're coming"), while the latter do their best to stem the undead masses, aided as you continuously replenish their ranks. Most levels require you to plant a wide collection of different plants (some shoot frozen peas, others penetrate special zombie defenses or "turn" zombies so they attack each other). All pit your fauna-deployment skills against multiple waves of drooling ghouls.

GHOULS RULES: If you lose a few times and tire from the shriek-inducing brain snack you become each time the game ends, stick with it at least till you get the Suburban Almanac; that compendium of all the various plant and zombie properties is a handy guidebook for staying alive.

MULTI-TOUCH: As you progress to some of the higher levels, don't forget to use a few fingers together to grab multiple ghoul-fighting tools from the screen-top, rectangular arsenal. For example, pick off a few fingers' worth of, say, rolling killer potato spuds and then plunk 'em into different rows.

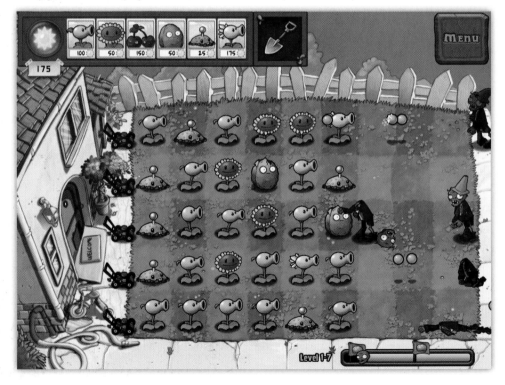

At Play

Best Pinball Game

Pinball HD
$1.99
Version: 2.0 | Gameprom

Attention, pinball wizard wannabes. Here's your chance to log hours of silver-ball fun without having to forklift multiple machines into your home. That's right, Pinball HD gives you a trio of wonder-worlds to flip through: Jungle, Wild West, and The Deep, each a breathtakingly illustrated, stunningly designed, wildly inventive take on iPad pinballing. The game action starts just as you'd expect: drag the launcher toward you and let go as the ball races northward and then rounds the bend into the land of beeps, bumps, and—since this is the iPad—about three dozen other effects most casual pinball players have never before seen.

BALL'S-EYE VIEW? In portrait view, the app begins zoomed in, with a closeup look at the ball's launching area. To pull back for an easier-to-react-to view of the entire table, press each side of the board with a thumb and then flick 'em both upscreen; or just flip your device to landscape.

FLIP TIPS: To flap the flippers (in either orientation), you can tap *anywhere* on the left or right side of the screen to control the levers on that side. Fingers tired? Tap anywhere on the top of the screen for pause and exit options. Cheesy music starting to grate? Head to the app's Settings menu, turn on the iPod option, fire up a playlist or song in the iPod app, and head back to Pinball HD.

Best App for Crossword Puzzles

Crosswords

Free lite version | $9.99
Version: 2.07 | Stand Alone

You know who you are: Sunday puzzle slayer, driven by an insatiable hunger for trivia and cryptic clue sleuthing, and tormented by a concern for journalism's well-being that—go on, admit it—has as much to do with fear that your beloved crosswords might perish as it does your concern for news. This, dear word hound, is your app. With it, you will not lack for choices. Even the free version comes with a decent stock of 40 puzzles. But serious word hounds will opt for the premium model, which comes with dozens of boards from as many different sources; you can even import your *New York Times* supply, if you're a subscriber.

SUPPLY SIDE: The lower-left corner's black-and-white four-square grid is your path to replenishment; tap it for a brain-bulging list of puzzle possibilities: more or less as many as you want in the premium version. You can even flip back through the built-in calendar to download historical puzzles.

HELPFUL HINTS: Tap and hold an empty cell and a wide variety of hints are one touch away: individual letters, completed words, even the entire puzzle, filled in (or a "peeking" option, whereby the solution flashes onscreen for about five seconds). If those aids pain your ego, try a memory nudge from a group of fact-gathering sites, including Google, Wikipedia, Answers.com, and OneAcross.com.

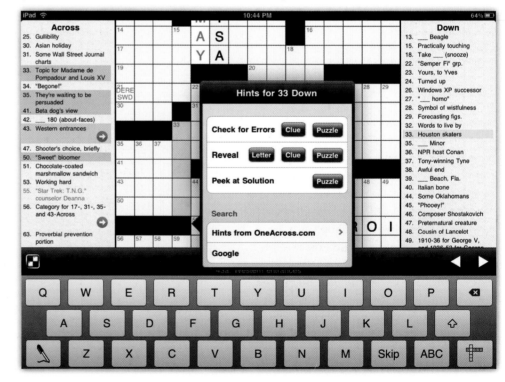

Best App for Sudoku

UniSudoku
Free lite version | $2.99
Version: 1.5.5 | David Ross Software

True to the game's minimalist, yet devilishly challenging nature, this Sudoku app's spare, elegant design is a perfect playground for those seeking maximal number-arranging pleasure. The challenge: arrange the digits from 1 to 9 in adjacent mini-grids without repeating any number in the table-spanning rows or columns. A simple number-entry and note-making system lets you concentrate on numerical reckoning rather than futzing with an administrative apparatus that competing apps seem incapable of hiding. Take the unlimited "easy" puzzles for a spin with the free version; if you find this particular grid groovy, the full version offers four more levels and lets you input faves from any book or newspaper.

9X9 PROBLEMS: The handwriting recognition system—scrawl any number you like—works impressively, mainly because it accepts only the digits 1 through 9, so it can keep an eye out for those patterns and play dumb when it comes to everything else. mark your "maybe" notes (the numbers you think *might* work in a cell) by single tapping the appropriate spot in the cell : 1 is upper left, 2 is upper middle, and so on. Double tap to get rid of a cell-filling entry you've changed your mind about.

⊕ HONORABLE MENTION

:) Sudoku
Free lite version | $2.99
Version: 4.0 | Jason T. Linhart

Perfect for those looking for a bit more hand-holding and maximum variety. You get more than a dozen difficulty levels, several tutorial lessons, and a healthy dose of in-game hints, some of which link to in-depth lessons on the Sudoku reference guide site *Sudopedia.org*. Most edifying is the way hints unfurl from slightly cryptic, gentle reminders to a detailed explanation of why, say, a 6 goes in the 8th row, cell 1. The graphics in this app come from the school of clip art, but for turning your puzzling hobby into a mind-improving habit, you can't do much better.

Best App for Scrabble

Scrabble for iPad
$9.99
Version: 1.1.74 | Hasbro

The competition in this category is slim: Hasbro's lawyers made sure there's only one app using the sacred eight-letter sequence. But Scrabble's worthy of this solo slot. The number of playing options is huge: against the computer, by yourself (odd, but possible), "pass and play" with up to three other competitors (opponents' racks are hidden between turns), iPad-to-iOS device over a WiFi network, or against Facebook friends. Those with iPhone or iPod Touch-toting friends can even download a free helper app and turn those mobile gadgets into privacy-protecting racks; the iPad serves as a ready-and-waiting board onto which you toss your tiles.

MIXING MATCHES: Three types of game styles are on offer: classic (the play-till-you're-finished mode of yore), point-based (first to reach 75 or 150 points wins), or a fixed number of rounds. Turn on the Duplicate setting if you want all players to pull from the same rack. Sounds silly, but it levels the playing field and leads to some eventful matchups. The gist: everyone submits their best play and the highest scoring one wins board placement.

TRAINING TILES: The Shuffle button is a helpful way of juggling the letters in your rack, if you're having a hard time envisioning words. You can also consult an in-app dictionary. Those in search of greater aid can tap the heart-shaped Best Word button. The app software magically figures the highest-scoring play for your current board; in exchange, you lose one of the hearts from your score box…and a small sliver of dignity.

GET SOCIAL: After quashing a copyright- and revenue-threatening blow from Facebook app upstart Scrabulous, Hasbro decided to host its own party. Whatever you think of the litigious past, this new effort's a fun way to face off. Invite pals you know or join games with strangers. Opponents don't need to have an iDevice; they make their moves online and you wage word war on the iPad. Go to the iPad's Settings app to turn on reminders when it's your turn to play.

TEACHER FEATURE: If you suspect that your latest move was more piddling than powerful, tap the left-side Teacher button. For your animation-watching pleasure, Professor von Wordsmith shows you the best possible play, delivering either a language lesson or a spasm of shame. Here the opening "even" (score: 14 points) pales against the jealousy-inducing "venge" (26 points), colored green to make sure you're properly envious.

More Apps for Scrabble

⊕ **HONORABLE MENTION**

Words with Friends HD

Free lite version | $2.99
Version: 3.1.3 | Newtoy

Credit John Mayer for much of this app's skyrocketing popularity. Back in 2009 the tabloid-troubled rocker tweeted: *Words with Friends' app is the new Twitter.* Whatever that meant, traffic exploded. Good news for the developers and good news for those not ready to commit to the official Scrabble app. Beyond the cheaper (or, with ads, free) price, the main lure of this no-nonsense app—you won't find nearly as many gaming options as in Scrabble—is its commitment to that title-touted friend feature. According to the developer, more than 1.6 million of 'em log on each day. In an instant, any one of them can be tapping tiles with you.

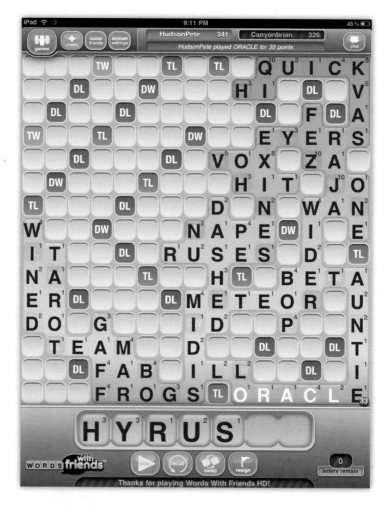

FRIEND FINDER: The Create button is your path to partnering up. You can invite someone you know or pick Random Opponent to get paired up. It's impressive how quickly it works; you've been warned. Gaming geeks will likely appreciate how few cheats are built into this app: no "find the best move," no dictionary. Just you, the board, and your opponent.

STOP & GO: Scrabble veterans might find the app introduces a peculiar rhythm. A quick volley might be interrupted by a long pause as your partner goes, say, to the dentist. If you'd like instant notification each time it's your turn, flip on the notifications in the iPad's Settings app.

Best App for Finding Hidden Objects

Little Things

Free lite version | $4.99
Version: 1.1 | Klicktock

If finding your keys drives you nuts, this treasure hunt may prove tough tapping. Then again, each puzzle's a beauty to look at and will likely entrance those wee-sized, non-key owners who don't yet associate hidden things with being late for work. A kind of visual acrostic, the game asks you to find various everyday objects—a guitar, scissors, a top hat—amidst a collection of hundreds of such things. Each layout is playfully arranged to itself resemble a familiar item: a horse, a dog, and so on. It's deceptively difficult (*why's the whale smaller than the fox?*) and the way it subtly forces you to mentally name your way through what your eyes scan across makes it a great learning tool for tots.

COLORFUL HAYSTACKS: Zoom in, pan around, tap. That's how to find stuff, but the twists between game styles keep the challenge fresh. Variations include: "speed stage" (find six different objects in 120 seconds), unlimited time challenges (similar but no time limit), and a tricky puzzle piece game. A nifty hinting mechanism shines a steadily shrinking spotlight on the region where the target resides.

HEALTH BENEFITS: Like the items you're looking for, the skills used in this app aren't immediately obvious. You improve memory (try keeping six nouns in your head while scanning for them), work on categorization (a sheep is still a sheep regardless of whether it's brown or black), and polish patience (stick with a plan of attack rather than skittering around, looking for clues pell mell).

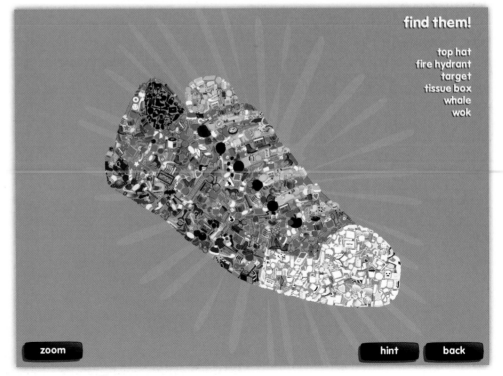

Best App for Word-Finding

The Ultimate Alphabet

Free lite version | $5.99
Version: 1.1.1 | Toytek

How's this for praise? Tough-to-follow instructions; annoying ads in the free version; and a puzzling decision not to Americanize British spellings. And yet: check it out if you're a crossword-loving geek in search of a new kind of fix, or want to peruse some of the oddest, artsy kitsch while bolstering your vocabulary. Each minutely detailed drawing is loaded with hundreds of visual clues that start with the same letter. So, on the "A" page, your job is to double-tap any item you recognize (*architect*, *aquarium*) and type in the corresponding word. It's as fascinating as it is frustrating. As one reviewer wrote: "If you want a cheap, easy game, go get Family Feud or something."

HELPING HANDS: Clues include both regular and cryptic ones familiar from normal crossword puzzles. There's also a jigsaw puzzle-style hinting device that nudges you toward the right answer the more times you try to assemble the word incorrectly. Tap the clue panel's question mark and then try to assemble the word by placing each of the word's scrambled letters in their appropriate spot.

MULTIPLE CHOICE: Many of the visuals represent more than one word. So you need to enter *adult*, *artilleryman*, and *apparel* to fully finish the guy in red standing behind the cannon. Really, there's no huge risk here: the initial app is a free download and gets you the letter A. From there you can decide whether this peculiar (and, some will say, peculiarly charming) app is meant for you.

Best Sliding Physics Puzzles Game

mentalBlock

Free lite version | $1.99
Version: 1.4 | Glowdot Productions

If you hated physics or those sliding tile puzzle games, do yourself a favor and pick another app. On the other hand, if spatial intelligence tests and reckoning the vectors of multiple moving objects delight you, you're gonna love this baby. It takes a little while to figure out the mechanics of this 21st century jigsaw puzzle, but once you get the hang of its rules, the gameplay is intriguing, even captivating. A Japanese stone garden aesthetic combined with an instrumental soundtrack that's one part underwater symphony, one part radio static infuses the game with an otherworldly quality that's soothing even as it challenges.

PLAYING WITH BLOCKS: Your main mission is to keep the green objects onscreen even as you clear the scattered, other-colored objects. Some of these disappear at the tap of a finger; others unmoor themselves only once neighboring blocks and bars disappear. What ensues is a series of careening shapes in motion, heading offscreen—all of which is perfectly okay, as long the sacred green boxes remain within the confines of the display.

RAINBOW POWER: Each color, as well as various direction-pulling arrows, imbue an item with its own moving properties: zap an orange bar that's restraining two inward-pointing blue blocks, for example, and the Brothers Blue spill headlong towards each other. The challenge grows as each level (55 in the full version vs. 15 in the Lite) presents a new, deviously placed arrangement. In each case, the green box resides somewhere in the midst, needing protection.

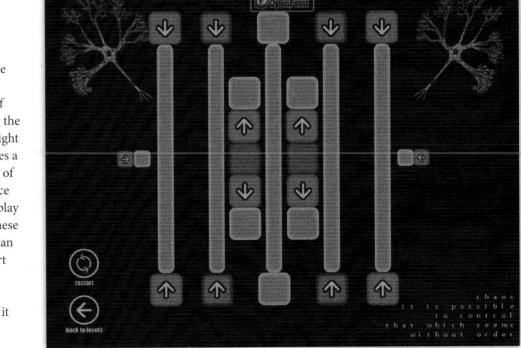

Best App for Racecar-Driving Traditionalists

Need for Speed: Shift for iPad

$12.99
Version: 1.0.1 | Electronic Arts

For old-school purists looking to log serious hours behind the virtual wheel, *Need for Speed: Shift* is fully worth the premium coin. Strap yourself in for a well-stocked ride: nearly endless car and track options (more of which open up as you rack up victories), some seriously escalating racing challenges (some races cut the laggard after each lap), and the sheer gorgeousness of insanely high-speed graphics. Upping the playability is an eclectic, adrenaline-infused soundtrack collection that won't make you want to fire up your own tunes.

DRIVER'S ED: The first time the app launches, check out the helpful tutorial to get up to speed on the basics. The short version: your iPad serves as a steering wheel—tilt it in the direction you want to turn. Acceleration is managed automatically by the app in Rookie mode; to handle acceleration and other controls (like gear shifting and braking) manually, switch to Pro or Expert.

PIMP YOUR RIDE: Keeping close to the green line and knocking fellow drivers off the track are two ways to beef up your budget when parts and car shopping. It'll take time to earn the $100,000-plus you need for the really cool rides, but after just a few moderately successful races (those you finish, for example) equipment upgrades like speed-boosting nitro are within reach.

Best App for Racecar-Driving Goofballs

Shrek Kart HD

$4.99
Version: 1.0.0 | Gameloft

If you're a four-hours-a-day gamer you'll probably grow bored with Shrek before finishing your first slice of 'za. But for those of us with, uh, jobs, this virtual auto arcade is the zippiest way to turn your iPad into an iCar. Pick from more than 10 racing machines and 15 tracks. Your basic mission, of course, is to complete the designated number of track loops ahead of your fellow racers. Knowledge of and affection for the movie franchise? Not required. Ability to enjoy yourself while maneuvering your iPad like a steering wheel, while dodging an ADD-inducing amount of onscreen stimulus? Mandatory.

SPEED TIPS: Tap the brake going into a turn for a boost of speed when you exit the curve (longer "drifts" get you greater speed boosts), and steer across on-track speed bands for quick jolts of mo'.

STEER CLEAR: Sitting some place where neighbors might not love your wild platter-waving steering gestures? Turn off the accelerometer and now you can simply tap the left and right side of the screen to move in those directions. If you opt for turn-by-tilting mode, go easy: as with most driving games on the iPad, wildly waving your 'Pad does only one thing—make you look silly.

HONORABLE MENTION

Parcel Panic

$0.99
Version: 1.3 | Mad Processor

If the thought of tooling around an oval bores you, consider adding a task to your racing regimen—say, picking up parcels, loading 'em in your pickup, and then speeding off to a designated drop point, all while the clock ticks. That's the core challenge in this charmingly illustrated app. Even more crowd-pleasing are its low price and dead-simple controls. Gas and break pedals are can't-miss clear and dummy-proof road and arrow markers show you where to head. For those who get frustrated quickly, here's a neat way to drive digitally.

Best App for Fighter Plane Combat

AirAttack HD
$0.99
Version: 1.0 | Art in Games

At just under a buck, Air Attack HD earns a bonus award for best price per screenful of graphical awesomeness. Your mission: steer an astonishingly nimble airship through a 3D-riffic missile storm of enemy fire. Eight levels await, each a new showcase for a Nazi-powered sea, ground, and air assault. The enemies you face range from standard fare (tanks, gunships) to physics-defying Franken-machines. It also richly rewards gaming fighter pilot newbies with a quickly grati-fying (experienced shooters might call it wimpy) rollup of enemy kills.

COCKPIT CONTROL: A generous "restart where you left off" op-tion means plenty of chances to hone your fighting chops. Experi-ment with the differ-ent control modes till you find the one that best suits your hand/eye skills. "Tilt" turns the iPad into a combo display/steer-ing wheel; "touch" lets you use finger-tracing control to pick your path. If you go the touch route, laying the iPad on a table makes it easier to sketch your plane's route.

ATTACK FLAK: The game favors pilots who bob and weave versus those who lay back and play a base-line, defensive game. Your plane's guns remain on auto fire, so all you need to con-centrate on is steering and controlling the special weapons you earn as you progress.

Best App for Helicopter Combat

Chopper 2
$2.99
Version: 1.1 | Majic Jungle Software

Helicopter legend Igor Sikorsky called the machines his firm manufactured the best chance we had to fulfill "mankind's ancient dreams of the flying horse and the magic carpet"; here's your chance to get a virtual taste of what inspired such rhetoric. Oh yeah, and while you're piloting your bird over multiple terrains (hills and valleys; desert; mountain and snow), you'll need to rescue civilians, ferry intelligence agents, and kill bad guys, all before time runs out or you crash. Aim your weapons by pointing the red line at what you want to hit; tap anywhere on the screen to fire. The stakes are high, but the overall vibe is, somehow, relaxing.

FLY THIS WAY: Three steering modes: tilt (towards and away from you control height; clockwise tilts propels you faster), touch (press an onscreen dial to control height; great if you've got airplane neighbors you don't want to elbow; lousy if you're a finger spaz), and remote. The lower you fly to the ground, the faster you go. But watch out: low altitude nuisances like trees, birds, and small weapons fire mean you can't just skim just above the surface.

OTHER ACTION: Special bonus for iPhone and iPod Touch owners: use your handheld to pilot your chopper. Worthwhile: pop in a pair of headphones and catch the nuances of a soundtrack that your 'Pad's speakers don't do justice ("Yes!", your rescued passengers cry; shrieks of agony from banged-up bad guys; the rustle of military drums). Kill tip: you can also scoop in and chopper-bash your enemies by bonking 'em with the nose of your bird. Ouch.

Best App for Air Traffic Controller Wannabes

Flight Control HD

$4.99
Version: 1.05 | Firemint

Sounds simple: safely land each plane by tracing its path to the appropriately colored runway. And sure enough, the first two or three arrive onscreen at nicely spaced intervals; the smokey lounge soundtrack and Fifties decor puts you in a martini kind of mood. But as more planes appear, the challenge behind this one-crash-and-you're-done affair becomes clear. You enter a state of aircraft-monitoring vigilance that's one part air traffic controller, one part chess player, as you try to reckon what the crowded airspace will look like as time passes. The fun lasts until a plane crashes, which, alas, always happens. Then it's just you, the groovy music, and the restart button.

INTERSECTION PERFECTION: The lines you draw can intersect, overlap, and pretzel through each other however you like…just make sure the planes themselves never collide. If you spot a problem path, the fix is a finger swipe away: just retrace a revised course. The app offers some help. It beeps and flashes red circles around planes flying too close for comfort.

ROOKIE REDIRECTS: Don't freak out each time you see the flashing red; wait and see if in fact collision appears inevitable. Top guns can speed up the action by tapping the lower-left fast-forward icon. And, hey, fly the friendly skies: multiplayer mode lets you split the screen and play against each other, or sync up with another iOS device and use each other's screen as additional landing pads.

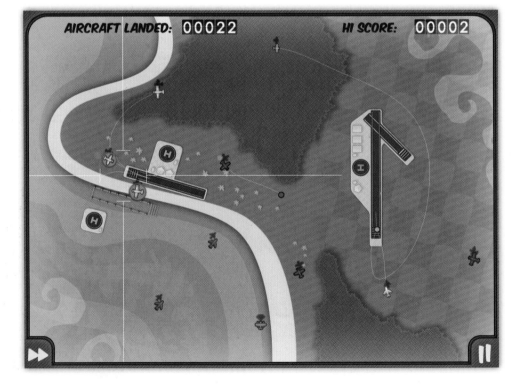

Best App for Flight Simulation

X-Plane for iPad

$9.99
Version: 9.621 | Laminar Research

Ladies and gentlemen, this is Cap'n iPad speaking. Please sit back and try to relax during what may be one heckuva bumpy ride. Unless you're wing certified, your first few takeoffs with this app are likely to be anything but smooth (the animated fire-fest crash gets a bit old). But devote a five-minute layover to the quick start tips on page 7 of the free manual (available at *http://bit.ly/xplane-ipad*) and soon they'll be calling you Captain Sullenberger at the office. And then, man, is this thing an aviator's dream. Forty planes, choppers, gliders—even a space shuttle—all ready for your flying pleasure. Flight spaces range from Alaska to Kathmandu. Wheels up!

UP AND AWAY: The short, short course for takeoff goes like this: set the flaps (the white knob in the lower-right corner) one-third of the way down from the top, turn off the brake by tapping its button, and slide the throttle (next to the flaps) all the way up. When you pick up enough speed, pull your iPad toward you, just like a regular pilot. To steer, tilt your iPad in whichever direction you want to turn.

TRAVEL TIPS: X-Plane'll kill ya for jerking the device around. Sloooowwly tilt it when turning, like you're trying to roll a jellybean across a silver platter. For a change of scenery (not to mention planes, weather conditions, and time of flight), tap the two-slider settings icon in the upper right; from the tabs that appear, you can fiddle with almost every flight feature imaginable.

Best Roller Coaster Design-and-Ride App

AirCoaster

$0.99
Version: 1.5 | Ziconic

Hands and feet inside the car at all times. And, for your stomach's sake, don't launch AirCoaster after a full meal. This roller coaster design-and-ride game is true enough to life to send any recently digested food in the wrong direction. Call it Reality Gaming. Most folks will opt to start by riding the app's demo track or sampling the sometimes rickety, occasionally insane creations of your fellow app owners. (Mr. AC Titan's "Death Trap" looks more like a nail bed on wheels than an amusement ride.) But once you tap around a bit, you might find the craft of track building its own draw. There's an odd charm in being able to build big things from what is, after all, still a pretty small device.

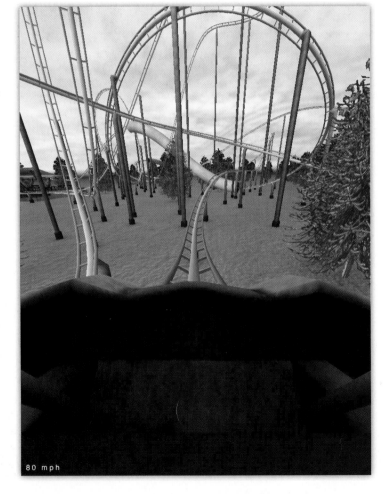

80 mph

TICKET, PLEASE: To sample the fun that awaits, start by taking a spin on the demo track (Tracks→Demo Track). For maximum real-life effect, pick in-the-car view; the icon on the bottom of the screen should show a track icon rather than the bird's-eye view's globe—that's what you see when you want to watch the ride from a distance.

HOP IN: The app also includes a full complement of share-what-you've-built and sample-others'-stuff tools: check out the Community button to get started and download some seriously stomach-churning and visually astonishing creations by your fellow 'Coasters.

DESIGN TIME: When ready, try your hand at track design: tapping the Editor button presents you with a box of controls only an engineer could love. Fear not. The basic idea: tap the track segment you want to edit, and then pick the control whose shape-shifting power you want to apply. Start, for example, with the spiral button which, yep, twists the track through as many loop-to-loops as you specify by using the slider.

ZOOMED IN: In general, it helps to zoom in (spread your fingers) and then tap and hold any of the big, blocky red, blue, or green arrows. Each darkens as it becomes movable. Once you've nudged any of the arrows, give the app a second to redraw the track. Move the control box out of the way by tap-and-holding the vertical lines atop the box; then move the whole shebang.

Best App for Dodging Slicing Swords

Hand of Greed

Free lite version | $2.99
Version: 1.0 | Branium Studios

You gotta give these guys credit for turning the Dungeon Dial up to 11 on this baby, a leader in the still uncrowded category of "tap the jewels before the swinging blades slice yer fingers" games. Consider what makes this Grade A Gothic: a Monks Gone Bad soundtrack featuring an apocalyptic choir chanting some kind of ode to darkness and misery; spurts of blood on your screen authentic looking enough that you might find yourself reaching for screen cleaner—if not a box of band-aids; and vaguely taunting, entirely cryptic slogans goading you into battle before each round: "As your life whithers/The crimson jewel heals." Shoot, even the typeface in this app looks medieval.

At Play

142

DOUBLE TAP: It's called *multi*-touch because you can jab the screen with more than one finger at a time. So peck those jewels with multiple digits. There's a miniature golf quality to the gameplay. Wait a beat to figure out the pulse of the swinging knives…but not too long. You have to complete each level before the fuse at the bottom burns out.

VILE VIAL: Keep an eye on the game's top-of-screen nick-meter: a gold-encrusted blood chamber whose contents represent, basically, the distance between you and death. Each time a blade slices your finger this receptacle empties a bit more, signaling your nearing exit to that great guillotine in the sky.

Best App for Golf on a Weird 2D Planet

Stick Golf HD

$2.99
Version: 2.4 | Jordan Schidlowsky

That golf is a game of reckoning trajectories and summoning your best inner geometer is nowhere more true than in this addictive, persistently ridiculous collection of golf courses. Want to test your ability to drive, say, upwards at an 85 degree angle so your ball careens off a cliff—magically hanging in the sky—and ricochets from there onto an adjacent, suspended-in-midair island, past the cactus tree and down the impossible-to-find-in-nature slope into the hole? Why not? Just remember not to toss your club in frustration—the iPad doesn't like hard landings.

RULES OF THE RANGE: Use the left and right arrows to control your shot's upward angle; then tap *Go!* twice: once to trigger the backswing, and again when you're ready to connect. Between theory and practice, however, sits more than a few traps. Most significant are the diabolical architectures practiced by this game's virtual course designers.

TRAPS AND HAZARDS: Perhaps trickiest of all is gauging the point at which to trigger the shot. Too soon and you'll dribble forward a weak mulligan; a Tiger slam, on the other hand, as often as not overshoots your target. As you work to calibrate the correct pressure, you'll no doubt rack up more than a few high-multiple bogies.

Best Multi-Colored Orb Squashing Game

Osmos for iPad

$4.99
Version: 1.6.3 | Hemisphere Games

You know how it goes: you're a tiny blue mote, trapped inside a digital petri dish and if you don't bulk up by hurling yourself into other blue motes, the red orbs will swallow you and the dreaded "Lifeform terminated" message appears. No one wants that to happen, and in this utterly original, finger-, mind-, eye-, and ear- captivating game, you'll quickly get the Newtonian-driven gist of how to control your micro blue sphere of life. Tap just to the *other* side of where you want to go and in true "every action has an equal and opposite reaction" fashion your blue guy skittles away from where you tapped (diminishing your mass with each energy burst). Welcome to life on Planet Osmos.

FINGER TIPS: Single finger swipes change the speed of time: to the left slows things down, to the right ups the tempo (the music's, too). For finer grained control, slow your swipe into a tap-and-slowly-drag motion in one direction or another. Zoom in and out with the usual pinch and spread; the latter especially can be useful early on in a level to get the lay of the land. Tap more quickly to increase your mote's speed, but the best advice is this: don't be a finger spaz. Slow, strategically placed taps are mostly what you need to keep yourself safe.

JOURNEYS, REWARDS: While the main objective in the dozens of levels in this game are to bulk up your blueness so that you, rather than your green or red foes do the squashing, this app is as much an exercise in mood soothing as it is a traditional survive-till-you die quest. Every so often, after completing a level, you may find yourself waiting, watching your mote and its sparkling, jellyfish innards career ever so softly around the screen. You're no longer a mote killing machine; it's just you and your iPad. Ohmmmmmm.

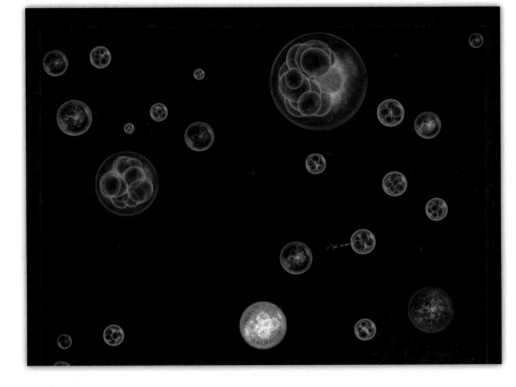

Best Crumpled Paper–Throwing Game

Paper Toss HD
$2.99
Version: 1.60 | Backflip Studios

Tossing crumpled paper into the trash might never qualify as an Olympic sport, but it's gotta be up there in terms of worldwide participants. Of course, that means including variants beyond the most popular, "I'm stuck in a cubicle and need to make sport of *something* in my life." PaperToss HD has got 'em all. Waiting in an airport, hangin' at a bar, and, of course: on the, er, can. The variables that separate chumps from champs are distance and wind speed (the latter controlled by a fan whose direction and velocity are represented by onscreen labels that change with each throw). Whichever camp you fall in, you're gonna need some serious screen cleaner after a few rounds.

TOSS AND TURN: For fan speeds under 1.00 or so, aim head on. More than 4.00 and it's time to summon your inner geometer. Like golf putters who aim up-slope, flick your trash drastically off course (or so it would seem). Then watch as the breeze catches your shot and curves it right into the receptacle.

RUBBISH ROOMS: Most venues have toughness settings hard-wired. Each come with a built-in collection of audio effects (random catcalls, ambient life noises); stick with it for awhile and you'll hear some entertaining gems. The scoreboard tracks how many consecutive shots you make; submit your high score online to see how you match up against fellow tossers.

Best App for Thinking Before Slicing

Cut the Rope HD
Free lite version | $1.99
Version: 1.0 | ZeptoLab

The App Store's brimming with so-called "physics games," which invite you to replicate real-world actions: pull a slingshot back and release it; bolt gears together to move stuff; squeeze air from a balloon towards a rope-dangled lollipop, thereby causing the candy to swing in a certain direction so that when you cut said rope its sugary charm drops into the mouth of a waiting frog. Sounds ridiculous, sure, but this wildly popular game has taken off for reasons that are as clear as they are charming: you really end up exercising your noggin trying to plan out exactly how and when to cut the rope in order to feed that dang frog and move on to the next level.

At Play

THE POINT? POINTS: Prior to feeding the frog, you need to rack up points. You do so by somehow pushing the dangling candy into the yellow stars—using balloon-pushed air, altitude-boosting bubbles, or plenty of other similarly silly methods. Spiked barriers often protect the frog; you need to navigate your shiny red circle around them.

TRAVELER'S AID: For help, enlist the travel services of those glistening bubbles: inject the candy inside one of those saviors and up and away you float till you puncture the thing at the point where you want it to descend. Speaking of: descents are what'll kill ya. If you send your circle southward and it misses the target mouth, it's level over.

Best Game for Killing Pigs With Birds

Angry Birds HD
$4.99
Version: 1.4.2 | Rovio Mobile

It's a rivalry born of an ancient wrong (though conveniently still viewable on YouTube at *youtu.be/1Bk_nqUQ0fc*): a band of birds gone mad with anger at a hungry pack of egg-thieving pigs. Their revenge? Slingshotting their bad bird-selves at the porkers wherever they seek shelter. You are their General, your finger the catapulting trigger that aims them. It's earned some of the highest ratings—over a half a million—in the App Store and three minutes in its company reveals why: this game is as hysterical as it is addictive. Something about the ridiculous sound effects and the just-right difficulty of figuring out how to catapult your birds at the right pig-slaughtering angle. Good times.

BIRD BOMBERS: Two ways to kill the porcine posse: bonk 'em with a slingshot-flung bird or deliver your death blow via some object whose collapse you cause by your airborne fowl. As you progress through each level, new birds become available, each with its own talents. For example, stroke the screen as your small blue chicks are mid flight and three new birds will emerge from the one that you launched. Or tap the screen to spring your yellow fliers into turbo mode.

PULLED PORK: Pinch your fingers together for a wider-angle view. You might get some advantage in rapid-fire launching, since the wobbling structures are more susceptible to toppling compared to waiting for them to stop swaying. Then again, you might want to take the time to recalibrate and aim carefully. These are the kinds of difficult decisions a chicken general must make in the war on pork.

Best Game for Ninja Wannabes

Fruit Ninja HD

$4.99
Version: 1.1 | Halfbrick Studios

The best apps get you to swipe, pinch, and spread fingers in ways that simply can't be done using a mouse or video game controller. At times, the action even beats real life, like when you're trying to samurai-sword slice an onslaught of fruit without triggering bombs falling in their midst. Perhaps the only downside to Fruit Ninja HD is its inexplicable—and, to some, inescapable—addictiveness. What on earth is going on here that compels otherwise gainfully employed, tax-paying adults to stay at this swipefest just to best their previous high score?

FRUIT LOOPS: The object is deceptively simple: finger swipe your sword through each banana, strawberry, and so on that some unseen juggler tosses in front of you. Three misses or an errant clank on one of the randomly appearing bombs and your ninjaness is no more. Don't forget that you've got 10 fruit-fighting weapons: use *all* your fingers…but don't give into finger flailing; skilled ninjas wield their weapons with grace and precision.

MULTIPLAYER MADNESS: Play on your own or, for fullscreen finger-swiping fun, face off against a fellow ninja. Multiplayer mode puts each of you in charge of one half of the screen, where you both slice off against a falling fruit salad. Wanna pimp out your sword collection? Visit the Dojo to select new styles, more of which become available the more you play.

Ninjatown: Trees of Doom

$2.99
Version: 1.5.3 | Venan Entertainment

How can you resist an app that promises to let you "fly on giant moustachios"? And who calls 'em "moustachios"? Who cares. This tree climbing, Ninja-themed romp will probably be most folks' first chance to indulge in arboreal antics since about second grade. Two tree trunks border either side of this portrait-mode orientation-only vertical race. Scamper upwards in either of two play modes: Classic (climb till you die) or Timed (hit checkpoints before the clock runs out). The goal is to accumulate points while avoiding game-ending falls.

TREE HUGGERS:
Trace your finger up a trunk to climb or tap the facing log to switch sides. Branch-flinging is another mode of transport. In between all that, you'll face an assortment of water-slicked stretches, hovering between-tree baddies, and barkless patches that'll send you falling to your mortal finish. As you get into the groove, the finger action resembles a stutter tap dance as you quickly jump, drag, and jump again.

TREETOP TIPTOE:
You gotta tap nimbly from side to side to make your way up the bare barkless patches. And, oh, about those 'stachios? It's the game's version of an express elevator: get aboard and you'll head north quickly.

Best App for Simon Says–Style Repetition

muBlip

$3.99
Version: 1.2.0 | para9

Can you tap your foot, chew gum, and mimic the trippy dippy arm snaking of that guy groove-walking in front of you? Would you want to? If you answered yes and have a modicum of A/V-friendly short-term memory, this "rhythm & shapes game" is for you. In each of a dozen or so increasingly difficult challenges, the geometrical shapes on your screen light up in a pattern that matches the accompanying techno-flavored beats. Your job is to replicate these movements—tap a lit-for-a-beat circle here, drag-to-connect two bars there—when the tune plays again. This game taxes your brain, which is exactly the point. Mesmerize your mind even as you build its memory muscle.

MIRROR MOTION: The thin timeline bar at the top of the screen is your guide from pattern rehearsal through live match. A white progress bar advances from left to right: in the red zone, you watch the objects below and try to remember the action. Each of the blue zones represents consecutive chances to get it right. Your score arrives as a percentage of all taps and drags done correctly.

TRAINING TAPS: It helps (and won't hurt) during the red watch-and-learn phase to finger the screen in an effort to etch the movements in your head. If you're having a hard time matching the rhythm, try the Moog Rock sequence. It's faster paced than many of the other levels, but its progression is more orderly—left to right, top to bottom—compared to the random Twister sequences found elsewhere in the game.

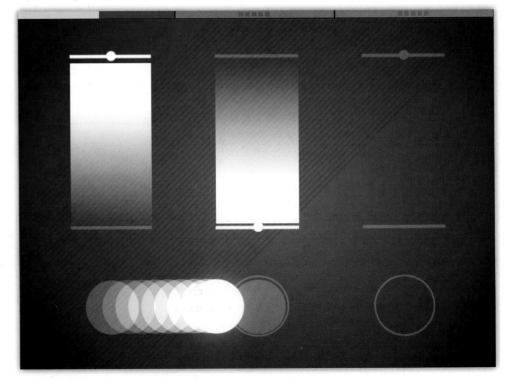

At Home

Its lightweight, easy-to-start-up nature makes the iPad just a click or two more convenient to summon for help than, say, a laptop. And in the opportunities created by that small improvement, we're starting to see the device and its supporting band of apps deliver a collection of aids that would make Martha Stewart smile. (That is, when she's not creating her own app: not covered in these pages, her iPhone-only *Martha's Everyday Food* is still a worthwhile download for fans of the diva of domesticity.) The kitchen category offers the most promise—jiminy, the riches that await a truly top-notch recipe app. But in keeping with our pledge to deliver only the highest quality-bar topping efforts, the first wave doesn't offer many gems to spotlight. On the shopping front, buying stuff online is something we're all used to by now; the iPad makes long product listings—not to mention checkout lines—disappear through apps that offer much improved browsing. And who doesn't want a way to sharpen the minds of kids and parents alike? For those in the mental minor leagues, app makers have done an impressive job in exploring the territory where education meets entertainment. Finally, lifelong learners aren't left out. A small but growing collection—including some jaw-dropping examples of how things like 3D presentations and video can help teach topics—give post grads a way to better their brains. All in all, a household niche is starting to emerge for the iPad, a kind of *Better Homes and Gardens* meets the Jetsons.

Best App for Craigslist Browsing

Craigslist Pro for iPad
$0.99
Version: 1.12 | Escargot Studios

Craigslist may have revolutionized the classified ad game, but it sure didn't win on the strength of site design skills. Here's a family-friendly version of a typical critique: it's a butt-ugly, user-unfriendly web surfing experience. Enter this app, which pulls off a stunning repackaging feat. Using big blocks of finger-friendly space, it presents you with an easy way to perform all of Craig's core activities: search, browse, and post. The site's home page is where you pick your location (adding more than one is fine), the type of thing you're looking for, and filter options like whether to include photos or, if you're looking for housing, minimum and maximum prices.

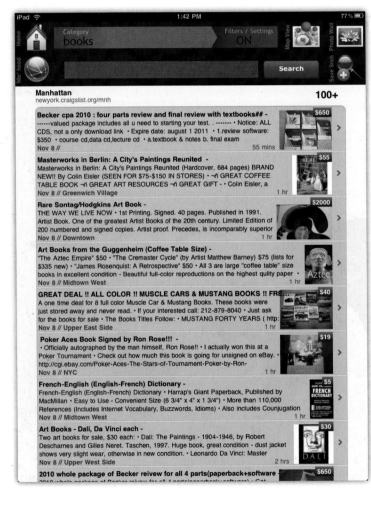

NEEDLE & HAY-STACKS: Searching and browsing are among the app's special skills. You can save custom queries for quick reuse, browse all the listings in one or more locations in a particular category, or hone in on a particular neighborhood in a big city. In-app tools let you email a reply or view the listing's location on a map.

PICTURE PERFECT: The Photo Wall button on the search results page alone is worth the price of the entire app. Tap it for a wall of pix, transforming what was a painfully slow, page-by-page browsing slog on the Web, into a quick scan for that porcelain mouse vase, vacation house, whatever. The List button gets you back to a more traditional text-heavy view, with a bit more description.

Best App for Amazon Shopping

Windowshop

Free
Version: 1.0.4 | Amazon.com

While Amazon's web shop more or less works by using the iPad's browser, this app version is a head-to-toe improvement—especially over those "not quite meant for tapping" multiple-level menu options on the site's left side. Instead, you get a fat-finger-friendly grid that's ready for swiping, panning, and flick scrolling. All of which makes category-based browsing one of the easiest ways to stroll through the store. Perusers can choose either from the readymade sections (Baby, Beauty, Books), or a Recommended For You option, which presents a complete replica of each area, stocked with computer-picked matches. Those who've got a specific item in mind can, of course, search.

DRAG & DISCOVER: In a potential first for grid-based layouts, you can actually drag the spread in *any* direction, not just vertically or horizontally. This kind of freeform, diagonal dragging offers a slightly more serendipitous way to wander the store's virtual aisles. Interested in a more conventional path? Tap the upper-left Browse button for the familiar list of shop categories.

ITEMS OF INTEREST: Individual product pages look pretty similar to their web-based brethren. Those who spring for Amazon Prime (pay in bulk for free shipping) get all their usual delivery options to pick from. And the one-click, quick checkout settings you set up on the site are all here, too. You can also read reviews, add to your wish list, and email product info to friends.

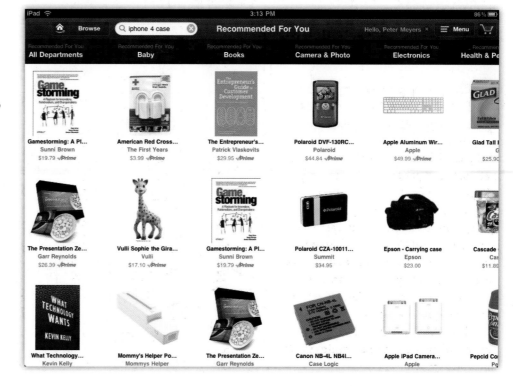

Best App for eBay Shopping

eBay for iPad

Free
Version: 1.3.1 | eBay

Like most people looking for a ladybug-shaped pencil sharpener/photo holder, your first instinct is probably: *someone's gotta be selling that on eBay.* But trips to the website, despite the company's best efforts to prettify its face and streamline its features, can be overwhelming. That's the purpose of this app: giving shopping mortals an easy way to navigate and buy. In other words, power users won't find their needs met (most notable omission: a way to post items for sale). But if you're in a deal-hunting mood—and these days, who isn't?—the app is a friendly way to step through a store that sells many more mainstream goods than it did back in the Purple Pez Dispenser Era.

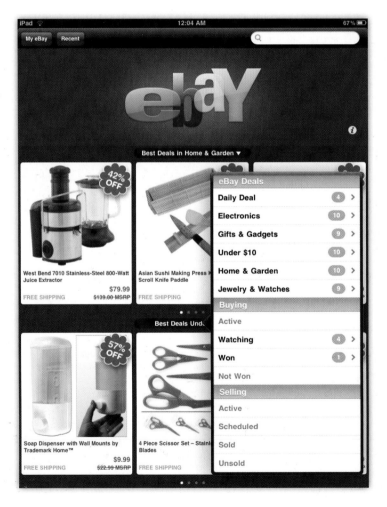

TWO-FACED APP: The home page features deals eBay is pushing (tap any "Best Deal" label's white triangle to pick a different category). To enter the belly of the beast, where the masses hawk their goods, slug in whatever you're looking for in the upper-right oval.

GO TIME: Placing a bid works just like it does on the regular site: enter the most you're willing to pay and the system takes over from there. The service starts by wagering your money just above the current high bid and then increments it automatically, as other bids arrive, stopping either when you've reached the limit you specified or the auction's end.

THE RESULTS: If your search turns up too many items, there are plenty of ways to narrow things down. The Advanced button controls search prefs like the seller's distance from you, time left in an auction, and whether to exclude items that charge for shipping. Press the upper left-corner's $-sign and a price range band appears at the bottom of the screen; drag either end to discard items outside the high and low targets you set.

DECISIONS, DECISIONS: Once you sniff out an item of interest, tap its photo on the results grid. The three-tabbed box that appears gives you tire-kicking info. Seller ratings (especially the volume of responses and those offered in recent months) are a good measure of reliability. The Watch button lets you add the item to your My eBay panel, where it remains for quick access: kind of like a Favorites shortcut for the auction crowd.

Best App for Stealth Mental Challenges

The Jim & Frank Mysteries: The Blood River Files HD

$2.99
Version: 1.3 | 99 Games

This is the *Deceptively Delicious* of brain-exercise apps: an adventure story vehicle for a series of mind- and finger-challenging quizzes and tasks. The app starts you off with simple stuff: you're asked to do things like chop wood by tapping your finger at quickly appearing bark markers. Soon enough, however, some of these suckers get tough: *Carla is four times her daughter's age. In 30 years, her daughter will be half as old as Carla. How old are Carla and her daughter now?* Up for dozens and dozens more of those cranial stretches? Take yourself a trip down the Blood River.

HINT MINT: Hints can be unlocked either by paying for them (cost: about 3 cents per hint, sold in dollar bundles) or using the hidden currency embedded throughout the game. These aren't flat-out answer shortcuts, but they do expose a route-to-progress that might strike old-school learners as unacceptably easy for young'uns who get easily discouraged (or who've got their own iTunes Store budget for buying in-app hints).

TALK NERDY TO ME: Some of the dialogue is as clunky and forced as that other popular entertainment genre in which the plot and characters' words are incidental to the, uh, main action. But let's be clear: the story here *is* secondary. If you don't like mental challenges, you're not gonna love these boys' scintillating conversations. Speaking of grating media: the Renaissance Faire Muzak soundtrack can, mercifully, be turned off in the Options menu.

Best App for Flashcards

Mental Case Flashcards for iPad

$4.99
Version: 3.2.4 | The Mental Factory

Pop quiz: what's the best way to turn your iPad into a flashcard-creating-and-reviewing machine? Mental Case, a great app for fans of the ponder-'n-check learning method. The "front" of each card poses a question; think, then swipe to view the flipside. Add audio to either question or answer and you've got yourself a learning tool that does what cardboard can't. Plenty of ways to get cards into the app: use the companion computer program (Mac-only, alas; see *macflashcards.com*), create new ones on the iPad itself, or from *Flashcard-Exchange.com*, a site filled with thousands of shared card collections—everything from anatomy to vocabulary.

SKILL DRILL: If you install the Mac-based program, when you sync the app with your computer (works over WiFi: nice), your progress is tracked on your Mac. The program is where you can configure "lessons": the order and frequency in which each card appears. (For those without the Mac program, head to the iPad app's Library, tap Edit, and then flick on Lesson Schedule; the app uses a "spaced repetition algorithm" to determine the most brain-enriching sequence.)

CARD TRICKS: The app makes it easy to customize any card in any collection: either ones you've created yourself or those downloaded from the online exchange. When you're ready to jump in and study, either tap the Library's Lesson (for a selection of cards that draws from everything stored in the app) or tap a "case" name, followed by the upper-right corner's Play icon, and then, finally, All Notes in Selected Case.

Best App for Pop-Up Books

Headspin
$0.99
Version: 1.1 | State of Play Games

Pop-up books seem at once perfect for and impossible to pull off on the iPad. There's that stubborn matter, after all, of the popping up. At least with the current iPad, that screen is forever flat. Headspin devotes its energies to high-end illustrations that have a nice jump-up quality. At heart, this book's really more of a pattern-matching game than a story; the narrative, such as it is, arrives on a series of cards that appear each time you finish a challenge, which consists of flipping paired items so they're symmetrically arranged. Not the most compelling gameplay, sure, but remember this app's mainly for kids— the same repetition lovers who watch one episode of *Blue's Clues* for a week in a row.

POP OVER: Every spread presents a new collection of items that spring to life, as well as a new timed challenge (the red pointer arcs from right to left, ticking off your available seconds). Success lies in tapping the objects on the right side whose orientation *doesn't* mirror the partner on the left. The little brown men? They skitter around while the clock is ticking, upping the difficulty of your work.

TICK TOCK: As you progress through the story, your available time shortens per challenge. The scoring's *Jeopardy*-style: if you keep getting things wrong, you soon find yourself in negative point territory. Since it is mainly for kids, though, the replay opportunities are generous. As for future books like this, the developer says more apps are in the works with more story, less game.

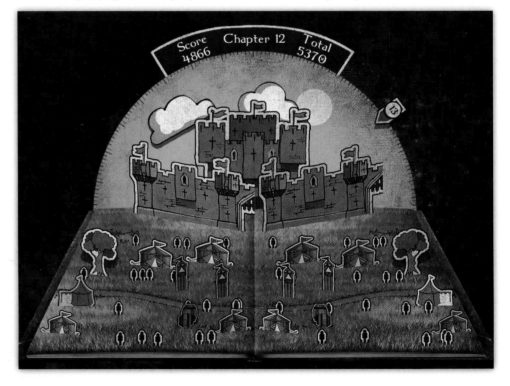

Itsy Bitsy Spider HD

$1.99
Version: 1.0 | Duck Duck Moose

Let's loosen, slightly, this definition of "pop-up", shall we? After all, the whole point of those print contraptions is to give kiddies a way to interact with the story—to touch the page and make something happen. And with the iPad, there's no shortage of ways to pull that off. Here the famous story unfolds on what's essentially one wide page. As your child taps on various things—the pivotal spout, the yard where Mr. Sun does his blow dryer thing—the spider crawls across the canvas. But don't consider this meager page count a shortcoming; instead, it's a seamless, rich stage, filled with activities, woven around the central ditty, all for the wee ones to explore.

READER REWARDS: This rendition sticks to the famous up-and-down-the-spout action that pretty much everyone knows. (Forgot the other verses? Ah, the joys of toddler-free living.) But the app's crammed full of tap- and swipe-triggered ways to explore this short, short story: kid-friendly lessons on the sun, birds, and banana slugs; a look at a caterpillar's journey from slug to butterfly; the endless thrill of puddle splashing.

SOUND STUDIO: The app even offers a way to let your little ones record their own voice as the narrator. Touch the start screen's note icon and sing away. Truth be told, though, this feature is better implemented on *Wheels on the Bus*, an app by the same developer, where karaoke-style prompts help chunk up each verse. The one-verse nature of this app doesn't lend itself as well to hearing the up-and-down verse over and over.

Best App for Kids' Books, Reimagined

Miss Spider's Tea Party for the iPad

Free lite version | $7.99
Version: 2.2 | Callaway & Kirk

Most kids' books on the iPad—at least in this first wave of the Great App Store Rush—are digital snapshots of a print edition. Maybe a little new media juju's been added (panning and zooming across pages are common tricks), but the pulp ancestry is unmistakeable. The same can't be said for *Ms. Spider*: a digital confection that betrays little hint of its print origins. To call it a book is only about a quarter right. You also get a handful of other thematically related but functionally distinct mini apps. Together, it's practically guaranteed to delight nearly any toddler susceptible to a charming tale about a friendless spider.

SWIPE FEST: You can hardly swipe a finger without running into some really clever, kid-friendly touches: in traditional read-the-book mode, as each page appears, bulls-eyes flash for a second or so over tappable hotspots (stroke Ms. Spider's brow, for example, to watch her cry).The reason? To remind where the kid can tap.

REPETITIVE TREATS: A whole new set of animations and audible trinkets lie waiting for kids who explore the Read version (vs. the watch-only video enactment, itself a marvel of well-synced music and animation). For an audience comprised of wee tots who *love* watching things over and over and over, the decision to present the same story repackaged with new, hidden treats is genius.

MIX AND MATCH: The Match game (a reimagination of Memory) adds a nifty can't-do-this-on-a-board-game twist: in addition to visual clues, tapped tiles trigger sounds, so kids burnish their audio memory, as well as their visual muscles. Pick between 16- and 30-card layouts, depending on how much memory your cranial computer is packing.

SAFE DRAWING: Don't miss the four drawing mode buttons at the bottom of the painting module. From left to right, they: confine wild finger jabbings to paint only inside the lines; unleash that same paint wherever the fingers land but preserve the underlying drawing; same as previous but colors cover up the base drawing; and present our nation's artists-in-training with a blank canvas.

⊕ **HONORABLE MENTION**

Bartleby's Book of Buttons Vol. 1

$2.99
Version: 1.0 | Octopus Kite/Monster Costume

This clever little interactive book really does justice to that typically meaningless term: you really must interact with the pages in this lovely tale to see the story unfold. What's going on here will likely outstrip the abilities of most toddlers, but should be a nice challenge for those tykes and tween types ready for their iBooks to do more. Each page in this shortish tale—about a button-bewitched boy named Bartleby—features a challenge, the solving of which requires a careful reading of the page's text and then a corresponding manipulation of the buttons, dials, switches, and so on that adorn each page.

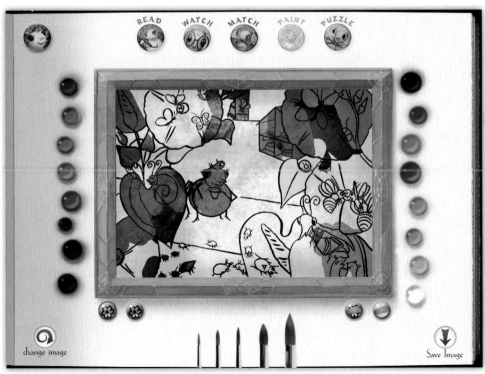

Best App for Practicing Math

www.thatquiz.org

ThatQuiz Math

$3.99
Version: 1.2 | ThatQuiz

Quick, off the top of your head: which is greater, −7 or −12? If that's a no-brainer, wise guy, how about figuring integrals like $\int_1^3 28x^3dx$? Fact is, though, this app isn't aimed at stumping or ego-boosting. It's a dependable, useful tool for students of all ages. Check out *thatquiz.org* for a before-buying preview of the exercises. Integers, fractions, concepts, and geometry are the main topics covered, and with almost 20 subcategories (inequality, probability, and so on), there'll be some real weight behind that threat: "Get a score of greater than 9 out of 10 on your exponents and then you can get back on YouTube."

MULTIPLE CHOICES: Each exercise comes with a left-side panel where you can customize things like number of questions, difficulty level, and topic-specific controls. Even in something relatively simple like inequalities, you can quickly flick on advanced settings that do things like add division and negatives to the values you're comparing, leading to challenges like: "(-22)÷(-2) > = < 36÷3".

FEEDBACK LOOPS: Get an answer wrong and the app helpfully displays the correct answer next to what you guessed. When the quiz is complete, a summary screen shows a list of your misses (again, with what you thought was the right response), plus offers a chance to dive back into the quiz, reviewing just the ones that stumped you.

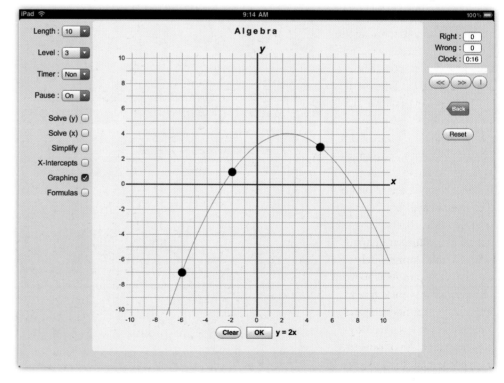

Mathboard

Free (MathBoard Addition) | $3.99
Version: 1.4.3
PalaSoftware

Practice, practice, practice. From foul-throw shooters to guitar virtuosos, repetition is the gateway to mastery. For your number crunchers in training, one way to make the path to math fun and reasonably instructive is MathBoard. A well-stocked collection of fill-in-the-blank and multiple-choice problems, the app's got all the hall of fame basics covered: addition, multiplication, subtraction, division, squares, cubes, square roots. The chalkboard motif is easy on the eyes and gets put to actual use in the scratchpad space. Timed quizzes help those SAT-aspirants who need to move their mental gears quickly. For muffed answers, Problem Solver is a step-by-step walkthrough of how to arrive at the correct answer.

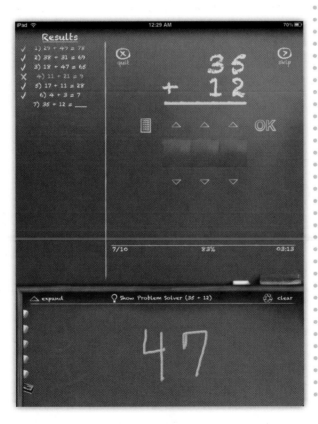

Math Bingo

$0.99
Version: 1.3 | ABCya.com

Kids like games. This app's a bingo-style math skills game. You can do the math on the thinking here. Addition, subtraction, multiplication, and division all get tested. Answer a question correctly to win a spot on the grid. Higher level challenges ain't cakewalks (quick: 17 times 16 is?). You'll also find a couple (marginally) math-related extras: Bingo Bug Bungee lets the wee ones play a Breakout-style video game—a bit of score-tallying needs doing at the end. And a tap-'n-move avatar playpen, well, maybe it helps them figure *x,y* coordinates while you soldier through another chorus of "wow," "wee," "yippee," chirped against a *Clockwork Orange*-y soundtrack that you can't silence (other than muting your iPad). What price your child's mental development?

Best App for Learning ABCs

Interactive Alphabet for iPad

$2.99
Version: 1.5 | Pi'ikea St.

Summon your inner three-year-old for this one. Remember that time when you could sing the A-B-C song but still answered questions like "What letter does *Apple* begin with?" by declaring: "Daddy, I found a booger!"? The target audience, in other words, for this visually appealing, aurally entertaining, and simple-to-operate app is wee tots whose brains are still a work in progress. Repetition, of course, is key for these li'l learners, and here they get a chance to tap, retap, and repeat through a flashcard collection of animated letters, each of which illustrates a common object.

ALPHA LEARNERS: Access an A to Z lineup via the "ABC" tab on top of the screen. That start page is also where you'll find options to cycle through different soundtracks (soothing, snip-snappety, sure-to-annoy-any-adult, and, blessedly, mute). On each letter's page subtle visual clues queue your kid about what to tap: the bobbing Jack in his signature box, a whale's waving tale and fins, and so on. Fun touch treats are never far away: the xylophone works more or less like its real-world counterpart.

ADVANCED TOUCHES: Some letters deliver treats to diligent, curious tappers. Drag the sun down to the horizon in "B is for Beach" and the scene goes dark. "Play" the goose and gosling: each one delivers a differently pitched honk and by "playing" the quartet, you can quack out a fun tune. Use the quill ("Q") to draw; lift your finger off the display to start a new line.

Best App for Learning to Write *A, B, C…*

Intro to Letters

$4.99
Version: 1.0 | Montessorium

Handwriting may someday give way to that MindMouse system that Apple surely must be working on. For now our littlest iPadders still need to learn how to wield a pencil for something other than jabbing their siblings. Intro to Letters is a Montessori-powered approach to the basic art of writing. Even if you're not a disciple of this occasionally humorless school of teaching (dudes, would it kill ya to include a bright color or two?) the craft that's gone into this app, which lets kids trace letters, hear spoken versions, and compare their own recorded audio, is clear.

LEARNING PATHS: The basic teaching method here is watch and repeat. A letter appears onscreen sporting a shadow-bubble icon; junior watches as the bubble animates its way across the proper drawing path. Next comes his turn to take a finger and trace the line for himself. The app's smart enough to know when wrong turns have been taken; gentle arrow reminders appear, nudging him to retrace and fix.

DIVERSE DRILLS: Five kinds of lessons help cover all aspects of the alphabet: pronunciation, letter recognition (including upper- and lowercase), even slightly advanced topics like phonograms (paired letter sounds like "ue" and "qu"). To help out, canned recordings play as each letter appears, distinguishing, for example, between a letter's sound and its name: "guh" vs. "gee". The audio practice module lets kiddies record themselves after hearing the narrator.

Best App for Brain Studies

3D Brain

Free

Version: 1.1 | Dolan DNA Learning Center

Meant for neuroscience students, this app's a worthy download for plain ol' noggin owners, too. In addition to civilian-friendly prose, you get a first-hand look at how digital textbooks really can do more than print. The showcase feature: two dozen-ish 3D renderings of various neural structures. Twirl, zoom in, and rotate till your own head spins. Start your exploration in Whole Brain view; the accompanying info is divvied up into the same chunks you get with other brain parts: an intro followed by details on things like case studies, associated functions, and links to current research. The brainiacs behind this work are the good people at the world-famous Cold Spring Harbor lab.

CEREBRAL SPIN: Don't forget to spin each model every which way: up, down, left, and right. The 3D drawings are richly illustrated at every angle. Especially cool are the structures that occupy both left and right sides. As you rotate the Corpus Callosum view, for example, each hemisphere turns transparent as it moves onto the foreground, giving you a better look at Mr. CC's center-straddling position.

BRAIN DUMP: Key parts in each view are colorized, but you'll want to tap the Labels button to see what's what. Once you've finished playing with the models, some serious learning awaits in the info panel. The case studies in particular connect human stories with brain science and the linked articles in the "Research reviews" section are great for deep dives into further reading.

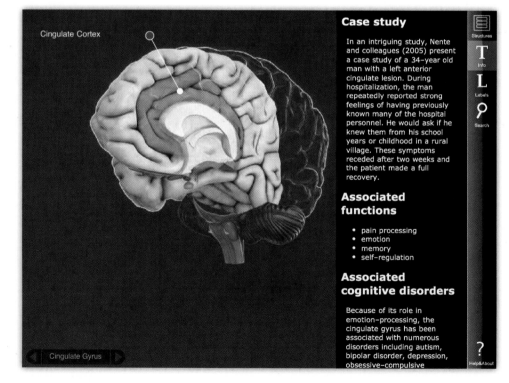

Case study

In an intriguing study, Nente and colleagues (2005) present a case study of a 34-year old man with a left anterior cingulate lesion. During hospitalization, the man repeatedly reported strong feelings of having previously known many of the hospital personnel. He would ask if he knew them from his school years or childhood in a rural village. These symptoms receded after two weeks and the patient made a full recovery.

Associated functions

- pain processing
- emotion
- memory
- self-regulation

Associated cognitive disorders

Because of its role in emotion-processing, the cingulate gyrus has been associated with numerous disorders including autism, bipolar disorder, depression, obsessive-compulsive

Best App for the Periodic Table

The Elements

$13.99
Version: 1.0.2.1 | Theodore Gray

High school chemistry may be a distant memory, but even English majors will wanna crack the spine on this digital book—a visual encyclopedia of the periodic table. It offers an early glimpse at how the book itself is likely to change as tablets take off. The main event is a pair of pages showcasing each element. What animates the learning experience are fab photos of each item in action in the real world (twirl to view from every angle) and a built-in browser hard-wired to a science and stats database for further study. For a deep dive to look up things like the current price of gold, tap the multiple-sided red star on the first page of any profile. This, in short, is one smart book.

BACKGROUND BASICS: Start with a look at the app's least sexy section: a plain prose intro to the periodic tables and the quantum mechanics behind its signature grid. There you also get a nice breakdown of what's in each element's right-side stats column. A quick preview: the far-right graphic shows the temperatures at which the element's state shifts between solid, liquid, and gas.

SPIN & LEARN: Page two of each profile is where you get to learn and twirl. Brief and lively essays offer accessible reads. Double-tap any of the images for a larger view. In most cases, you can give objects a lazy Susan look, but for some of the video images your horizontal swiping acts like a slo-mo rewind and fast-forward slider.

Best App for Keeping Time

Night Stand HD
Free lite version | $1.99
Version: 1.5.2 | SpoonJuice

Like the calculator app, a built-in clock is another freebie Apple withheld from the iPad (both come on the iPhone). Travelers especially will want to plug this gap in order to bypass that 6th circle of hell ritual: hotel room clock radio fiddling. Developers have flooded the App Store with options, including displays in binary code, time floating in a sea of bubbles, and, of course, equations that you first have to solve in order to figure out what time it is. Please. Nightstand HD gives you the goods: a world display for tracking multiple cities, a stop watch; no-frills weather reports, and, yep, a simple-to-set alarm clock. Stunning graphics make these clocks a pleasure to watch.

VERSION VARIATION: Budget travelers will probably want to go for the perfectly fine Lite version, which offers the world clock lineup (six displays appear) and an LED readout for the main clock. Customize the latter's color or adjust it or any other clock's brightness with an easy to remember, middle-of-the-night gesture: the double tap. Premium-only benefits include waking to iTunes music, those tiny weather reports, and the stopwatch.

ALARMING NEWS: If you haven't yet installed the multi-tasking version of the iPad OS (version 4.2 and later) then be sure to put your 'Pad to sleep after setting the alarm (as opposed to switching to another app). Those who have the new OS, go alarm crazy: even if you switch to another app, this is one nudge that'll come get you. Softening the blow is the lovely assortment of sounds (birds, glass, modern)—unless you opt for Scream.

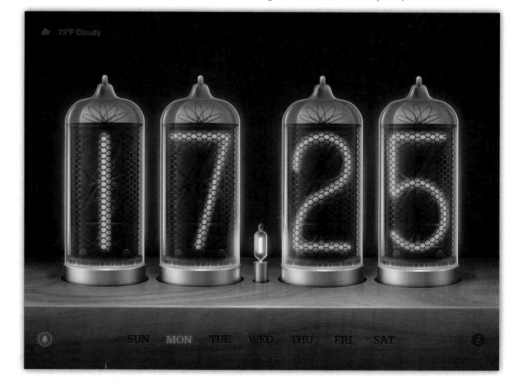

Best App for Measuring Stuff

Multi Measures HD

$0.99
Version: 1.0 | SkyPaw

This guy's the Ginzu Knife for those who need to measure the world around them. It not only serves as a ruler, but it also does duty as a protractor, level (surface and spirit!), plumb bob, and seismometer. Most folks will get their money's worth from the ruler alone. Measuring the short stuff's easy. For objects under 7 3/4" (the horizontal width of the iPad screen) simply situate your post card, wood screw, or whatever, move the slider, and you're good to go. For longer items, a measure/move/swipe three-step does the trick (tap the "i" button for details). You probably won't want to use this app for mission-critical assignments, but for common questions it'll do just fine.

ON THE LEVELS: The surface and spirit tandem can come in handy. The spirit version is the one you probably know from hanging pictures around the house. A one-tap simple calibration button lets you establish a baseline measure; from there, just use the thing like the carpenter's mainstay. The surface variety works the same way, except its Holy Grail is horizontal flatness.

MOTION CONTROL: The seismometer is probably useless for most people, but it's a heckuva lot of fun to play with. In this capacity, the app stands guard, monitoring any kind of movement on your iPad and registers its findings on a lie detector–style graph. Should your device move beyond the boundaries you've selected (you can monitor any or all x-, y-, and z-axes), an alarm sounds.

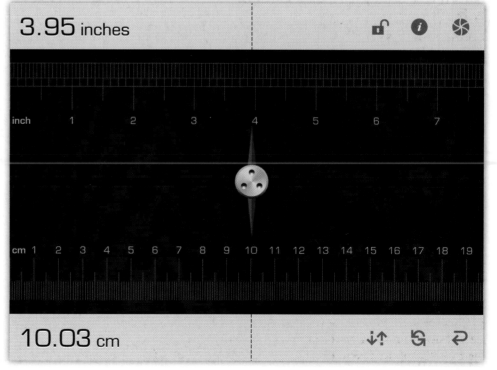

Best App for Grill-Side Guidance

Weber's on the Grill for iPad

$4.99
Version: 1.0 | Weber-Stephen Products

Pay for a recipe app from a grill manufacturer? What's next—a monthly shopping fee from your fridge? But wait a sec before shutting the lid on this virtual grilling companion. It's a beautifully designed, nicely cooked app, loaded with recipes, easy to navigate, and brimming with the kind of in-app tools (portable grocery lists, embedded timers) that justify the developer's choice to go app rather than ebook. Add in the iPad's ample screen size (and a suitable holder or stand) and this guide will help you shine no matter what logo's on the side of your grill.

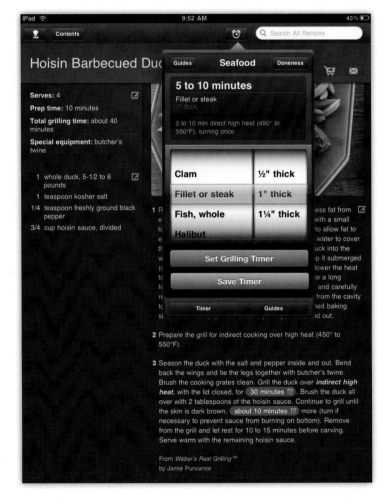

GOOD TIMING: Saved Timers let you store a custom timer for, say, 1 1/2" thick filet mignon. Each canned setting comes with its own cooking tips (when to shift from direct to indirect heat, for example). These and other built-in timers make it easy to keep track of your food's progress. Set these clocks and a countdown tracker appears top of screen.

NIFTY NOTES: Another great idea: easy-to-access "make a note" icons, so you can jot down tips that inevitably occur when cooking in the field ("Water down Edna's gin fizz *before* she slices the mango.")

At Home

LIST MASTER: The app's stocked with user-friendly touches: the emailed recipes are the real deal (compare that to the ad-soaked "come to our website" teasers that other apps deliver when you use their "share this" tools); the "save to grocery list" option groups your items to match common grocery store sections and gives you at-a-tap checkboxes, so you can track your shopping progress within the store. It even tallies up ingredient amounts when you're shopping for multiple recipes.

GRILL, BABY, GRILL: A well-stocked collection of how-to guides help you get your grill on: the usual topics are covered (red meat and poultry each get a handful of entries), plus a nice helping of barbecue basics (fire configurations, measuring heat) for cooks just getting started. And get this: some of these tutorials include video explanations and, in a possible first for app developer-kind, some don't, for the simple reason that a photograph next to the text works just fine. One small step for topic-appropriate media selection.

Best App for Collecting Online Recipes

Paprika Recipe Manager

$9.99
Version: 1.1.0 | Hindsight Labs

Today's cooks probably get as many of their ideas from the Web as they do traditional cookbooks. Easier than copying and pasting your online faves, Paprika helps grab, organize, and tuck into your recipe collection. It's equipped with everything you need to input index card favorites gathering dust in the kitchen, but where it really shines is with its custom-rigged web browser. Use it to trawl and scoop up nicely formatted recipes from pretty much any site. The icing on the cake? How easy the app makes sharing. You can email everything from ingredient shopping lists to favorite recipes—perfect for when it's time to put those sous-chefs in your life to work.

KITCHEN AID: The app is outfitted from head to toe with cook-friendly design touches. The main recipe screen lets you flick through an easy-to-scan list. Tap any entry's shopping cart icon to add the ingredients to an email-ready shopping list or hit the envelope button to fire off the instructions to a friend.

GET ORGANIZED: The Categories pane helps as your collection grows. Add your own custom groupings by tapping the "+" button. If you need to blow through a batch of categorizing work, start from this screen and tap the "i" next to anywhere you see "Uncategorized". Then make your pick from your pop-up list.

COOKBOOK BROWSER: Paprika kicks things off by bookmarking a handful of well-stocked cooking sites. Dial up a recipe on any of these sites to see where the app earns its keep. Tap the upper-right Save Recipe button and, presto, it's all there waiting for you: ingredients, preparation instructions, even a photo (if there's one on the web page). If the insta-pluck doesn't work, try the manual workaround: tap and hold the recipe section you want to copy (ingredients, for example) and then pick the corresponding pop-up tab (Copy Ingredients).

ROLL YOUR OWN: Creating or customizing recipes is pretty easy. Just fire up a new recipe holder (buttons for that are throughout the app), fill out as many of the info categories as you like, and then add ingredients and instructions. The app's keyboard is topped with common recipe terms like ¼, ½, and *cups*. Here's a timesaver for any favorites you've already got on your computer: email it to your iPad, then copy and paste into the new recipe template. Bump up the font size by tapping the gear-shaped Settings icon.

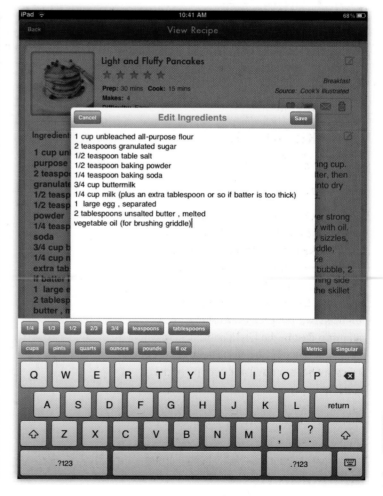

Best App for Browsing Big Recipe Collections

Epicurious Recipes & Shopping List

Free
Version: 2.1.1 | Condé Nast Digital

Gourmet chefs and those who saunter into any ol' kitchen and whip up a meal: move along. But for us food soldiers facing five empty tables a week, this one's a no-brainer. Stocked with 30,000 dishes from *Gourmet* (may she rest in peace) and *Bon Appetit*, it's perfect for finding your next meal. Some get bundled under seasonal banners (Oktoberfest); others target finicky or restricted food types (School Lunches, Passover). Sharing options made it past the bean counter brigade: you can email any recipe. A nice grocery list feature tops it all off (compiles ingredients into a master list), making this one of the best, least expensive kitchen aids ever.

TRUFFLE HUNTING: Start in the left-side search pane, pick a meal type (dinner, say), and then narrow that further by entering in the upper-right oval the ingredients you have on hand. That gets you 23 dinner choices where, say, truffles, star. A 1- to 4-"forks" ratings system also lets you see how your fellow foodies ranked the recipe. (Alas, it's view only; to cast your vote, go to *Epicurious.com*.)

OPEN BOOK: It's a bit of a "living" cookbook: continuously updated to include new recipes and seasonal suggestions (Halloween Treats). The downside: because the app downloads its haul from HQ's servers, you need to have an Internet connection to roam freely among those many recipes. The app does, however, store most of what you've recently browsed, making it ready for offline viewing.

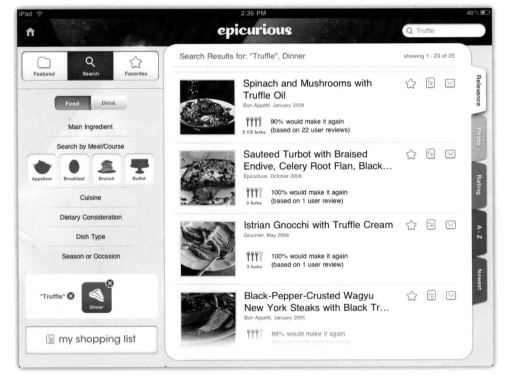

At Home

Out and About

The smartphone, it's clear, is the Swiss Army Knife for those who travel. You really can't beat its miniaturized, multiple talents: from phoning home to finding emergency watering holes, these mobile app kits have changed the way we move around. But trips happen in multiple phases and not all steps on that path are best served by such a small screen. For instance, you're probably not gonna whip out your iPad at a restaurant to calculate the tip (you wouldn't do that, would you?). It is clear, however, that as a traveler's aid, the iPad can help plan, manage, and for those who've shelled out for the 3G version, even do a bit of mobile navigating. Sometimes the help you need is in navigating your own neighborhood, or those nearby. From finding restaurants to "staycation" sightseeing, your iPad stands ready to serve as your own personal Julie McCoy. When it's time to venture farther afield, your little black pad's got plenty of ways to ensure you travel right: find cheap airfares and hotels, manage those many-tentacled itineraries, and make reservations so a good seat's ready for you upon arrival. And when you get there—whether it's Zanzibar or Albania—a fleet of virtual point-of-interest guides and translators are on call. As are some stunning worldwide photo tour collections for those who want to make believe they're tripping from, say, inside the office. And, of course, cyberspace introduces the chance to travel not just around the world—other planets beckon, too. Astronomy fans, prepare to be wowed: movie directors aren't the only ones who've caught the 3D bug. Some outerspace guidebooks are truly outtasight.

Out and About
Best apps for here and there

download 'em all

Photo: Daniel Silveira

Best App for Finding a Restaurant

Urbanspoon for iPad

Free
Version: 1.1 | Urbanspoon

Ten million downloads ago, Urbanspoon began its quest to add slot-machine-style fun to the chore of restaurant picking: click Spin and it randomly rung up a reco for you. The service started on the iPhone, where its popularity exploded (you could shake to spin…neat). Now's your chance to whirl the famous wheel on the big screen. Truth is, the fancy finding mechanism is only a small part of what makes this app a winner. It's really the huge database of listings this service now draws from that makes it a useful tool. About 800,000 restaurants are covered and not just in big cities: from Altoona, Pennsylvania to Zeeland, Michigan, good eats await.

SPIN-FREE ZONE: That red Spin button is so darn compelling, it's hard not to tap. But other methods work, and many of 'em are better suited for those with an inkling of what they want to eat and where. The lock icons are the key. Manually scroll your way through one or more of the neighborhood, cuisine, and price columns; tap and hold the lock till it lights up. You've just told the app to find, say, ultra-cheap Italian restaurants in Grosse Pointe.

TIME TO TWIRL: You can also enlist Mr. Spin's help once you've narrowed down your options. Set the golden locks on, say, location and price, and then, when you tap Spin, the app auto-flicks just the cuisine wheel. Spin again, of course, for another suggestion. The map's Show Popular button is helpful, too, especially if you're viewing a neighborhood stuffed with blue restaurant pins. When tapped, this button thins out the herd.

Out and About

TRAVEL TIME: You can have the app use the iPad's location-finding skills to sniff out your current whereabouts, or pick a destination yourself from the "Choose a city" window if you're planning a trip. You'll see about 50 major cities listed, but don't forget that's just the top of the pancake stack. Enter any city or town's name and chances are you'll find at least a few blue pins.

THE ENTREE: Your main course awaits once you actually tap a restaurant's name. A quick finger on any blue pin gets you key stats like contact info and the percentage of reviewers who liked the joint. Tap the "view details" option for the full story: a web page loaded with the works: a menu, a map, restaurant reviews, blog posts that mention the eatery, and a chance to pen your own.

177

More Apps for Finding a Restaurant

Zagat to Go
$9.99
Version: 4.0.2 | Zagat Survey

Long before "crowdsourcing" became every firm's favorite manufacturing method, Zagat people powered their famous red books. Everything you know about the guides is here: ratings in four categories (food, decor, service, and cost), contact info, and terse and to-the-point reviews. About 40 cities are covered (mainly the U.S. biggies, but also some international hotspots like London and Paris). The app also gives you the company's coverage of nightlife, hotels, and shopping. Flip a switch in the Settings menu and download for offline viewing the whole honking 100 MB collection. Perfect for that flight to L.A. Just remember to do the deed before takeoff.

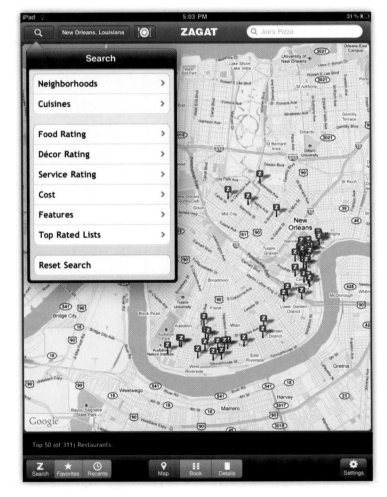

VISUAL BROWSING: Map mode helps eyeball the neighborhood you're headed to—great for spotting which restaurants are within range. Compare that to those typically frustrating web searches for, say, "Harlem restaurants"; here you simply pan and zoom to where you want to visit and in an instant you see red Z's pop up.

THIS NOT THAT: All the search categories you'd expect are here, including finicky filters ranging from Children Not Recommended to Crayons & Games Available. On the downside: coverage doesn't quite measure up to other apps, not to mention what's out there in the real world. (Three Italian restaurants in all of Brooklyn? Yougotta-bekiddinme.)

BOOK MARK: Book mode replicates the classic print edition layout. Tap any of the gray page-top tabs (food, decor) to sort what appears according to that criterion. Since you're often viewing multiple pages' worth of listings, and there's no simple way to flip through the pages other than one at a time, here's a tip: swipe right on the first page and you'll cycle back to the last page.

DETAILS, DETAILS: Each review page lists, of course, location, contact info, and ratings. (Tap the "i" for a refresher on the service's opaque number scale: it runs from 0 to 30, with a few letters thrown in for cost info when price data's not available.) You'll also usually find built-in links to OpenTable's reservation maker, and menus. The map is live: pinch to zoom out for a bird's-eye view.

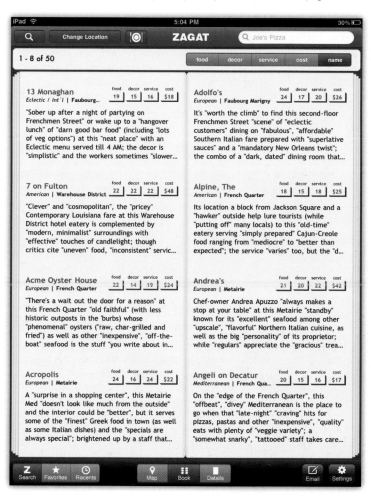

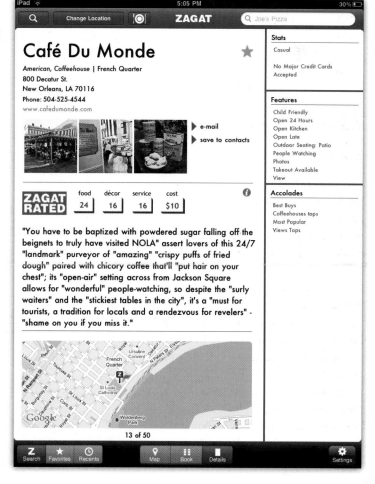

More Apps for Finding a Restaurant

Speak4it

Free
Version: 2.3 | Yellowpages.com

Warning: after using this app you may never want to search the "old" way—by zipcode, restaurant name, or category listing—again. The novel idea here is actually a joint venture between your iPad's voice recognition capabilities and your own ability to finger paint across the area you want to search. You simply sketch a line around where you want to hunt, speak your request (no special mic necessary), and voilà: the telltale red pins appear. Perfect for those times when you wanna meet for a drink near that building that's across from that park. No problem: sketch, speak, done.

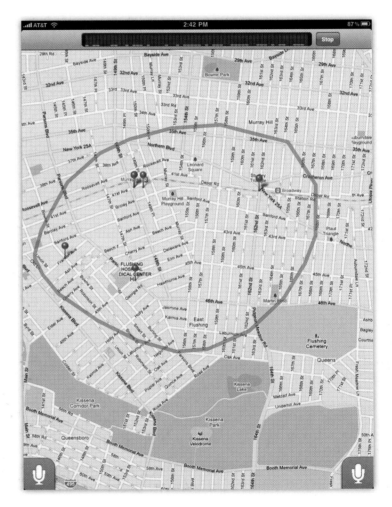

SEARCH BETTER:
You can enter what you're looking for the ol' fashioned way (tap the search oval, enter your query), but where's the fun in that? Recite your request instead. Start by tapping either of the microphone icons; when the recording panel appears at top, trace whatever boundaries you like: could be a straight line down Main Street, a circle around campus, whatever.

HEARING TEST:
The app's a good listener. Of course it can handle basics (*pizza, sushi*), but even slightly odd locutions (*peruvian greenwich connecticut*) it nails. Nice. You can also tap the address book icon in the search oval to reissue previous requests or save faves for one-tap access.

Out and About

Best App for Reserving a Table

OpenTable for iPad
Free
Version: 1.1 | OpenTable

Some folks like quiet dining. Think of this app as quiet restaurant searching. How's that happen? First, only restaurants who pony up for the firm's reservation-handling system are included. *Sloppy Sammy's Taco Truck*, in other words, ain't here. And yet the list tops 14,000 spots worldwide. Next, user reviews are amazingly fresh and helpful (which is not to say all positive); old posts get phased out quickly and 200,000 new ones arrive, the company says, per month. If you're fed up with trawling, want to rub virtual elbows with those who dine above the fray, and like a seat with your name on it, this app's for you.

THE JOY OF LESS: You'll find more listings in Yelp and UrbanSpoon, but if you don't mind missing the handful of establishments that don't use the OpenTable system, what you get in return is what some would call a blessing in these info-overloaded times: *fewer* choices. Use the app either to nab a rezzy at a specific spot (tap "Find by Name") or conduct a neighborhood search.

HOW TO HUNT: Start by picking from any of the dozens of metro areas the app covers. Pick a neighborhood, a specific restaurant if you've got one in mind, and then enter info about your party's size and when you want to dine. Search listings show when tables are available.

Best App for Finding Cheap Airfares

Kayak HD

Free
Version: 15.2.1 | Kayak Software

By now, everyone's used to hitting the Web when it comes to flight planning. So a fare-finding app needs to somehow improve upon your average browser-based trawl. Kayak's app glides ahead of the pack with a better-than-browsing user interface and a handful of great planning and cheap-o friendly tools. In case you're not familiar, the firm built its loyal following by wide-scoping most *other* big travel ticket sites (they do hotels, cars, and so on, too). Most useful are the parameter-tweaking tools; invoke 'em with a satisfying set of finger swipes: here, not there, then, not later. Much faster than mouse, click, and reload.

DESTINATION ANYWHERE: Round-trip and one-way searches work just as you'd expect: enter destination and dates. Build a multicity trip and watch the flight pin-and-path its way across the map in the lower-left corner. Flesh out your findings with transportation and lodging by using the buttons at the bottom of the screen.

POPULAR PICKS: Scroll through the Hot Searches list to see other recent finds from fellow Kayakers who've searched from your home airport. (Change this setting by tapping the left-side From label and then entering a new departure airport.) If you like their itinerary but need different dates, tap the listing and change the left-side column's calendar info.

Out and About

GET OUT OF DODGE: The Filter panel is a super powerful way to customize your search. Summon it by clicking the main screen's big honkin' Search button. Don't like flying through a particular airport? Nix it by removing the check in the Layover Airports list.

PICKY, PICKY: Tap the Explore button for an entirely new way to put on your best deal-hunting binoculars. Punch in your particulars in the When, What, and Flight tabs, then select a budget range using the slider at the top of the screen.

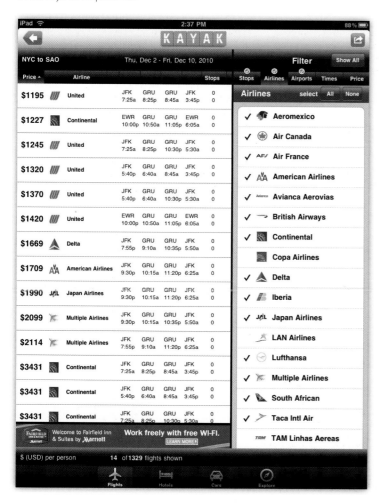

Best App for Fighting Traffic

Beat the Traffic HD

Free
Version: 2.0 | Triangle Software

You won't get step-by-step, point-to-point guidance with this app, but as a traffic-fighting sidekick to a dedicated direction-giving service, Beat the Traffic is invaluable. It presents a map that's forever-fresh, fed by traffic data pulled from a network of public traffic-reporting sources, mixed together with some software-powered predictive magic (used in the traffic forecasts you can dial up before leaving home). It's the same service many local TV shows use, and it's got goodies like a nearly continuously updated stream of roadside traffic-cam images and accident alerts ("on Merric Rd Eastbound, East of Central Ave")—many of which are 10 minutes-or-less fresh.

FOREWARNED, FOREARMED: Equipped with this all-seeing traffic-cam, you can quickly course correct. Color coded roadways make at-a-glance decisions easy to make: red stands for traffic clots moving at less than 25 mph, green is all good (50+ mph, to be specific), and orange is in between. Tap any camera icon for a recent shot of the road.

CRYSTAL BALL: The screen-top Forecast button is great for plan-aheaders: tap it and you can skip in half-hour increments (up to two hours from now). And show your fellow commuters some love: the Report button lets you add to the network's knowledge by sharing what you see. For-pay extras include personalized routes and auto-alerts for commuters (those'll cost you $20/year).

Out and About

Best App for Tracking Your Trip

TravelTracker Pro
$8.99
Version: 4.01 | Silverware Software

Your flight info's in your jacket pocket, the rental car confirmation is (probably) tucked in that folder marked "Trip Stuff," and who knows where the hotel directions are? Here's a chance for the iPad to virtually suck up those random trip logistics, so that never again will that desk clerk watch in smug silence as you pat yourself down and plead, "I know it's here *somewhere.*" What you can track and view with this app is pretty comprehensive. All the usual suspects like flight, hotel, and car info, but you can also keep watch on a secondary cast of characters: meeting and expense notes, directions, and even those random activity details ("relish factory tour starts at the pickle stand").

TRIPIT TRACKER?: Truth be told, this app should probably be called TripIt for iPad, since the bulk of its value comes from syncing with that popular web-based itinerary tracking service. (Why no app from them? They've got an iPhone-only version that gets creamed for a variety of shortcomings.) In any case, the partnership works well: set up a TripIt account online and the app makes it easy to pull or push info in either direction.

ADD 'N GO: If trackable events arise when you're on the road, add 'em to your dossier by using the New Item button. As far as app-only features: there is—make sure you're sitting down for this—a flag guessing game (tap to reveal which country) and, more usefully, an awards program file (store your account number and info on companies that accept these points).

Best App for Driving Directions in Your Car

MotionX GPS Drive HD

$2.99
Version: 7.1 | Fullpower Technologies

Designed specifically for the 3G iPad (WiFi-only iPads can't even download it), this app alone may well be worth the extra $100 or so that Apple charges for its cellular-powered tablets. Certainly that's true for regular road trippers. You've now got more reason than ever to ditch—or not buy in the first place—a single-purpose GPS device. Cost is one reason: even with the extra voice-guidance fee ($25/year, $3/30 days), you'll come out ahead of most subscription-based systems. But even more valuable is how this app/hardware combo turns auto-nav-powered trips from a painful visit to the land of poor software design and balky touchscreens to a system that works like Apple built it.

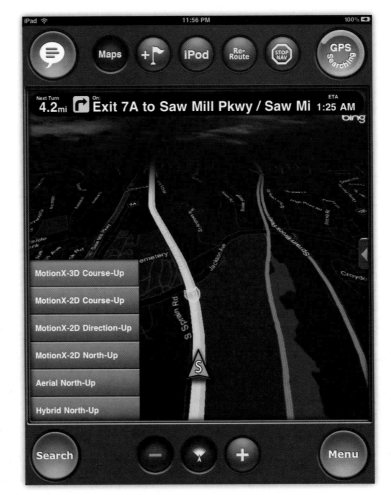

PRE-TRIP PLAN: Take a virtual spin before hitting the road—great for seeing which route the app has selected. Don't like its gameplan? Switch on or off "Use traffic data" (in Settings→Driving & Traffic Options) to seek out an alternate route.

DRIVER'S AID: Live Guidance is the optional service you pay for (after an initial freebie period of 30 days). What you get is turn-by-turn audio—essential for solo drivers. A nice assortment of map views (2D, 3D, aerial, and so on) lets you pick the visual that best matches the kind of map-reading you like to do. Nice.

MULTIPLE VIEWS: Once you're underway, a split-screen layout gives you three main sources of guidance: a visual of the route, a list view of mainly text directions, and a big honkin' "what you need to do next." For the left-side map portion, you can toggle back and forth between bird's-eye view and up-close with the usual pinch and spread gestures.

CUSTOM RIDE: The app's Settings area is worth a pit stop. Music lovers will appreciate an option to mute the music when an audio prompt plays. A "night mode" presents maps in darkness-friendly high-contrast colors. And if you find yourself regularly using the pre-trip simulations, you can speed up the rate at which the show unfolds.

Best App for Translation Help

Travel Interpreter

$9.99
Version: 1.4 | Jourist Verlags

Learning the local lingo is a noble goal, but let's be realistic: who's got the time? Here's a chance to venture into parts less known with at least a *little* language. Covering two dozen tongues, from Arabic to Turkish, this talking phrasebook can boost your immersion efforts…not to mention help out in case of emergency. Navigation options include a decent search tool and browsable categories thoughtfully chunked up into real-world requests. On the top level, things kick off with "Basics" (subcategories include: "First need phrases"). Other big groupings cover topics like dining, shopping, repairs, laundry, health, and the drugstore. Bon voyage.

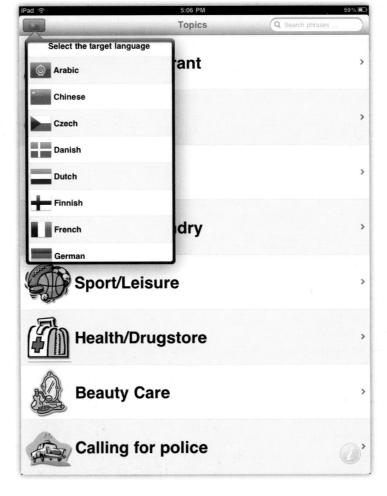

HELPING HAND: Big, easy-to-read type is perfect for quickly scrolling through each list of phrases. Then you can either show or have the app speak your selection. The illustrations are playful but accurately drawn, making for handy pointing aids (show the waiter you want chicken wings rather than breast meat).

OTHER TONGUES: If you find you're in a multilingual region—the border between Little Italy and China-town, say—it's easy to quickly get the same phrase translated two ways. Just tap the upper-left corner's globe icon and pick from the menu. One overall downside: offline access to the collected works means you're in for a 650 MB download.

Out and About

Best App for Wikipedia-Style Travel Guides

Wikihood for iPad

Free lite version | $6.99
Version: 1.3.1 | Dr. Stephen Gillmeier

You know that concierge you've been meaning to add to your domestic staff? The one who'll do things like prepare helpful info dossiers about all those places you're planning to visit? Hold off 'til you've had a chance to test out Wikihood, a nifty roundup of Wikipedia articles related to specific locations. In truth, it's not just for travel: dial up insta-reports on your own or nearby 'hoods to learn historical trivia or plan fun outings, check out what the world's biggest encyclopedia has to say about the town you grew up in, or even just use it as a way to tour the site's ever-expanding article trove in a geographically driven, fun way.

THE SEARCH: How it works is simple: use the iPad's location-finding tool or punch in wherever you're interested in; the app returns in a jiffy with its article haul. (Tip: leave off country names when searching.) If you sorta/kinda know where you're looking for but haven't got a name handy, switch over to the Map tab. From there, drag so the spot you're interested in sits within the blue viewfinder icon's crosshairs; then tap the "load selection" button and you're off to the articles.

THE RESULTS: Go ahead, plan a walking tour: red pins indicate entries relevant to various locations. When tapped, each pin sprouts a summary snippet of text; the blue arrow-in-a-circle on the right end is your path to the full Wikipedia article. Tabs below each listing divide the app's wiki-catch into distinct categories, including People, Culture & Buildings (available in both app versions), and Geography and Economy (paid only).

Best App for Finding Wi-Fi Coverage

Wi-Fi Finder

Free
Version: 2.5.0 | JiWire

Road warriors face lots of foes, but iPadding without Internet access has to be one of the biggest buzzkills. Until universal coverage arrives, add this freebie to your must-download list. Loaded with pointers to over 300,000 free and paid hotspots in close to 150 countries, it ranks up there with your favorite creature comforts. (That goes for stay-near-home types, too; check out nearby coverage and you're likely to find a few surprise spots.) Simple to navigate map, search, and filter tools make pre-trip planning a snap. And an option to download the full list means this dog will hunt even—or perhaps better said—especially when you need it most.

Out and About

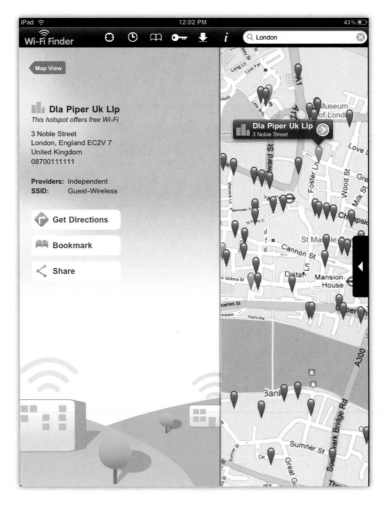

SIGNAL FINDER: You get three finding options: GPS-sniff any spot near your current location, conduct a worldwide search, or download the full collection for offline use (your initial install is a lightweight shell). Once you've homed in on an area, green (free) and blue (paid) teardrop markers show the Wi-Fi spots. Drag the map around and it refreshes its finds automatically.

SITE STATS: Tap any marker for detailed info on the listing. "SSID" tells you the network name to look for once you've arrived. (Go to the iPad's Setting's app, tap Wi-Fi in the left column and then pick the network you want to join from the "Choose a Network" list.)

FOCUS FEATURE: The Filter tool is particularly helpful when you're in a city crammed with options. You can narrow down by venue (hotel, restaurant) or provider. Another way to winnow: in the right-hand results list, tap either Paid or Free.

OFFLINE OPTIONS: Downloading the full collection (38MB) solves the dilemma of how to find hotspots when you're out and don't currently have a connection. Only caveat: you get a text-only list (as opposed to a map). To keep your listings fresh, tap the menu bar's "i" button and pick "Check for Offline Database Update".

191

Best App for House-Hunting

Zillow Real Estate Search

Free
Version: 3.0.9 | Zillow.com

One silver lining to the housing crisis: there's never been a better time to go home shopping. *Zillow.com* has been around for a few years now, rolling up publicly available data on 90 million-plus U.S. homes, and serving it up to real estate gawkers everywhere. (A common first search: how much is my childhood home worth?) With this app, snooping's never been easier. Serious shoppers will love the trove of cold, hard data (historical sales prices, taxes, neighborhood trends). Tire kickers and coveters can graze on speculative goodies (guesstimated market value). Everyone will like the app's bevy of visual search and browse tools.

FIGURES & FACTS: The Details tab rounds up key info on each listing. Most fun (or depressing) are the 1-, 5-, and 10-year charts showing the firm's "Zestimates": algorithmically generated market value guesses based on publicly available data. Zillow admits these are only software-powered conjectures, but you will find real-world stats above and below most charts on data points like last sale, tax info, and sales of comparable properties.

COLOR CODED: Map markers come in different colors: red (for sale), yellow (recently sold), purple (for rent), and "Make Me Move" blue, whereby you declare (on *Zillow.com*) what you'd sell your house for…without actually putting it on the market. For listings you want to keep an eye on, tap the arrow till it bulks up, then drag to the right-hand pane; it now resides in the Favorites panel, where you can also save neighborhood-wide searches.

Out and About

MODEL HOMES: Tap the Gallery button on any page and you'll see a grid of photo cards for all the listings in the area you're viewing. Photo stacks indicate multiple shots of the property; swipe left to see additional pix or tap for a page dedicated to the listing.

FINDING KEEPERS: Thin the results herd by filtering your search. Tapping the Filter button curls back the main page and gives you ten or so ways to winnow. Be sure to come back here if you're sightseeing and coming up empty; a likely culprit is you've left a filter in place and need to turn it off.

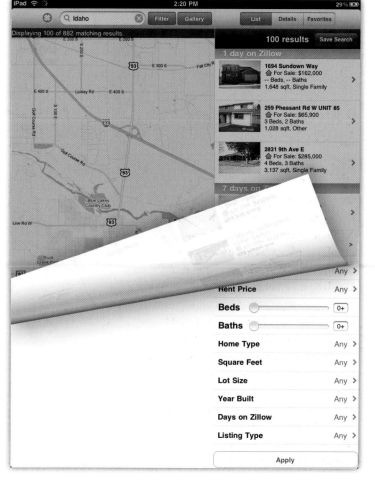

Best App for Jaw-Dropping Photo Tours

Fotopedia Heritage

Free
Version: 2.0.1 | Fotonauts

The French have an expression for window shopping (*leche-vitrine*) that, literally translated, means "window licking." For those with wanderlust, this is one screen-licker of an app. Spend more than 10 minutes, as you almost inevitably will, browsing through this gorgeous collection of worldwide travel photos and you'll not only go wide-eyed at its pix, but you'll probably soon start travel planning. The app's user interface is as attention-grabbing as its photographic eye candy. You're never more than an intuitive swipe or tap away from browsing through or discovering new destinations. You won't find a big Help section in this app, and the reason's simple: because you don't need one.

BAD APPLE FREE: The app's powered by a clever act of curation: it takes only those photos in the Wikipedia-like Fotopedia database that match up with UNESCO World Heritage sites. The most notable distinction between Fotopedia, which describes itself as a "photo enyclopedia," and its forefather is high quality: a community-powered voting process does a great job of weeding out the duds.

DEEP DIVES: The titlebar's caption lets you know how many other photos are in this particular site's collection. Tap the filmstrip icon at right for a handy browsing tool for what to gawk at next. The usual left- and right-ward swiping gestures also work if you just want to move between the big pix. For a work-soothing slideshow, tap the upper-right play icon.

PURPLE PINLAND: If you're a fan of map-based browsing, tap the main screen's globe icon. Everything you know about touchscreen map controls works here: pinch your fingers to zoom out, spread 'em to zoom in, tap-and-hold to pan left or right. The pins indicate spots with photos. The magnifier glass search icon in the upper right is another handy browsing tool. Its pop-up menu lists a regional hierarchy that's easy to step your way through.

PIX PLUS PROSE: The info on display in this right-side panel (tap the main page's "i" button) comes from UNESCO and, naturally, the related Wikipedia entry. You can also try to lure a travel pal by emailing or posting vacation bait to Twitter or Facebook. And if all these pictures really have sparked your travel interest, a built in TripAdvisor tool helps you start planning a trip.

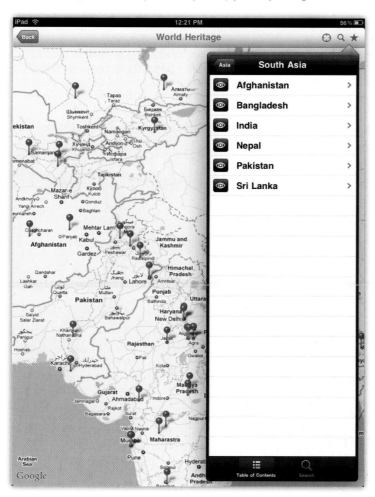

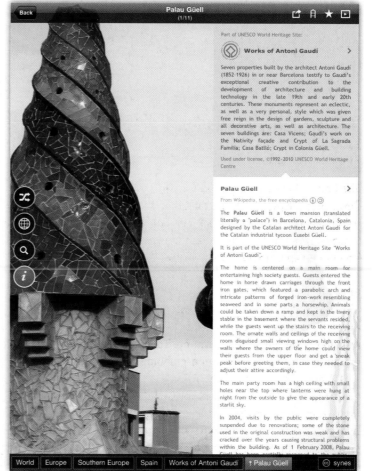

Best App for Country Dossiers

The World Factbook for iPad

$1.99
Version: 1.1.4 | Fuzzy Peach

Who knows which apps will be on the next James Bond's iPad? One safe bet: the World Factbook—a fascinating group of country research reports that the snoops in Langley update every two weeks. That's right, the insights in this collection are gathered by our very own CIA (public domain status lets anyone republish it). Each of the 220-plus dossiers are divided into categories: people, government, the euphemistic "transnational issues." The app's comparative tools are what makes browsing fun: Anguilla is half the size of Washington D.C.; Uzbekistan has the world's fourth lowest unemployment rate.

AKROTIRI BOUND?: If you can think of a country (territories and "dependencies" too), it's almost definitely covered. More than just a collection of dry facts, each country's entry kicks off with a backgrounder that's as informative as it is devoid of any overt political slant. Learn, for example, in a couple hundred words, about Afghanistan's last hundred years, including a sober take on its current challenges.

COMPARE & CONTRAST: Tap the bar graph icon wherever you see it for a look at how a country ranks against others in a particular category (infant mortality, GDP growth, population below poverty line). Or click the World Location's Comparisons tab for a lengthy list: Internet users, military expenditures as a percent of GDP, education expenditures, iPad app usage (okay, not yet, but that can't be far off).

Out and About

Best App for Downloading Maps

OffMaps

$1.99
Version: 4.2 | Felix Lamaroux

The iPad's built-in Maps app is great—except when you don't have an Internet connection. Wouldn't it be nice to have a worldwide guide that zooms from city-wide to street level and requires neither Web access nor folding skills? OffMaps gets you pretty close. Among its most useful services: a feature that lets you, prior to leaving home, draw a selection box around an area and download its maps. The app draws from the Wikipedia-ish *OpenStreetMap.org*, which means you get tips on dining spots and bars, but also occasional errors. With that caveat in mind, as a complement to your travel team, OffMaps is a good bet.

WHERE TO GO, WHAT TO DO: You can download base maps and/or guides. The former contain just what you'd expect; the latter are an additional layer that gets superimposed on the map and identifies points of interest. The app gives you two freebie guides; after that you can either pay $1 for three more or $9 for an unlimited number. (Both plans also get you updates.)

MAP QUEST: So here's what you need to do: before your trip to wherever, navigate there using the main map. Tap the download arrow, draw a selection rectangle around the city, and bump up the level of detail to the max (that way you get micro-street level detail). Then go pour yourself a cup of tea; these downloads tend to be hefty and the server that's on duty is sluggish.

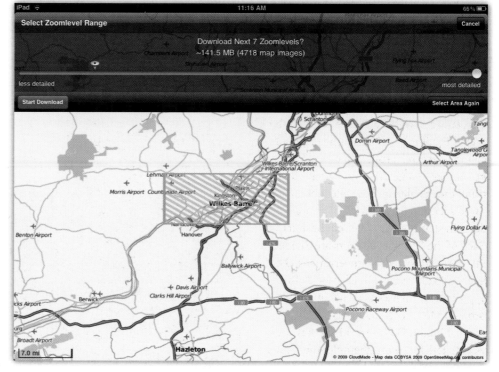

Best App for Assorted Maps

Maplets
$2.99
Version: 1.4.1 | Zaia Design

Here's one solution to Crumpled Map Syndrome: the annoyance of devilishly difficult-to-fold maps, afflicting travelers from amusement park visitors to zoo gawkers, from bus riders to mountain climbers. Offering an easy-to-search database of more than 2,000 maps, this app serves as a kind of giant back pocket for those in need of visual directions. Unlike the familiar Google Maps, Maplets specializes in collecting those site-specific guides that contribute to the aforementioned condition: parks, ski resorts, trails, subways, buses, and so on. Each map is downloadable, so what you grab is handy wherever you are; regular updates keep your collection fresh.

TRAVELER SPECIAL: If you're about to hit the road—especially for parts unknown— the visual map-finding tool is killer. It lets you set your sights on a general area (northwest Arkansas, for example); then simply tap the "Search in Area" button and down drops green pins wherever the app's got resources ready for you.

MAP OF THE MAPS: Once downloaded, the map immediately appears; you're basically looking at a scrollable, zoomable PDF. Other ways to search for available maps include by keyword (*Paris, Disneyworld*) or browse a list of location names near you. For the full list, check out *http://bit.ly/maplet*. City maps are one area where the service is spotty.

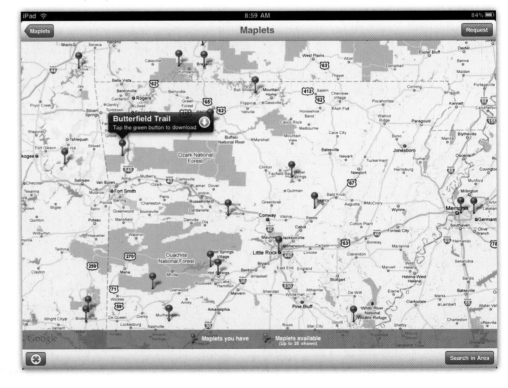

FIND YOURSELF: If a map is souped up with GPS coordinates (not all are), you'll see a location-finding icon in the lower-left corner; tap it to find where you are on the map. Some maps, like the one shown here, are actually collections of related mini-maps. The menu in the upper-right gives you a list.

MISSING PIECES: Maplets doesn't have everything, but judging by a test, the firm is quick to respond to special requests (the Graceland map was added two days after a request was submitted). Hunt down the app's Request a Place button (on the Find a Maplet screen) and submit a simple form.

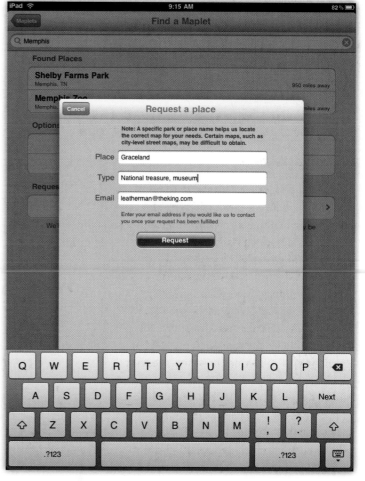

Best App for Touring the Globe

Google Earth
Free
Version: 3.1.1 | Google

Everyone's first instinct is to grab this app, zoom in, and play Spot My Home. But before jumping to that bit of fun, take an astronaut's-eye view—pinch your fingers together till you see our big blue mottled marble. Then swipe your finger across it and watch the world whirl. Whee! Sure, there are practical benefits to be had (that vacation home you're about to rent? See for yourself whether the beach really is "within walking distance"). But this app's as much about globetrotting entertainment as it is utilitarian value. And with an ever-improving photo tapestry at its heart, this is one road trip everyone will want to take.

GETTING AROUND: Figuring out the navigational gestures can take time. Some highlights: drag one finger to pan (swipe quickly to speed up); spread and pinch two fingers to zoom in and out; turn two fingers (like you're twisting a lid) to rotate. If things aren't quite moving the way you want, flick Autotilt on (in the settings menu); now tilt the iPad back and forth and watch the map move.

LAYERS OF INFO: Your dashboard in this Earth rover is filled with a few hidden gems. The Layers menu lets you flip on a diverse group of labels and icon annotations: businesses, geo-tagged Wikipedia entries, locally shot photos. The My Maps option lets you tour a bookmarked list of favorite destinations; set that up by heading to the maps section of *Google.com*.

FROM THE SWISS ALPS…: Enter hot or cold spots you want to check out in the search oval. If you mistakenly select a place that launches you on a long-distance journey, and the app starts whisking you across the globe, just tap the screen with one finger and you'll stop. The extra-info symbols overlaid on the map are all tappable. Mini in-app browser windows funnel in additional web-based info connected to each type of icon.

…TO THE SUBURBS: At up close and local zoom levels, the image quality is stunning, (not to mention spooky for those folks worried about living in Surveillance Nation). Enter an address in the search oval for a quick trip to a specific spot. Once you've arrived at your destination use that same oval to find local joints: *pizza*, *hardware*, whatever. A horizontal stack of three bars on its right side means a list of results are waiting.

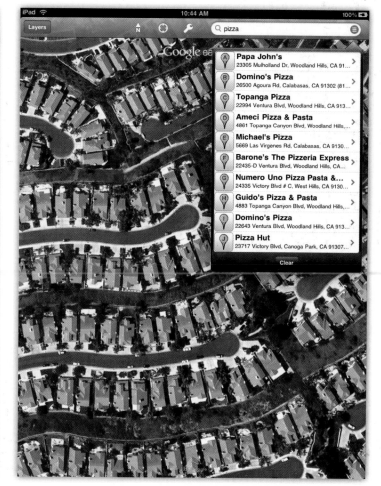

Best App for Astronomy

Star Walk for iPad

$4.99
Version: 5.0 | Vito Technology

Two pieces of advice for first-time users of this app: 1) When testing out "star spotter" mode, which you do by looking at your skyward-pointing iPad and watching the display change to reflect what's above you, make sure you and your engrossed self don't trip over any dogs, crawling children, or fire hydrants. 2) Try to use your "inside voice" when screaming: "Holy cannoli! This is frickin' cool!" Star Walk is an astronomy tool even for people who don't like astronomy (a condition that may change after a few hours with this app), an endlessly fascinating resource for people who do, and a must-have for showing off your beloved iGadget to non-iPad owners and stoking their jealousy.

SKY PILOT: Basic browsing is tap-and-drag simple. Hold one finger on the display and drag in any direction; watch as a full range of stars, constellations, meteor showers, and so on come in and out of view. For details on what you're looking at, tap-to-select nearly any object. When you tap the green label, a sidebar window pops up with key stats and background.

ZOOM WITH A VIEW: Got a spot in mind somewhere else on Earth from which you'd like to gaze starwards? Just use the Settings tool to summon a globe that you can spin to the place you want. When the stick figure icon is positioned where you want, tap the lower right corner's li'l dipper icon. Now you're looking up at the sky.

Out and About

TIME TRAVEL: Take a trip in either direction—past or future—and watch an animation of the sky's changing tableau. Start by tapping the Time Machine's upper-right clock icon; then swipe in either direction on the vertical timeline bar. How fast you swipe controls the speed of the animation; tap the bar again to stop the time travel. To view just those objects visible to the naked eye, head to Settings and adjust the brightness slider all the way to the left.

DAILY DASHBOARD: The Sky Live button (tap the lower-right corner's bullet list icon to access) presents a handy dashboard of heavenly activity of special interest to Earth dwellers—including day length, the sun's elevation, and lunar tidbits like when things are waning or waxing. Construct an on-the-fly flipbook-style animation of recent and pending days by tapping the back or forward arrows (respectively; upper-right corner). Notice how, for example, the moon photos change each day, like slowly advancing frames on a filmstrip.

203

Best App for Exploring the Solar System

Solar Walk

$2.99
Version: 1.5.1 | Vito Technology

What with NASA's new carry-on limits, trips to Mars are getting to be a pain. So, grab your iPad and take a virtual tour instead. This app presents not just the Red Planet, but its eight big-league neighbors and the key moons. The visuals here are the crowd-pleaser: a 3D-style model that's fun to finger navigate around. (Speaking of 3D: bring your own glasses—anaglyph red/cyan are what you'll need; buy 'em on Amazon for about $5—and you'll get a multidimensioned glimpse of the show.) The writing ranges from clear science-speak to, uh: "Looking like a giant pizza covered with melted cheese and splotches of tomato and ripe olives, Io is…" Grab a slice and come have some fun.

SPACE & TIME: Pinch and spread gestures let you take lightspeed trips: move two fingers apart and get an up close look at, say, Saturn's moon Iapetus. You can rotate 30 planets and moons—good news for Iapetus, since its dark side is pretty uninteresting. Use the clock in the upper-right corner for time travel; tap the year, for example, and whisk through historical sky views by scrolling down the timeline.

TOUR GUIDE: The pop-up info panels (tap the upper-left corner's "i" button) offer brief dossiers on each planet; swipe from right to left to make your way through the whole explanation. Spend some extra time on the Internal Structure section, which is where you get a nifty visual of the innards of whichever planet you're viewing.

SOLAR WALK
3D SOLAR SYSTEM MODEL

© 2010 Vito Technology, Inc.

Music by Astropilot

Out and About

For Your Health

 Where, when, and how an iPad contributes to a healthy lifestyle is a topic that someone should be studying. On the one hand, the pint sized-pad gets you away from the hunched over environs of your desktop PC (even sitting at Starbucks in front of a laptop ain't much better, hunching-wise). What could be more nourishing for mind and body than propping your feet up and computing in comfort—the beautiful people in the Apple demo videos seem to be in strapping shape...same should be true for all of us, no? But then there are those clear instances we're already starting to see of people spending *way* too much time on their tablet; whatever the ergonomics of couch surfing turn out to be, that can't be a great thing. So, with "all things in moderation" as our marching motto, we finish up our app tour with a few examples where it's clear the iPad can help pave the path to healthier living: quick medical advice lookups, data tracking (diet, blood pressure), even as part of a workout—though it's not yet clear any developer has cracked the challenge of solving the "I'm sweating far too hard to actually swipe the screen" problem. And as long as you're willing to pledge not to actually curl up with the dang thing, you'll learn about some helpful sleep-inducing apps and a close cousin: meditation and mindfulness aids, for those in need of winding down. Finally, what value would a book be if it didn't deliver help to those who'd...just delivered. Baby stats tracking, baby. You may not be sleeping, but that doesn't mean your knowledge of your kids' key statistics should suffer.

For Your Health
Best apps for your body

download 'em all

Photo: Thomas Hawk / thomashawk.com

205

Best Portable First Aid Reference

WebMD for iPad

Free
Version: 1.1 |WebMD

Is there an iPad in the house? Hey, 911 is still your best bet for emergencies, but for everyday nicks, dings, and pains, why not carry around the Web's most popular healthcare resource? What you get here is mainly a subset of what's online. (Fair warning, the deeper you dive, the more likely you are to meet mini web pages sucked down from the site.) But there's utility in having a streamlined version of the site's jumbo collection. For one, it's all a bit easier to navigate, further evidence that a pared-down app is often more pleasurable than an ad-laden, info-overloaded website. And there are also some app-specific diagnosis and searching tools that do what can't easily be done on the Web.

HURTS HERE: A smart symptom checker lets you tap on any part of the body and then pick from a whittled down list of ailments connected to that region. Tap the head, for example, and the pop-up list includes everything from anxiety to "warm to touch." Some of the symptoms even come with a short series of questions to further customize the diagnosis. (Is your earache "sharp or stabbing," "dull or achy," and so on.)

HELP HERE: The hospital locator tool could be helpful, especially if you're in an unfamiliar neighborhood, though it remains to be seen whether turning to an iPad is the tool of choice for those in need of hospitalization. Perhaps more practical is the pharmacy finder, which lets you use the iPad's built-in location finder (a watered-down version is available for wifi-only devices) to pinpoint nearby drugstores.

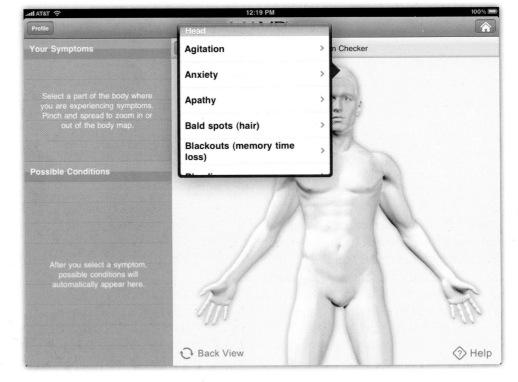

Best App for Studying the Heart

Heart Pro

$17.99
Version: 1.01 | 3D4Medical.com

Truth be told, this one's likely to serve the specific needs of a small group of readers: med school students, heart surgeons, and, perhaps, vampire killers. But for the rest of us, the queasy lure of watching a beating heart *and* getting a glimpse of how video-enriched references can change the game for all kinds of learners might be enough of a draw. The videos are actually only one of the pulse-quickening features. You also get a visual index (tap a heart part name and see it ID'd on a model), the ability to rotate the 3D images, and even a chance to "cut" most of 'em open to peer further inside. Eeew. Neato. Exactly.

SEARCH & DISCOVERY: The Pins tab lists dozens of spots, both on the surface and buried inside the heart. Tap any label's "i" button for an info pop-up. Especially for those sub-surface elements, you'll want to use the floating menu bar's transparency button, which lets you adjust that setting for arteries, veins, tissue, and nerves. It's a great way to fade items you're not interested in, so you can focus on the ones you are.

SHOWTIME: The movies (on the tab of the same name) aren't simply digitally rendered action sequences. Thanks to stitched-together 3D photos you're seeing what amounts to a nearly anatomically perfect look at a beating heart. Ten or so different clips give you zoomable looks from a wide variety of angles (anterior, right lateral). Intrigued by all this but not enough to spend $18? Check out a demo video at *http://bit.ly/heartpro*.

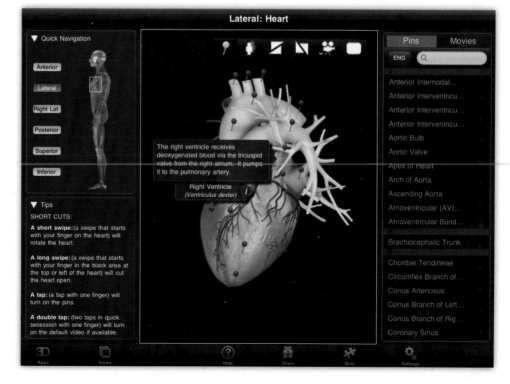

Best App for Dieting and Weight Loss

MyNetDiary HD

$9.99
Version: 1.3 | 4Technologies

Ahh, the American Dream: buy a house, have 1.7 kids, lose the bellyroll bear hugging your tummy. MyNetDiary won't supply willpower, but it'll lead the way, especially for those committed to good eating, decent exercise, and honest data entry. The service's core is a food- and activity-tracking journal that changes on-the-fly to track progress towards preset goals (lose 10 pounds in two months, say). A huge database of 100,000 food items makes one big dieting challenge—how many calories did that Cobb Salad have?—a snap. Fully synced web-based and smartphone versions (available with premium extras like data exporting) provide a full-frontal assault in the weight loss war.

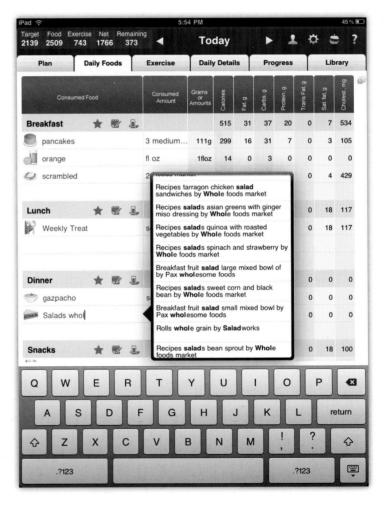

FOOD FORECAST: Log meals for any day in the future. At first this sounds like a system for wishful thinking, but it makes sense: you can map out an eating and exercise plan that helps you keep on target. Got big Friday night plans? Chart those buffalo wings and offset the difference with an extra 30 minutes at the gym.

SHORT CUTS: When entering amounts, you pick between common units (ounces, grams) or servings (great for salad bar regulars). Speaking of, simply entering a phrase like *salad whole* triggers the appearance of a long list of pre-entered dishes, so you can pick from, say, Whole Food–specific choices, all of which appear with their nutritional info filled out.

208

ATHLETE SHEET: The exercise tracker is as comprehensive as the food catalog. Pretty much any activity you can think of has a preset entry. All you need to do is enter, say, *elliptical* and then punch in minutes logged on the machine. Other activities, like the ones shown here, reveal the honest reckoning one faces when you open the app. How hard, in other words, did you try?

THE PAYOFF PAGE: Use either of the first two areas to enter diet-related notes. The really good stuff is in the Daily Analysis section: that first figure is how much you ate, the second how much you burned, and the total is your over/under against your goal. Don't like what you see? Head back to the other tabs and either bump up your shakin' or cut down the bacon.

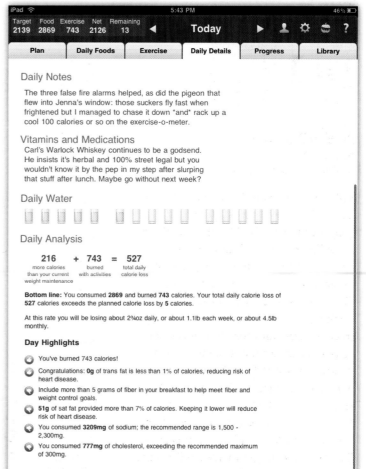

Best App for Tracking Health Stats

Heartwise Blood Pressure Tracker

$2.99
Version: 3.5.1 | Jonathan Lartigue

Everyone knows regular exercise is important, but for some folks, data tracking's a close second. Serious athletes, of course, want to monitor stats like weight, but just as often it's rank-and-file patients—those with a heart condition, for example—who need to keep an eye on a few key numbers. A PC-based spreadsheet could work, but then there's Excel to wrestle with, not to mention getting to the computer when it's data entry time. This app saves you from both by focusing on two things: making it easy to enter your numbers (blood pressure, heart rate, weight) and instantly serving up trendspotting-friendly graphs.

210

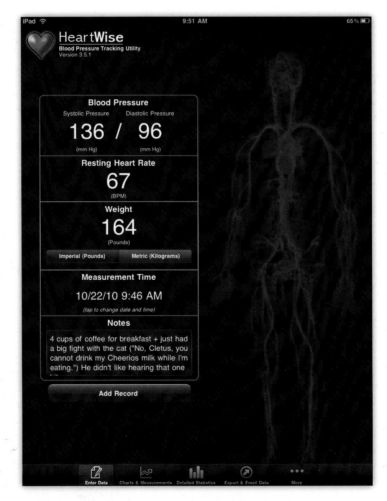

DATA ENTRY: To log your stats, tap any pound sign. (Obviously you'll need a blood pressure cuff to track the systolic and diastolic figures.) To key in historical data, tap the time to adjust that setting. Notes are an optional entry but can be helpful if you're reviewing records with a doctor and want a reminder of things like diet or exercise.

BACKGROUND: Before your first entry, head to the More tab and punch in your weight and height; the app can then calculate BMI. You'll also find a risk factor chart that lays out American Heart Association recommended blood pressure levels—useful if you want to know where you fall on the normal-to-hypertension spectrum.

BIRD'S-EYE VIEW: The big payoff comes a week or so into your efforts. On the Charts & Measurements tab, you'll see a dashboard that lists, from top to bottom: blood pressure, resting heart rate, and weight-related charts. Tap any data point to see a pop-up note showing an entry's key info. To grab the whole collection and dump it in a spreadsheet, use the Export & Email Data option.

THE DETAILS: You can drill down into any of the main data sections by tapping one of the graphs. That brings you to this page, where you get a line-by-line history of the measurements you've entered. You also get max, min, and average stats—perfect for when the doctor asks, "So, how have you been feeling?"

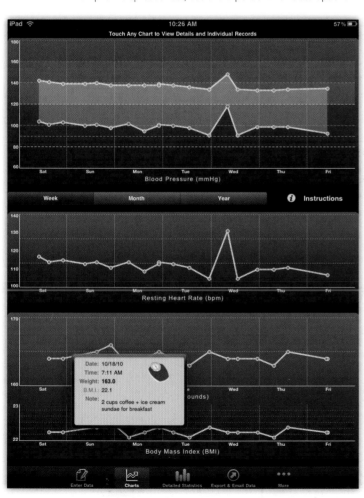

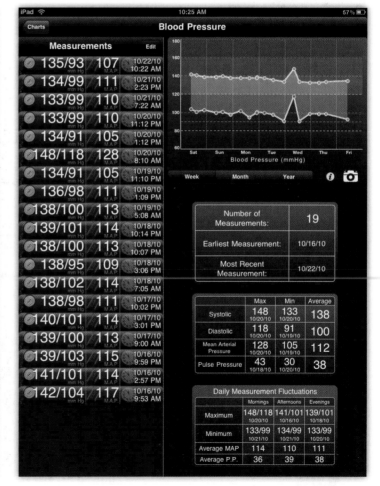

Best App for White Noise

White Noise Pro

$3.99
Version: 4.6 | TMSOFT

Add electronic noise machine to the list of devices iPad owners *don't* need. What makes this app the best way to go from in bed to asleep? Let us sheep count the ways. Large catalog of high-fidelity, true-to-life sounds? Check—those raindrops and frogs and air conditioners sound like the real deal. A useful sleep timer? Check-plus, since you also get the option to add a "fade" period (from 30 seconds to 5 minutes) to help eliminate that jarring blank of sudden silence. And most unexpected, and potentially most useful of all: a Mix List feature, in which collections of background noises combine to speed you along to the Land of Nod. Sweet dreams.

SOUNDS OF SOMNOLENCE: Pick from mechanical objects like clothes- and hair dryers. (New parent tip: this last one's great for soothing crying infants, since it sounds like the swooshing fluid that's in heavy rotation on WOMB). Or cue Mother Nature and summon some ocean waves, running water, or Amazonian jungle jingles.

SLEEPY SYMPHONY: Use the Mix Pad to orchestrate custom combos. Tap *Empty* in the Mix List and then pick from the Sound List. Each noise you add shows up first as a circle atop an illustrated stick figure. The size of the circle, which you control by pinching and spreading, represents the variance (roughly: the sound pattern's diversity).

Best App for Relaxing & Sleeping

Relax Melodies HD

Free lite version | $3.99
Version: 1.2 | Logiciel

The name of this app captures perfectly the special service it aims to provide. Yes, it's got a bunch of mechanical noise replicas (white noise, train tracks), but what it's really good for are all things melodious. Wind chimes, zen tones, flutes, and on into its more subjective but thoroughly pleasing interpretations of themes like Immersed, Night, and the slightly tautological Melody. Play each sound separately or mix 'em together by using the simple tap-to-activate controls. A built-in sleep timer and favorites list make this some easy listening that you'll actually want to turn on.

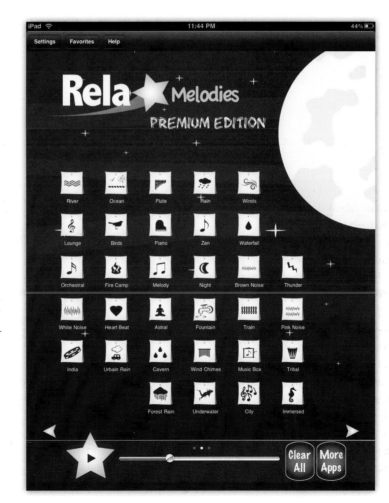

MIX MAESTRO: Activate any sound you want by tapping its icon; the volume bar that appears temporarily at the top of the screen controls that particular track. (The volume bar at bottom is for all the tracks you've activated.) Maximize your melody mix with the Premium Edition: it's ad free and offers about 50 more tracks than the free version.

SAVE 'N SLEEP: The Favorites menu is where to head when you're ready to preserve any multi-track gems you've polished up good and soothing. Start by picking your track mix, open Favorites, tap the Save tab, and then hold down any question mark (or overwrite a previously saved composition by holding down its number).

Best App for Tracking Baby's Stats

Baby Connect for iPad

$4.99
Version: 1.8.6 | Seacloud Software

In addition to diapers, you know what else babies fill alarmingly quick? Notepads. That's right: when, for example, was the last time you gave her the medicine? And what dosage did Doc prescribe? Other track-worthy topics: milestones (crawling, walking), sleep schedule, vaccinations, growth rate. Put away your notepad: this parent-friendly app tracks it all. Plenty of input options—aside from the iPad app, there are iPhone and web-based versions—mean you can record events wherever and whenever. And sharing features (email, downloadable spreadsheets) give you a chance to post something other than cute photos for the data wonks in your family.

For Your Health

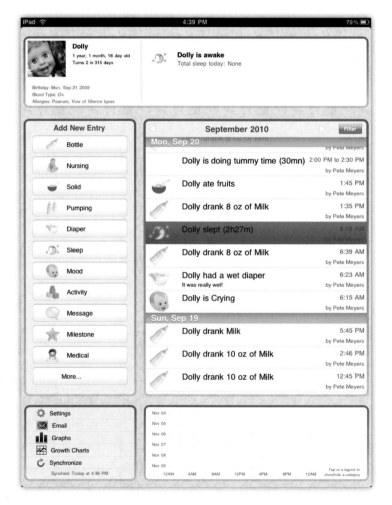

DATA ON BOARD: At heart, this app is a custom-rigged database: pick the event or milestone you want to capture, enter its particulars (start time, duration, date) in the pop-up menu that appears, and view a running log. (Tap the Filter button if you'd like to filter the log to show different time periods or categories.)

WEB LINK: A free online account is worth setting up. Everything that's on your iPad gets synced automatically with the site. Input a vaccine record online, say, and a minute or so later you'll see it on your iPad. Co-parents and other caregivers can join the datafest: set up accounts for as many people as you want (ditto: babies).

MADE TO MEASURE: Spare the kitchen wall and monitor your kid's measurements pencil free on your iPad. Growth charts let you track the Big Three: weight, height, and head size, with key percentile curves showing for comparison's sake. The Percent tab at the bottom of the screen shows percentile ranking over time, if you're into that sort of thing.

TRACK IT: Especially with multiple caregivers, making sure baby gets the right amount of bottle can be a challenge. The app gives you a graphical way to make sure you're on track. Same goes for sleeping, diaper changing, nursing, and pumping: as long as you keep your data feed fresh, the app rewards you with some pretty tracking pictures.

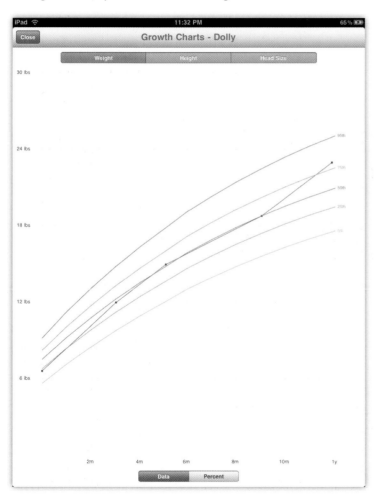

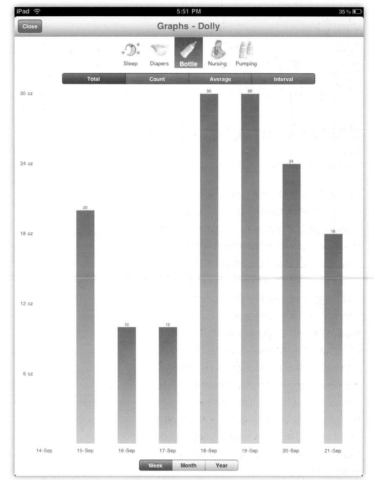

Best App for Drawing Up Plays

PlaybookBball
$9.99
Version: 1.3.2 | Daren Chow

Eight seconds on the clock, your team's down by two with the ball. Coach, how you gonna pull this one out? Suddenly you remember: the Elevator Play (Google it). It'll never work, you think. Then again: it just might work!!! Grab your iPad, fire up this app, and show your crew what to do. What you've got here is basically a stripped-down animation program, custom rigged for coaches (other sports covered in companion apps include football and soccer). Most users will opt to design their plays prior to the game but, truth is, this system's simple enough to whip up a quickie court side. The game changer? Play mode shows your Xs and Os in action. Swish.

PLAYER PLANNING: Start by positioning the players wherever you want them (you can show either or both teams). Then drag one or more of 'em along whatever routes you have in mind. At any point, players can execute different actions: a simple run from one spot to another, a dribble, a screen, a pass, or a shot. Add as many steps as you like for each play you design.

BONUS POINTS: You can tag (label) any of the plays in your collection, making it easy to pull related ones for special situations ("three-pointers," "Two-Minute Drill"). Other handy options: add on-screen notes to remind you of key tips, step through the action move by move (as opposed to letting the whole animation run), and pick from different court dimensions (NCAA women or men, NBA).

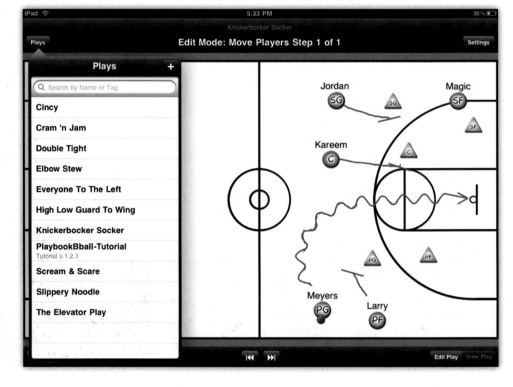

Best App for Improving Your Golf Game

Golfplan

$0.99
Version: 1.2 | Shotzoom

Video tutorials are old news to golfers, but their fatal flaw is the distance from TV to green. This video guidebook app delivers great advice whenever and wherever you're in the mood. Your instructor is PGA veteran Paul Azinger, whose teaching skills are right up there with his golf talents: he speaks and explains clearly and benefits from pro-caliber camera work. Sixty or so one-minute lessons pack in easy-to-follow specifics that take advantage of the show-don't-write format (video truly is better for teaching topics like posture and movement). Each ends with a summary screen recapping key takeaways. Coverage is coursewide: driving, short game, bunkers, putting—it's all here.

TEE TIME: Head to the Videos tab for a pick-your-path tour of the learning catalog. Or set up a semi-custom study plan in the Golfplan tab, where you choose which aspects of your game need work and answer a few basic questions (do you tend to miss fairways left or right?). A four-week lesson awaits.

GOLF PARTNER: iPhone and Android owners may want sibling app Golfshot, a scorekeeper and shot tracker that includes thousands of course maps and even a distance finder. As you collect data (sand saves, for example) the iPad app's Analyze tab gives you a nice visual of what you need to work on.

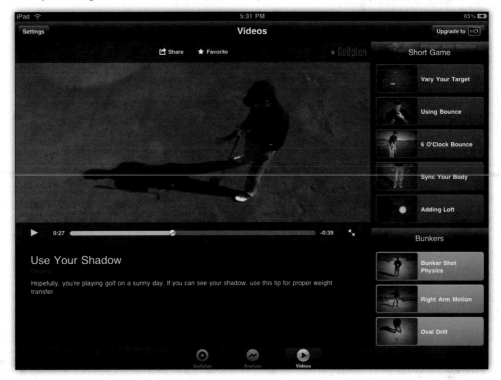

Best App for Birdwatching

iBird Pro HD

$29.99
Version: 1.2 | Mitch Waite Group

For serious birdwatchers, a field guide is essential. This app threatens the printed variation of that species with extinction. Cataloging close to 1,000 North American fliers, this multimedia reference works for browsing and in-the-field birding alike. Showcase features include fine-grained searching, crystal clear maps (and writing), and playable chirps. The five hours worth of audio—bird songs and calls—is a showstopper. Not only do these chirpings help make sense of what used to be rendered phonetically, but you can even use these audibles to lure feathered friends a bit closer for some photo fun.

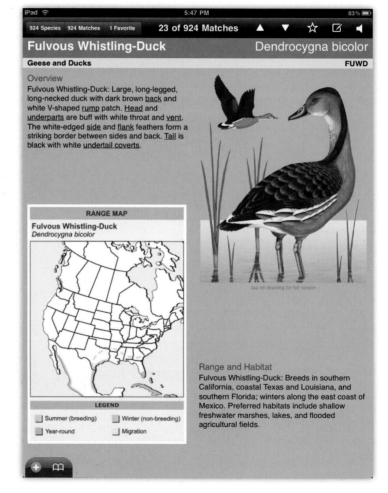

PROFILE PAGES: Each bird's Overview delivers an introduction, a habitat map, key stats, and beautiful illustrations (more than 1,300 throughout the app). Pop-up glossary definitions in the text offer quick refreshers on the difference between, say, *underparts* and *upperparts*.

SPEAK, BIRD: Tap the upper-right speaker icon to hear recordings (pulled from Cornell's famous and enormous collection). Many of these pop-up audio panels have detailed commentary and even alternate variations to help you distinguish, say, an in-flight call from one uttered during a dispute.

EAGLE EYES: The Search screen offers what the geeks call "parameterized searching". Translation: find what you're looking for, quickly. You move across the page from left to right, first picking the main attribute (primary color, song pattern) and then the corresponding search value (red, squeak-shrill). Your database plucked results appear at right. Bonus: after picking your first attribute, head back to the left column, and pick another.

COMPARE & CONTRAST: Birding's not *American Idol*—at least not yet. But sometimes you do want to see how your favorites stack up against each other. Head to the app's Compare section and dial up a database-style listing of up to three birds. Use the Compare Attributes button at top left to select which features get tallied and then mix and match your lineup by tapping the "Compare with" button.

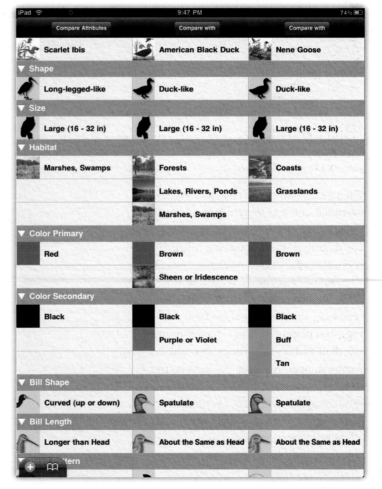

Best App for Weather Watching

WunderMap

Free
Version: 1.1 | Weather Underground

Friend, you know who you are: a weather geek, and darn proud of it. This app's for you. The basics are here, of course: pop-up boxes with info on current conditions and detailed forecasts. But it's the world-wide network of volunteer field agents that's turned this service into a weather wonk favorite. From nearly 15,000 of these worldwide monitors, you get instant updates on everything from dew point to wind gusts. This community-powered meteorology rides side saddle to a more traditional set of offerings like radar and satellite shots of cloud coverage. Combine all that with breaking alerts and forecasts and you've got yourself enough info to man the meterological mic yourself.

MAP FEST: The Layers button lets you add a handful of special purpose map visuals—things like precipitation, clouds, and, for disaster-philes, "Severe weather." Flick this last one on and, if Mommy Nature's brewing trouble, you'll see a patchwork of orange (fire weather warning), yellow (severe thunderstorm), green (flood), or pink (heat advisory). A regular 10 plagues roundup.

PICK A PIC: Turn on the Webcams option in the More button and your map is now dotted with photos from the field, also supplied by the volunteer weather stations—a nifty way to flesh out a picture of what's happening. These pix get updated on a more or less minute-by-minute basis. One final app-only bonus worth mentioning: it's blessedly free of the website's ad clutter.

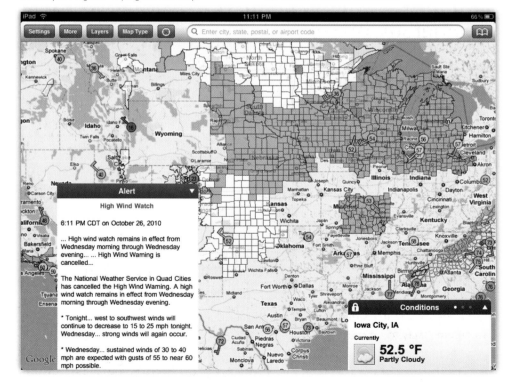

WeatherStation Free

Free
Version: 2.0 | Bigsool SARL

Those of us with an easily satisfied weather report jones will likely appreciate this straight-to-the-point information designer's dream screen. It's definitely not meant for those who crave lots of details or travelers who need to track multiple spots in one day (you can track only one spot at a time and switching requires a slightly clunky pinch and pan gesture). But boy howdy is the key info here easy to digest. Chunked into quickly distinguishable main sections (Current, Today, Tonight, Forecast), this one-pager spotlights everything that weather-following civilians are likely to care about.

WHAT YOU GET: Temperature, of course, but also useful tidbits like chance of rain and a NOAA-powered prediction of whether clouds, sun, or some combo awaits. It's like a Presidential Daily Briefing for those who need to know what's happening outside, but don't have time for details. Location-changing requires you to move around a Google map to pick a new spot.

GREEN SCREEN: The "Change theme" pop-up menu makes it easy to try out any of the dozen different background colors. Alien is fun when you're trying to keep cool, Pinky lends some romance to your weather report, and Digital Watch is a sober palette for those who share space with the boss.

Best App for Chimers and Timers

Zen Timer for iPad

$2.99
Version: 3.2.1 | Spotlight Six Software

An iPad app for meditation? Isn't that what you do to get *away* from the clatter of technology? Sure, but the ultra-soothing tones here are worth a listen, thanks to their easy-to-customize options and the unobtrusive way the iPad lets you tap, trigger, and then forget it's even there. Equipped with a half dozen-ish richly rendered sounds, the app lets you set start, stop, and interval bells. If you want to tweak settings like timing (of the pause between sequential bells, for example), go for it. If you want to spend about 10 seconds on setup and then forget about this app till it's time to touch the Start button: no worries.

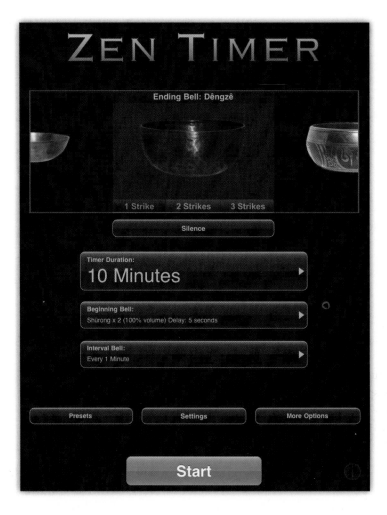

SIMPLE SETUP: Audition the various tones by horizontally swiping through the photo gallery of bowl types. Use the same one for all three points (start, stop, interval) or pick different styles for each. A nice-sized Silence button appears whenever a bell rings, giving you a one-tap way to go back to blankness.

YOUR WAY: Use the Presets button to save any combo for quick summoning. Personalize the app even further by importing your own background image to occupy the screen. You can even put your iPad to sleep (press the button on the top edge of the device) and you'll still hear the interval and ending chimes.

Zazen Suite: Meditation Timer & Mindfulness Bell

Free lite version | $1.99
Version: 1.04 | Nathan Hangen

You'll find fewer sound styles here than Zen Timer (and the four options you get are a tinge less elegantly recorded), but a couple extra features make this a better fit for some meditators. The app's Mindfulness Bell is a pleasant way to receive reminders on a regular basis. Prod points could range from posture checks for back sufferers to randomly spaced mental audits for 12-step types. And, as a universal app, iPhone and iPod Touch owners will have a version to ring up when they're away from their iPad.

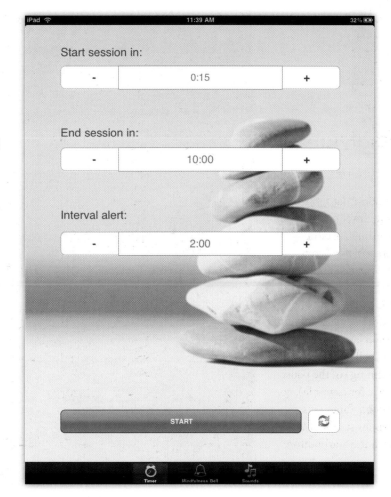

SET AND GO: Tap the plus or minus buttons to adjust the timings for the three types of alerts shown; pick your tone type in the Sounds tab. The pair of arrows chasing each other's tail icon lets you quickly reset each of the three timers to 10 seconds (start), 10 minutes (end), and 5 minutes (interval).

MIND THE TAP: The Mindfulness options cover a pretty nice range of likely uses. Those in need of regularly scheduled reminders can set the chime to play at minute intervals or pick a specific time from the clock selector. But if you want to make sure you don't fall into a tune-it-out rut, a random setting lets you get gently jostled a set number of times per hour.

223

Best App for Better Breathing

Health Through Breath
Free lite version | $2.99
Version: 4.0 | Saagara

Time, at last, for a deep breath amidst this app overload. This program helps put you back on the path to how life was before we gadgetized ourselves. Ironic to use technology to counter its effects? Sure, but there's no denying the visuals you get here make it easy to correctly funnel the air through your nose, down several body levels into your abdomen and back up, past your chest and out your mouth. The ecto-pulmonary view of the breathing model, its innards exposed, might not be as visually peaceful as, say, that Brazilian health spa you went to last year, but then again, it's easier to take out your iPad on a lunch break than it is to go to South America.

For Your Health

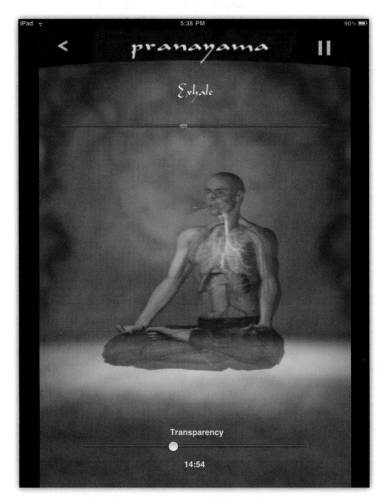

IN AND OUT: The choices you make, before practice, determine how many breaths you take per minute and how long you hold each breath. The ratios you pick from indicate length of inhale, followed by exhale; Timing is how long you hold the ratio for. So a setting of 1:2 with a 4-count means you inhale for four seconds and exhale for eight seconds.

DEEP BREATH: The Custom area is where you assemble a personalized and, if you're up for it, extra challenging program (we're talking, like, two-breath-per-minute challenging). To make things harder, flick on the Retain counter for either the inhale stage, the exhale stage, or both.

Index

Symbols and Numbers

Get even more for your money.

Join the O'Reilly Community, and register the O'Reilly books you own. It's free, and you'll get:

- 40% upgrade offer on O'Reilly books
- Membership discounts on books and events
- Free lifetime updates to electronic formats of books
- Multiple ebook formats, DRM FREE
- Participation in the O'Reilly community
- Newsletters
- Account management
- 100% Satisfaction Guarantee

Signing up is easy:

1. Go to: oreilly.com/go/register
2. Create an O'Reilly login.
3. Provide your address.
4. Register your books.

Note: English-language books only

To order books online:
oreilly.com/order_new

For questions about products or an order:
orders@oreilly.com

To sign up to get topic-specific email announcements and/or news about upcoming books, conferences, special offers, and new technologies:
elists@oreilly.com

For technical questions about book content:
booktech@oreilly.com

To submit new book proposals to our editors:
proposals@oreilly.com

Many O'Reilly books are available in PDF and several ebook formats. For more information:
oreilly.com/ebooks

Spreading the knowledge of innovators   oreilly.com

Buy this book and get access to the online edition for 45 days—for free!